Meet the Pug

For Years of Happiness

by Louise Gore
with Marcy Heathman

The Pure-Bred Series

Doral Publishing
Wilsonville, Oregon
1990

Published by Doral Publishing, P.O. Box 596, Wilsonville, Oregon 97070. Printed in the United States of America.

Copyedited by Luana Luther, Beverly Black and Anna Marie Wilson
Book Design by Tracy Warren
Cover photo by Judith A. Crowe
Typesetting by Oregon Typesetting, Lake Oswego, Oregon 97035

Library of Congress Card Number: 89-050236
ISBN: 0-944875-01-7

To the novices of the Pug world this book is lovingly dedicated in the hope that you will find some of the answers to the questions that I am asked all the time. This is the best way that I can share my knowledge with all of you. Enjoy.

CONTENTS

CONTENTS

CONTENTS

SECTION VIII—The Register of Merit Sires and Dams

SECTION IX—Bibliography & Index

ACKNOWLEDGEMENTS

The authors would like to thank Mrs. Betty Weston for allowing us to make use of her records and collection in compiling the listings of the Register of Merit Sires and Dams.

It is also necessary to thank Mrs. Anna Marie Wilson for her support, editing assistance, interest, and general enthusiasm for this project. She is a credit to the Pug breed, and without her help this book would not have been possible.

To Mrs. Philomena Doherty, who generously donated many photographs and pedigrees from her personal collection, as well as her knowledge, our sincere thanks.

The American Kennel Club Gazette has granted permission to use part of Dr. Grossman's article on Genetics.

B & E Publications has given kind permission to quote extensively from Frank Sabella and Shirlee Kalstone's book, *The Art of Handling Show Dogs.*

To the editors of *Akita World* magazine, many thanks for permission to use numerous quotes from a variety of issues.

To Michael Allen, editor of the *American Cocker Magazine*, for permission to use numerous quotes from a variety of issues.

To Lynn Lowy, editor and publisher of the *Great Dane Reporter*, many thanks for permission to use significant material from a number of issues.

To Susan Coe, editor of *The Basenji*, for granting permission to use special material for this text.

To Joe McGinnis, of Doll/McGinnis Publications, for kind permission to use material from the "stable" of magazines he publishes.

To Marie Tayton, widow of Mark Tayton, for permission to quote from his book, *Successful Kennel Management.*

Many thanks to J. B. Lippincott Company for permission to quote from *The Human Pedigree* by Anthony Smith.

Permission has been granted by Donald Sturz Jr., editor and publisher of the *Golden Retriever Review*, to use specific material from a variety of issues.

FOREWORD

It would be difficult to find anyone who was involved as deeply with Pugs over such a long period as Louise Gore—or one who had a greater knowledge of or devotion to the breed.

Her marriage to Herman Gore was a most fortuitous match for it turned out that he was no less devoted to the breed than she. But that was not always so. One evening, while bowling, Herman saw a Pug and was fascinated by it. Shortly thereafter, somewhat to Louise's dismay, he came home with three Pug bitches, all of whom had been bred. Some years earlier, Louise had been quite taken by a Pug statue that was featured in the Broadway production of Life With Father, but Herman's headlong plunge into the breed was nevertheless a bit of a shock for Louise. However, she was soon as deeply involved and committed as her husband. And, from one of those first bitches came Louise's first champion, Ch. Sally of Blossom Lane.

In the years that followed, the Gore's put together one of the finest Pug breeding kennels in the country, and Louise carried on after Herman's death in 1967. During this period, Gore Pugs became known for their standard of excellence, and it was difficult to examine a pedigree or read a show report without seeing one or more Gore Pugs prominently featured. As a means of sharing her expertise, Louise was active in the Pug Dog Club of America, the Pug Dog Club of Greater Cincinnati, the Louisville Kennel Club, and the Great Lakes Pug Club. She served on committees, assisted at shows and judged matches and sweepstakes.

In later years, debilitating illness curtailed Louise's breeding and showing activities, but she continued to share her store of knowledge through a series of articles published in Pug Talk and elsewhere. Encouraged by friends, she devoted recent years to recording her lore of the breed in this book. It is tragic that her death on February 23, 1990, deprived her of the pleasure of savoring the great success this book is bound to enjoy.

One cannot exaggerate the impact that Louise and Herman Gore have had on the breed of Pugs, and difficult, too, to find anyone with a surer eye for the Pug or a surer sense of selective breeding. This book is a distillation of Louise Gore's knowledge of the breed. But it goes beyond that, embodying essential information on the breed's history, the story of its growth in popularity in this country, the origins and progress of the Pug Dog Club of America, and a review of the outstanding show Pugs—sires, dams and breeders. To this is added valuable data on genetics, dietetics and other technical aspects of breeding and rearing pure-bred dogs, to which co-author Marcy Heathman has made valuable contributions.

Meet the Pug—For Years of Happiness is a definitive work by a uniquely qualified breeder, and is a "must" on the library shelves of fanciers and judges alike.

Dr. Edward N. K. Patterson
Destin, Florida
February 28, 1990

SECTION I

Background

- *Pug History*

- *The Pug Dog Club of America with Specialty Results*

CH. ABBEYVILLE PERSONALITY

CHAPTER 1

Pug History

The very first days of the Pug breed cannot be pinpointed with any accuracy. Official literature from the Pug Dog Club of America concedes that the Pug most probably came from China where it is known to have existed for over 1800 years. Pugs were probably then brought to Holland through the Dutch East India Trading Company, hence the term, "Dutch Pug." Just as the breed is physically unusual in having a number of unique traits, it is also historically unusual in having a number of purported origins! The stories of the Pug's origin are so numerous and contradictory, it would be impossible to list them all here.

The first reliably recorded instance of the Pug as a breed in history occurred in 1572. A Pug saved William the Silent by barking and warning

CH. ROWELL'S SOLO MOON RISING

him of a night attack by Spaniards. Pugs were then considered heroes throughout Holland for many years. It is known that William and Mary brought Pugs with them from Holland when they ascended the throne of England in 1688. They established the Pug as the breed of choice among the English royal circle as well. It is easy to see why the English labeled the breed the Dutch Pug. Pugs remained popular in England until the late 1800s when the breed was replaced in popularity by the Pekingese during Queen Victoria's reign.

In 1868, two short-nosed dogs were imported into England by the Marquis of Wellesley. These two were named Lamb and Moss. Together the pair produced a male offspring known as Click. When Click was bred to Pug bitches, he produced quality puppies with decidedly Pug features and became the founding father of the modern breed. Many of today's pedigrees, if traced back far enough, can find Click among the ancestors.

From the late 1800s there were two dominant strains that continued, in one form or another, until the mid 1900s. These were the "Morrison" Pugs, which were known for their apricot-fawn color, and the "Willoughby" Pugs, which had a grey-fawn color, almost entirely black heads, and abnormally wide traces, or saddle-marks (not something Pug breeders look for today!). For many years, breeders prided themselves on having pure Morrison or pure Willoughby Pugs. Today the strains have been thoroughly interbred and a pure line no longer exists.

Watson's Dog Book, published in 1910, has pictures of a number of Pugs that could, with some difficulty, be identified as members of the Pug breed today. The breed has experienced many changes since the turn of the century!

The American Kennel Club recognized the Pug Dog as a breed in 1885 and one Pug was registered that year, Ch. George. George was bred by Miss Lelia Tegvan of South Carolina and owned by Mrs. E. A. Pue of Philadelphia.

For twenty-five years the numbers of Pugs registered and bred hovered just above zero. Two prominent breeders, Mr. A. G. Eberhardt of Ohio and Mrs. L. C. Smith of California, were responsible for helping keep the breed alive during these early days. But it was Mrs. Sarah Given Waller and her Sigvale Kennel who, in the 1930s, helped establish the popularity the Pug enjoys today. She imported many dogs, especially from the Broadway Kennel of England. The Sigvale Kennel provided the founding stock for the other notable kennel of the day, Mrs. Frothingham Wagstaff's Udalia Kennel. Mrs. Wagstaff later bred Ch. Udalia's Mei Ling, who was for many years the only Pug bitch to have won the Toy Group at Westminster (1945) — having done so at only eight months of age!

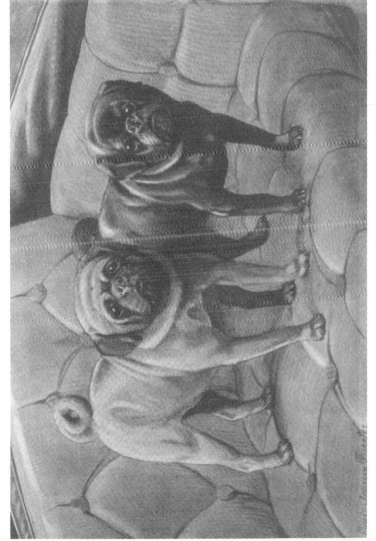

Painting by Louis Agassiz Fuertes, © *National Geographic Society*

There are two other important names from the 1930s and '40s that should be remembered as well: Winifred Steggall and James Trullinger. Miss Winifred Steggall and her Winna Pugs, a Canadian Kennel, had great impact upon America's dogs, especially in the northern and northeastern states. The Winna Pugs were a dominant influence in the bloodlines of all the major kennels of the fifties — and their influence is still seen in today's pedigrees. James Trullinger, author and well-known breeder-judge, captured the Best of Breed at Westminster in 1940 with his Ch. Diamond Jim. Mr. Trullinger eventually became a noted breeder/judge and his opinion was sought after and respected.

For further information on the early days of the Pug, the reader is advised to read *The Complete Pug* by James Trullinger (©1947, Howell Book House) and *The Book of the Pug* by Joan McDonald Brearley (©1980, T.F.H. Publications Inc.).

In the 1950s the Pug breed began to truly catch fire in America, and it was Ch. Pugville's Mighty Jim who fanned the flame. Owned by Mrs. Filomena Doherty, he was an American, Canadian, Cuban and Bermudian Champion. He was the first Pug to be campaigned on a national level, week in and week out. With eight all-breed Best in Shows at the time of his retirement, Jim let the dog world know that a good Pug could win anywhere. Following on Mighty Jim's heels was Gus and Esther Wolf's dog, Ch. Wolf's Li'l Joe, who began a show career that would also lead to BIS wins. This furthered the reputation and success of the breed throughout the nation.

Others who were instrumental in improving the breed in the 1950s include Clinton Allen, who imported Ch. Philwil Cherub of Glenva from England, the Pugholm Kennel of Frederic and Elizabeth Soderberg, Mrs. Mary Shipman Pickhart and her Sabbaday Kennels of Connecticut, Mr. Fred Jacobberger of Blondo Hill Pugs, and Mr. and Mrs. Rolla Blaylock who produced the incomparable Ch. Blaylock's Mar-Ma-Duke. All of these people bred and campaigned top notch dogs in different parts of the United States, giving the breed necessary national exposure.

The 1950s also saw the establishment of the modern Pug Dog Club of America. The parent club of the breed was begun for the explicit purpose of promoting the breed throughout the country. Mrs. Filomena Doherty, president of the Pug Dog Club and also the owner of the best known Pug in the country, made many public relations appearances. Mrs. Doherty's Pugville Kennel was associated with many popular motion picture stars, and even was a favorite of royalty! This exposure served to greatly improve the popularity of the Pug breed in the United States.

From then until now, there has been a steady stream of Pugs in the national eye: Ch. Bassett's Dapper Dan of Gore, winner of Best in Specialty at the PDCA National Show of 1966 and Best of Breed at the Westminster Kennel Club Show the following day; Ch. Cappoquin

Kewpie Doll, a fine bitch who finished her championship at the Westminster show and then went on to Group placements in both America and Canada; Ch. Pug Pen's Captain Midnight, an excellent Group winning black dog owned by the popular actress, Sylvia Sidney; Ch. Pug O'My Heart's Vandal, a west coast dog who was a Best in Specialty winner and a multiple Group winner as well. In the 1970s came Ch. Gore's Jack Tarr, a prolific black sire as well as a winner in the ring for over three years, and Ch. Belcrest's Aristocratic, who dominated the Pug breed in the early '70s, being number-one rated in 1971, 1972, and 1973. He was ranked as the number eight Toy Dog in the entire U.S. by Kennel Review magazine in 1973. The Best in Show awards, seen so rarely during the days of Mighty Jim and Li'l Joe, became more common as better specimens of the breed were nationally campaigned. By the late '70s, the names Ivanwold, Harper, Sheffield, Bonjor, and Dhandy all appeared on a frequent, if not regular, basis. They, along with many others, old-timers and newcomers, have maintained the breed at the high level of visibility that it still enjoys today.

But there was one dog who placed the Pug at the pinnacle of the modern show world. This was Ch. Dhandy's Favorite Woodchuck, the all-time top winning Pug in his day, and the top Toy dog of 1981. His winning career began in 1979 with one Best in Show and 33 Best of Breed wins. From there his winning escalated, culminating with his victory as Best in Show at the Westminster Kennel Club in 1981. Today, he still holds the record as the all-time top winning Toy dog in the Kennel Review System.

Registrations of Pugs continued to rise during the 1980s, placing Pugs 28th among all breeds reported by the AKC by the late 1980s. And the numbers continue to increase at the astounding growth rate of over twelve per cent per year! Demands on breeders by a growing number of new buyers may cause a "population boom" that could be more detrimental to the breed than any inherent defect ever has before. It is in the hands of today's breeders to ensure that this once rare dog does not become one of the newest "fad" breeds. After all, "unique" is part of the Pug mystique!

CHAPTER 2

The Pug Dog Club of America

The origin of the Pug Dog Club of America is just as mysterious as the origins of the Pug breed. According to records of the American Kennel Club, the Pug Dog Club of America first became a member of the AKC in 1931 and held its first show with the Morris and Essex Kennel Club in 1937. A book published by the American Kennel Club in 1935 used information about the breed that was provided "By Courtesy of the Pug Dog Club of America." But, earliest available records from the club archives show only that there were dues-paying members in 1949 and 1950, and this is based on a financial statement of 1953! There are no official records of the Club prior to that time and unfortunately, none of the original members are still alive.

The first dated minutes of the modern incarnation of the Club come from a meeting held at the Penn-Sherwood Hotel in Philadelphia on December 10, 1954. There were 11 members present, including James Trullinger, Agnes Miner (Even So Kennels), Mrs. Thelma Baker and Miss Winnifred Stegall of Canada (Winna Pugs). That evening the following people were elected to serve on the PDCA Board of Directors: Charles Barto, Arthur Cassler, Mrs. Filomena Doherty (Pugville), Dr. Nancy Riser (Vikiri), Fred Jacobberger (Blondo Hill), James Trullinger, Mrs. Sewall, John Marsh (Pugtowne) and Walter Foster. Mrs. Doherty served as Secretary-Treasurer, and Walter Foster was President. Dr. Riser was appointed Annual Specials (Awards) Chairman.

The second meeting was scheduled for February 13, 1955, the day before Westminster, to encourage out-of-town members to attend. With 22 members present, the agenda included discussion on the possibility of dividing the open class by color.

By the late 1950s, the membership of the PDCA had grown to eighty members and three regional clubs. The 1958 National Specialty was a star-studded event. Noted celebrities in attendance that day were Mr. & Mrs. Ricardo Montalban, Richard Burton, Lena Horne, Countess Kontozow Tolstoy, Mrs. Frothingham Wagstaff (owner of the first Pug bitch winner of the TOY Group at Westminster), and the Duke and Duchess of Windsor.

Three generations of Cynthia Young's Rydens Pugs

In 1960, the office of Secretary-Treasurer was split into two separate offices and the decision was made to publish a semiannual bulletin for the members. But the big news of 1960 was the ballot to separate blacks and fawn pugs into two varieties. After much discussion a vote was held and the result was 34-19 against separation.

In 1962 for the first time, an application was received for the highest average Obedience score. It went to Button's Little Lottie, C.D., with an average qualifying score of 198 1/3. The owner-trainer was Mrs. Bonham B. Barton.

The Club received notification from the American Kennel Club in 1964 stating that the AKC would not accept the separation of the breed into two varieties. While that should have ended the discussion, a few people would continue to raise the issue for some time. A poll was taken, and the results indicated that the majority of members who desired the separation were fawn owners, and that the black owners wanted their dogs to compete against the fawn color.

In 1966, the Club began bestowing Annual Awards for Sire, Dam, and Breeder of the year. New rules defining who was eligible to receive these awards were made. In essence, all breeders, owners and co-owners had to have been a member for at least one full year.

By 1967, the PDCA had grown to 229 members and 4 affiliated

regional clubs. Members by now included Jack and Mimi Keller (founded the breed magazine, PUG TALK, which still publishes Pug news on a national level.).

The PDCA held its first futurity also in 1967. Mr. James Trullinger judged an entry of 25. As well, 1967 saw publication of the club's first Handbook, a small magazine which included articles by Mrs. Doherty, Mary Shipman Pickhardt, Mary Lou Mann, Dr. Nancy Riser, Agnes Miner and James Trullinger. Topics included whelping, the origin of the Pug, a Breeder's Credo, what to look for in a show Pug, old age in the breed, and the Constitution and By-Laws of the Club.

The Pug Dog Club of Greater New York was approved for member status in 1969, making it the fifth regional club, and the Bluebonnet Pug Dog Club made an application to hold its first Specialty Show. Also, 1969 marked the last Year of the Futurity, and the beginning of the National Sweepstakes.

In September of 1971 the PDCA National Specialty offered its first class in obedience. Many PDCA members felt that the required obedience jump heights were too high for Pugs. So a letter was mailed to the AKC, requesting a lowered jumping height for Pugs. The request was denied.

Oliver James Hart Jr., drew a total of seven entries for obedience, and four Pugs earned legs in their pursuit of obedience degrees. Highest Scoring Pug in Trial, with 191 points from the Open Class, was Ch. Dougan's Silver Jo Jo, C.D., owned by Glen Wells. Highest scoring Novice Pug was James Wellington, with 190 1/2 points.

In 1973, the Pug Dog Club of America was incorporated. Memberships were accepted for the Greater Milwaukee Pug Club and the Tampa Bay Pug Club, bringing the total number of member clubs to eight and the club designated as its first breed columnist for the American Kennel Club Gazette long-time breeder, Mrs. Romola Hicks.

The PDCA Sweepstakes was held in conjunction with the Cincinnati Club Specialty in May. During a three-show weekend, all of the breed judges were PDCA members, believed to be a first. Also a first was an "Educational Symposium" planned and presented by Mrs. Bonna Webb of Bonjor Pugs. Topics at the symposium concerned the effects of the health and care of the sire and dam at the time of mating. Several very experienced members shared their knowledge while remarking on different aspects of the subject.

By 1976, there were a total of nine regional clubs and over 250 members of the PDCA. During the following ten-year period membership expanded to 368 members. That number has remained fairly constant. Forty-five states are currently represented, as well as international members from Brazil, Canada, England and the Netherlands.

In 1982, the Constitution and By-Laws of the parent club were rewritten to include some major changes. These allowed voting by the members on issues previously handled only by the Board, including voting on judges for the Specialty shows, opening of the Board meetings to members (they had been closed in 1976), and revisions to the process of nominating and electing Board members. Some of the changes made then are still being worked out today, including the nominating/election procedures. But, the 1982 Constitution, and its 1985 amendments were giant steps in the modernization of the PDCA.

In 1985, the Board, working with its members and the AKC, produced the slides and text of the Pug Slide Presentation. Later, this slide show was videotaped. At present, the Illustrated Standard, a project from 1985 as well, is awaiting the results of the AKC's Standardization of the Standards program before continuing on.

The 1989 Board of Directors of the PDCA include Mrs. Marilynn Ellis, a breeder-judge, Mrs. Mary Moxley of Charlamar Pugs, Mr. Ronnie Plott, PDCA Delegate to the American Kennel Club, Mrs. Margery Shriver of Sheffield Pugs, Mrs. Lorene Vickers-Smith of Wisselwood Kennels and Pamela Weaver of Pamajo Pugs. The officers of the PDCA are President Pat Scully, Vice-President Charlotte Patterson, Treasurer Roger Perry, and Secretary Ann White.

There are currently thirteen regional clubs in the United States that are members of the PDCA, as well as five non-member clubs.

The member clubs include: the Bluebonnet Pug Club, (Dallas, Texas); the Central Indiana Pug Club, Inc., (Indianapolis, Indiana); the City of Angels Pug Club, Inc., (Los Angeles, California); the Greater Atlanta Pug Dog Club, Inc., (Atlanta, Georgia); the Great Lakes Pug Club, Inc., (Chicago, Illinois); the Missouri Valley Pug Fanciers, (Nebraska); the Pug Dog Club of Greater Cincinnati, (Ohio); the Pug Dog Club of Greater New York, (New York City); the Pug Dog Club of Greater San Antonio, (San Antonio, Texas); the Pug Dog Club of Maryland, Inc., (Washington, D.C.); the Puget Sound Pug Dog Club, Inc., (Seattle, Washington); the Tampa Bay Pug Club, Inc., (Tampa, Florida); and the Yankee Pug Dog Club, (Connecticut). Non-member clubs known at this time include the Columbine Pug Club (Denver, Colorado), the Greater Milwaukee Pug Club, the Mid-Michigan Pug Club, Inc., the Pug Dog Club of Northern California, and the newest club, the Pug Dog Club of Southern Florida (Miami).

Information about the Pug Dog Club of America can be obtained by writing the American Kennel Club, 57 Madison Avenue, New York, New York 10010, and asking for the address of the current corresponding secretary of the PDCA.

WINNERS OF THE PDCA NATIONAL SPECIALTY

The Pug Dog Club of America has sponsored a National Specialty show every year since 1957. For the first ten years the shows were held in February, around the date of the Westminster Kennel Club show. This, it was hoped, would allow those members of the club who travelled across the country to attend the Westminster show to also attend the National Specialty and Annual Meeting.

In 1967, National Specialty was changed to fall, with September eventually settled on. It continued to be held in the greater New York City vicinity every September in conjunction with the Annual Meeting of the Pug Dog Club of America.

A new feature to the Specialty, the Top 20 Showcase, has recently been added. The Showcase invites the top 20 dogs in the nation to participate in an exhibition where Awards of Merit are given. In this way, many of the top dogs of the country are gathered together for comparison. Only one dog, Ch. Blaylock's Mar-Ma-Duke, has won the National Specialty three times. He did it in the early years, 1958–1960. Since then, four other dogs have managed to win twice: Ch. Sabbaday Echo (1962 & 1963), Ch. Ivanwold Senator Sam (1978 & 1979), Ch. Dhandy's Favorite Woodchuck (1980 & 1981), and Ch. Bonjor Peter Parker (1983 & 1984). In the thirty-two years of the National Specialty Show, only four bitches, Ch. Satina (1967), Ch. Sheffield's Kitten On the Keys (1982), Ch. Sheffield's Spitfire (1988), and Ch. Neu's Enchanting Sorceress (1989) have managed to win this prestigious event.

Following is a list of the winners of the Pug Dog Club of America's National Specialties. The date is followed by the name of the dog winning Best of Breed and its owner. Following the BOB winner is the name of the winner of Best of Opposite Sex and its owner. The letter (B) indicates the name of a bitch winning Best of Breed, while the letters (Blk) indicate a black dog of either sex.

Feb. 10, 1957	Ch. Tarralong Phillip	S. V. Bellinger
	Ch. Hazelbridge Regina	Dr. Stubbs
Feb. 9, 1958	Ch. Blaylock's Mar-Ma-Duke	G. Winders
	Minuet of Pugeen	J. S. Kosvic
Feb. 8, 1959	Ch. Blaylock's Mar-Ma-Duke	G. Winders
	Ch. Cielo's Spring Bokay	P. Earle
Feb. 7, 1960	Ch. Blaylock's Mar-Ma-Duke	G. Winders
	Pugtowne's Calico Sue	Z. Frisina
Feb. 12, 1961	Ch. Star Jade of North'boro	Sabbaday Kennels
	Fy. Bell's Fashion Plate	M.M. & N.J. Sokcevic
Feb. 11, 1962	Ch. Sabbaday Echo	Sabbaday Kennels
	Ch. Bartel's Diana	Mrs. Florence Bartels
Feb. 10, 1963	Ch. Sabbaday Echo	Sabbaday Kennels
	Ch. Oya's Toffee	Pugville Kennels

Feb. 9, 1964	Ch. Fiesta Fahey	Mrs. L. Fahey
	Ch. Cerrone's Mr. Dante	Dorothy Cerrone
Feb. 14, 1965	Ch. Fiddler Fahey	Mrs. L. Fahey
	Ch. Pol's Apple Pan Dandi	Peter & Polly
		McLaughlin
Feb. 13, 1966	Ch. Basset's Dapper Dan of Gore	Mr. & Mrs. Bassett
	Ch. Wheatland's Little Sue	Mrs. A. Gries
Sep. 11, 1966	Ch. Basset's Dapper Dan of Gore	Mr. & Mrs. Bassett
	Ch. Cappoquin Kewpie Doll	Mr. & Mrs. Peter
		Standish
Sep. 10, 1967	Ch. Satina (Blk.B.)	Richard Paisley
	Ch. Pugville's Bashful Beau	John R. Pratt
Oct. ll, 1968	Ch. Crowell's Little Joe of Gore	A. Crowell
	Ch. Honey of Martlesham	Sarah R. Wall
Oct. 10, 1969	Ch. Belcrest's Jim Dandy	Belcrest Kennels
	Ch. Baronrath Tara (Blk.B)	S. Kennedy &
		M. Hecht
Sep. 11, 1970	Ch. Heritage Tom Cat of Gore	Barbara Minella
	Ch. Reinitz Frantic Joy of Gore	Dr. & Mrs. A. Reinitz
Sep. 17, 1971	Ch. Baronrath Baron of Kokusai (Blk)	M. F. & Y. Davis
	Ch. Whispering Lane's Le Lanai	M. L. Shaw
Sep. 15, 1972	Ch. Carbon Copy of Ju Lims (Blk)	J. C. Fischer
	Ch. Miller's Imperial Ballerina	M. & D. Miller
Sep. 14, 1973	Ch. Belcrest Aristocratic	Belcrest Kennels
	Ch. Sheffield's Sure-Fire	Margery Shriver
Sep. 13, 1974	Ch. Bleuridge's Link	B. Braley & E. G.
		Willard
	Ch. Miller's Imperial Tami	M. & D. Miller
Sep. 12, 1975	Ch. Bonjor's Tuff Jorge'll Do It	B. Webb &
		D. Huffman
	Ch. Sheffield's Constant Comment	Margery Shriver
Sep. 11, 1976	Ch. Sabbaday Kidd's Capricorn (Blk)	Sylvia Sidney
	Ch. Sheffield's Constant Comment	Margery Shriver
Sep. 16, 1977	Ch. Shep's Li'l Golden Tom Boy	Colleen Hertzler &
		June Bradley
	Ch. Harper's Star Sapphire	Norma S. Harper
Sep. 15, 1978	Ch. Ivanwold Senator Sam	Mrs. Robert Clark Jr.
	Ch. Sheffield's Country Cousin	Margery Shriver

Sep. 14, 1979	Ch. Ivanwold Senator Sam	Mrs. Robert Clark Jr.
	Ch. Waterside Blackberry Imp	S. & L. Burnham
Sep. 12, 1980	Ch. Dhandy's Favorite Woodchuck	Robert A. Hauslohner
	Ch. Ivanwold Panhandle Pixie	Carol & Walter Dederick
Sep. 11, 1981	Ch. Dhandy's Favorite Woodchuck	Robert A. Hauslohner
	Ch. Sheffield's Country Cousin	Margery Shriver
Sep. 17, 1982	Ch. Sheffield's Kitten On The Keys (B)	Margery Shriver
	Ch. Bonjor Clark Kent	Doug Huffman & Bonna Webb
Sep. 16, 1983	Ch. Bonjor Peter Parker	Bonna Webb & Alan Harper
	Ch. Fahey's Fancy Pants	Mrs. Jane Fahey
Sep. 14, 1984	Ch. Bonjor Peter Parker	Bonna Webb & Alan Harper
	Bornfree Let's Dance	E. S. Van Tassel
Sep. 13, 1985	Ch. Bonjor Clark Kent	Bonna Webb & Doug Huffman
	Ch. Youngford's The Tempest	Mrs. Virginia Warner
Sep. 11/12, 1986	Ch. Paulmar's Little Luke	Martha J. Pratt
	Neu's Enchanting Sorceress (Blk)	Sonja E. Neu
Sep. 10/11, 1987	Ch. Blaque's Streakin Deacon	Blanche C. Roberts
	Ch. Bornfree Princess Mee-Too	Marjorie J. Bauer
Sep. 15/16, 1988	Ch. Sheffield's Spitfire (B)	Margery Shriver
	Ch. Corporal O'Riley Of The Pines	Jim & Cindy Tomsic
Sep. 14/15, 1989	Ch. Neu's Enchanting Sorceress (Blk.B)	Sonya E. Neu
	Wagener's Bocephus of LK	Tammy Collins

SECTION II
What Makes Up
A Standard

- *Blueprint of the Pug — Standard with Clarification*
- *Form Follows Function*
- *A Standard Needing Inspection*

CHAPTER 3

Blueprint of the Pug

What follows here is the text of the Standard of the Pug, as well as personal clarification written many years ago to help novices visualize the breed.

The standard itself is in regular text while the clarification of the standard is italicized.

The Standard

Symmetry—Symmetry and general appearance decidedly square and cobby. A lean, leggy Pug and a dog with short legs and long body are equally objectionable.

The pug should have a boxy, balanced appearance—a dog of heavy bone compactly put together. A tuck-up is not desirable. The dog should give the appearance of a square from any angle. Viewed from above, the dog should appear rectangular from shoulders to hips.

INT. CH. MIRANDUS INVADOR OF HARLOO

Size and Condition—The Pug should be "multum in parvo," but this condensation (if the word may be used) should be shown by compactness of form, well-knit proportions, and hardness of developed muscle. Weight from 14 to 18 pounds (dog or bitch) desirable.

No one feature of the Pug should be so prominent as to cause the Pug to appear out of proportion. Preference should be given to the Pug nearest the desired weight, when the quality is equal. The Latin phrase, "multum in parvo" translates into "a lot in a little."

Body—Short and cobby, wide in chest and well ribbed-up.

The Pug should be wide both front and rear to insure the desired cobbiness. The back should be neither roached nor swayed.

Legs—Very strong, straight, of moderate length and well under.

The legs should be well-muscled to give balanced support. Pasterns should be well-up on the front legs. The hind legs are well-thighed and with hocks well-up from the toes, thus insuring a firm gait, neither plodding nor paddling.

Feet—Neither so long as the foot of a hare nor so round as that of a cat; well split-up toes, and the nails black.

The foot of the Pug should be slightly oval in shape. Toes that turn neither in nor out are desirable.

Muzzle—Short, blunt, square, but not up-faced.

The nose should be short, black and wide. Jaws are broad and square. The bite should be very slightly undershot or even to insure squareness. Chops should completely cover the teeth and tongue without lippiness, yet not long enough to cover the chin.

Head—Large, massive, round — not appleheaded, with no indentation of the skull.

"Round" means from both front view and in profile. Size of head to be determined by the size of the complete Pug. Nothing should detract from the symmetry. Head should be carried gracefully on a short neck, slightly arched.

Eyes—Dark in color, very large, bold and prominent—globular in shape, soft and solicitous in expression, very lustrous, and, when excited, full of fire.

The eyes should be set well apart and should look forward, i.e. NOT "east-west." Nor should eyes be bulging, as these affect the Pug's expression.

Ears—Thin, small, soft, like black velvet, there are two kinds — the "rose" and "button." Preference is given to the latter.

Markings—Clearly defined. The muzzle or mask, ears, moles on cheeks, thumb mark or diamond on forehead, back-trace should be as black as possible.

Mask—The mask should be black. The more intense and well defined it is, the better.

Wrinkles—Large and deep.

They should be clearly defined. The large, single over-nose roll wrinkle is desirable to enhance the roundness of the head. It also allows the Pug to have a small amount of nose hidden underneath.

Trace—A black line extending from the occiput to the tail.

Tail—Curled tightly as possible over the hip. The double curl is perfection.

The tail set high on the rump is desirable to give squareness to the Pug. A tucked or drooping tail should be penalized as this fault spoils the symmetry of the Pug.

Coat—Fine, smooth, soft, short and glossy, neither hard nor wooly.

Some fawn Pugs have black-tipped hairs in their coats. These are NOT "smutty" colored Pugs.

Color—Silver or apricot-fawn. Each should be decided to make the contrast complete between the color of the trace and the mask. Black.

The color of the black Pug should never exhibit signs of rust or gray (except in an older dog, of course). Fawns should always display clear color, without any smuttiness.

CHAPTER 4

Form Follows Function

The function for which dogs were originally bred is not the function for which they are utilized today. Most Pugs are kept in a house or apartment as the family pet and seldom have the opportunity to demonstrate their specific skills.

To go along with the function we have established breed types. That is a physical form which allows the dog to perform its function and around which we can weave an artistic word description. The definition of breed is type. The division of animals into groups of their species, according to differences in physical type, is the basis of breeds. A definite recognizable type must be common to all members of the group. For, without BREED type there is no breed. A BREED is the highest form of a species, that over a number of generations of controlled breeding, has developed definite physical characteristics that, taken together, are the consistent type of that species.

Organic Engineering

You can get a better understanding of the functional aspects of a breed of dog if you think of them in terms of engineering. Consider, for example, the role of the early breeders in England. They had two kinds of jobs. First, they tried to design a useful product: a dog who could go after upland birds, stay close to the hunter, have a good nose, be steady and have the ability to go all day long in the field. Originally these hunting dogs had to put food on the table, only later were they hunted for sport. Then these early breeders had to find a way to manufacture these products. In bringing a new product into being, an engineer first lays out a method of operation. He might even design and build a new tool just for making this one product. With the breeder, he might bring in another breed and cross it and re-cross it and introduce others until he got the correct mixture. The breeder might have to go through dozens of developmental stages before turning out a satisfactory replica of the designed product. But no matter how many steps you must take, a good product engineer (breeder) never departs from the intent of the basic design. He recognizes that the design has a special purpose which his efforts must serve. The farmer in England, who had to protect his live-stock and fowl against the incursion of foxes who holed up in dens in rocky lairs, invented a sturdy little dog to take care of that problem. This dog had to get along with the pack of hounds who were to be used to run the fox to ground. Added to the design was the necessity of having a skull and rib cage that were flat enough to allow him to squeeze into any crevice the fox could. Finally, to have punishing jaws to dispatch the fox and haul him out. This little dog was called the Lakeland Terrier. He is about the same size as the Cocker but certainly built for an expressly different function.

But whether we are talking about a dog breeder or an engineer, they both design their products or devise techniques to make use of certain basic designs. For example, an engineer must use only those geometrical figures that would yield desired structural strength. He must also use shapes that will conserve on materials and yet provide for the greatest efficiency. Futhermore, he must also concern himself with simplicity of design. Therefore, whenever possible he must construct simple machines (levers, pulleys, and inclined planes) rather than intricate combinations of these machines.

Obviously, a dog—or any living organism—is its own engineer. Throughout its life, it constantly refers to a basic design and manufactures the product it needs. In so doing, it makes use of the same principles of design that men use in building machines and other conveniences. The dog also makes use of the same mechanical principles that underline the operation of man-made devices. Consider, for example, the transmission of force. When an animal moves its movable parts, it transmits force in much the same way that machines do. In so doing, the animal uses its built-in, simple machines. You can see this quite clearly in locomotor structures and that is why judging the gait of a dog in terms of its ability to perform its function is so very important in the overall approach to judging dogs.

Movement

For many years vast majority of dog people, and even physiologists, believed that animals running at higher speeds would exact a higher "cost" in terms of energy burned—it didn't turn out that way! Recent studies have shown that animals use up energy at a uniform, predictable rate as the speed of movement increases.

As if that shattering piece of information wasn't enough—they found out that for any given animal, the amount of energy expended in getting from point A to point B was the same regardless of how fast the trip was taken. A Cheetah running 100 yards at a top speed of 60 mph, uses the same amount of energy as it would *walking* the same distance. The running is more exhausting because the calories are used up more quickly.

Size, however, does make a difference. Small dogs require much more energy per unit of weight to run at top speed than a Great Dane would. Small dogs appear to have higher "idling" speeds. The cost of maintaining muscular tension and of stretching and shortening the muscles are higher in small animals.

These same series of studies suggest that as much as 77 percent of the energy used in walking comes, not from the operation of the muscles themselves, but from a continual interplay between gravity and kinetic energy. From an engineering standpoint it seems that the body tends to rotate about a center of mass, somewhat like an egg rolling end on end or the swing of an inverted pendulum. The 30 percent of effort supplied by the muscles is imparted through the limbs to the ground to keep the animal's center of mass moving forward.

At faster speeds, four-footed animals appear to be capable of calling into use a work-saving scheme that relies upon the elastic storage of energy in muscles and tendons. Some are better at it than others. Some are capable of storing more energy per stride than others.

During running or trotting the built-in springs for propulsion are the muscles and tendons of the limbs. When the animal has need to move even faster, he has the ability to use an even bigger spring. As the dog shifts from the fast trot to a gallop they tend to use their bodies as a large spring to store more energy. They do *not* change the frequency of their strides, rather they increase the length of them.

Simple Bio-Machines

Let us now consider how the dog compares with man-made machines. The dog can be compared to combinations of simple machines and other mechanical systems you might find in any factory. A few familar examples will quickly clarify this analogy. The dog's legs for example. You could diagram them as levers. The appendages of all animals in fact, serve as levers. If laid out side by side, they would present a rather special array of "machines." As we have certainly seen dogs—from the Chihuahua to the Great Dane—present a wide variety of angles and levers.

Of course you would expect this, for their owners have widely different ways of life. Modifications in such bio-levers reflect the animal's way of life. So you would expect the Saluki's leg to be the kind of lever that gives the advantage of speed and distance. By the same token, you would expect the design of the front legs of the Basset "a burrowing animal," to provide for the multiplication of force, rather than the advantage of distance or speed.

Another simple machine that is easy to detect in nature is the pulley. You will find the living counterpart of the pulley wherever you find a muscle-tendon joint apparatus. Whenever a tendon moves over a joint, it behaves like a pulley. Such mechanisms enable the dog to change the direction of force. A notable example of an application of the pulley principle is the action of the tendons and muscles in the dog's neck. When the handler "strings the dog up" on a tight lead, the ability of the dog to use that pulley correctly is gone. What you have looks like a spastic alligator moving.

Inclined planes are prevalent in all living things, but their presence is not always obvious. They frequently appear as wedges, which are made up of two inclined planes arranged back-to-back. The incisors of the dog, for example, are wedges. The cutting action of these teeth is an application of the wedge principle in nature. The terrier-type of mouth is vastly different from that of the sporting dog. The sporting dog mouth is designed to hold a bird gently without crushing it. Therefore, its construction does not allow for great force to be generated. In contrast, the terrier jaws are punishing and can generate enough force to kill game. Another illustration is when a standard calls for a sloping topline in movement. The sloping plane from withers to tail is designed to harness the thrust or drive from the rear quarters and move the dog along a straight line with power.

Hydraulics and Life

Any person who has tried to dam up a creek, or in some other way tried to manage moving water, has had experience with hydraulics. It involves the application of energy to practical uses. Frequently, therefore, hydraulics deals with the transfer of mechanical energy of moving fluids to the powering of machinery. It also deals with the the use of pressure created by fluids (hydraulic pressure). All this, of course, finds an application in biology, wherein fluid is of paramount importance. Applications of hydraulic pressure are evident in dogs. Certainly the pumping action of the heart (as being responsible for the movement of blood through the circulatory system) is an appropriate example. A standard asking for a deep chest and the front wide enough for adequate heart and lung space is telling us we need room for a pump big enough to keep the dog going under pressure all day long. This pump exerts pressure, directly or indirectly, on all body fluids. As you know, when the heart is in need of repair or is worn out, the blood pressure of the animal varies abnormally. When this happens, the animal finds it hard to maintain a proper fluid balance of its tissues and organs. The final result is interference with the movement of the materials of life. Death can occur if the equipment designed to maintain hydraulic pressure fails in its function. As you may recall from your school studies of anatomy, it takes more than the pumping of the heart to maintain normal fluid pressure in an animal. The condition of the arteries and the veins is equally important. If these circulatory structures do not have the proper strength or elasticity, this condition could cause abnormal variation in the hydraulic pressure of the body. The arteries and veins are fluid conduits. Therefore, they must have a structural design that will enable them to withstand and adjust to sudden changes in hydraulic pressure.

From your studies, you may recall how effectively the design met the need. The walls of the arteries are designed to have heavier muscular construction than the veins. That's because the blood being pumped under great pressure from the heart goes out through the arteries and returns under less pressure through the veins. Thus, the arteries can withstand greater pressure than the veins can tolerate. The arteries tend to be more elastic than the veins so they can react more quickly to changes in pressure and so regulate the movement of fluid to compensate for the change in the situation.

Organic Architecture (Type)

The shape of a building usually reflects its function. The design of its various parts (roof, doors, ventilators) also relates to special functions. So it is with the shape of the dog. In a large dog, the design often calls for a shape that will provide the necessary strength, compactness and capability to perform certain functions. For example, dogs such as the Malamute were used to haul heavy loads. They were designed with a shoulder construction and balanced size that would enable them to perform this function. On the other hand, for example, a long and slender shape characterizes the coursing type of dog (Afghan, Greyhound, Borzoi and Saluki). This shape facilitates the faster movement of energy from place to place. The Cocker, on the other hand, is designed with a balanced shape to be neither a hauler or speed demon, but to go at a moderate pace for a sustained period of time.

In all cases we need to consider how we recognize the shape we are dealing with. First we must consider outline. Outline encompasses every aspect of the individual animal, making it immediately clear as to what breed or species it belongs.

Structure, Shape and Symmetry

As we have noted, overall body shape has a definite relationship to a dog's way of life. It related, for example, to the use of energy. It also has to do with the animal's ability to relate to its environment and to perform the function for which it was originally bred. As you continue to study dogs, you will see more and more how the shape of things facilitates their function. Take the opportunity to see how the smooth functioning of an animal or of its parts, relates to its function.

A major identifying characteristic of a breed is its head. The head and expression is the very essence of a dog. Without proper breed type, an individual is just a dog, not a Pug, a Springer or even a Great Dane.

Balance is also very important. No part should be longer, shorter, larger or smaller than is compatible with the whole. Everything must fit together to form a pleasing picture of "rightness."

Most breed standards call for a short back. Rightly so, for this is where the strength is. However, a short back is not synonymous with a short dog. The back is actually that small portion of the topline which lies between the base of the withers and the loin. A dog with a long sloping shoulder and a long hip may give the impression of a longer dog. A dog which gives the impression of being taller than it is long, is a dog badly out of balance. This dog is quite likely to have such a short croup that it appears to have none at all. A short steep croup will straighten the leg bones and leads to a highly ineffective and inefficient rear movement. A dog properly angulated at one end, but not on the other, is in even worse balance.

The too-upright shoulder is probably the worst imbalance of all because it affects every other part of the body. It puts great stress on a moving dog, making is pound its front feet into the ground, or crab sidewise to avoid interference with its hind feet.

As you look at your dog in the yard at home or in the show ring, look for the features of its design that might account for its survival and popularity. Look for the relationship of structural design to vital functions. Ask yourself: "How is this shape most suitable for the function of this structure?" "How is the body shape of this animal related to the environment in which it has to live?" In searching for answers, go beyond the obvious facts and look for subtle relationships. Look for special problems. For example, in reading many of the breed magazines today, we find breeders bewailing the promiscuous breedings and the terrible things that have happened to their breed. They often point out their breed is no longer able to perform its primary function because of straight shoulders, over-angulated rears or too much coat. Their claim is the breed is no longer functional. FORM NO LONGER FOLLOWS FUNCTION!...What are the breeders of today going to do about it?

CHAPTER 5

A Standard Needing Inspection

The previous chapter covered the current standard of the Pug that is accepted by the American Kennel Club and a personal interpretation of that standard. At this time though, the American Kennel Club is requesting all breeds currently registered with them to revise their standards to conform with a "standardization" policy. This policy requests every breed standard to address the same fundamental aspects of their breed. Every standard should now mention the conformation of the head, legs, topline, rear, tailset, etc. It is hoped that this will assist judges in uniformly judging the breeds, as well as fill in gaps in some standards.

This standardization comes at a time when many breeders and judges throughout the country claim that Pugs have serious problems, especially in the following areas:

1. Overall poorly constructed rears, and subsequent faulty movement.
2. Toplines not level. (The standard makes no mention of toplines.)
3. Overemphasis on the head; lack of attention to the body.

This analysis from people within the breed as well as observers, is too serious to overlook. The thinking at the current time is to have changes incorporated into the new, standardized standard. But the true question of the matter is, should the Pug standard be changed because the dogs produced today are different, or should the breed (and its standard) remain a constant? After all, the standard for Pugs has remained relatively unchanged for over 100 years. From looking at old drawings and photographs, though, we can see that the breeders concept of the Pug has definitely changed in 100 years!

As an example, Pugs of the early 1800s had long bodies with a head that more closely resembles the shape of today's American Staffordshire Terrier. There was much less wrinkling, less bone, and only a single loop on the tail. By 1900, the Pug that appeared in drawings had more bone and more of a curl to his tail, but was still very long in body in comparison to today. The "black mask" of the day covered more of the entire face than currently acceptable. While the dogs of 1900 are obviously Pugs, there are none that would be seriously considered for use in a breeding program today. The conceptual Pug of the beginning of this century is much different from the concept of the Pug today.

CH. IVANWOLD MARGARET ROSE

The American Kennel Club launched its "Standardization of the Standard" program to eliminate major omissions, errors and inconsistencies in all the breed standards, and to make it easier for judges to learn about the breeds. The duty of changing the standards fell onto the shoulders of the parent club, in this case the Pug Dog Club of America. The requirements of the program have pointed out obvious deficiencies in the Pug standard. In the order they occur within the standard, they are:

1. *Bite.* The Pug standard does not mention the type of bite a Pug should have, although many people "know" that an overshot mouth detracts from the true Pug expression and facial shape. The natural bite of the Pug is very slightly undershot with the lower incisors just slightly in front of the upper incisors. Both front rows of teeth should be straight between the incisors. Where will the standard mention the wry mouth that leads to the lolling tongue seen so many times in the ring? If the dog cannot keep his tongue in his mouth, then he should be dismissed from the show ring.

2. *Neck and Topline.* The current Standard lacks any mention of these important structures. Interestingly enough, topline is one of the aspects many judges have decided for themselves. As previously mentioned, they demand a level topline in the breed, even though the Standard omits any reference to it at this time. It has been obvious for some

time that the neck of the Pug must be strong and carried high with dignity. A proper neck determines the cobbiness of the back, and should have a muscular crest for proper carriage of the massive head.

3. *Hindquarters.* The Pug Standard makes no reference to hindquarters. The Pug needs strong hindquarters to propel himself in the proper manner. Legs should be straight and well muscled. The stifles, when seen in profile, should be rounded and not protruding. The Standardization process will hopefully correct these oversights. The lack of a hindquarters description ties in with:

4. *Gait.* This is where it should be decided whether or not a Pug should roll, a characteristic often mentioned as distinctive of the breed. I believe that a properly put together Pug, with strong front action and a propulsive rear, will roll when moving in coordinated harmony.

The Schedule of Points that the Pug standard has incorporated for so many years will no longer be used. Another way must be found to inform judges that the head of the dog should count for 40% of the total. Or should it? If the breed is "overdone" in the head, as so many people believe, then the removal of the point scale should benefit the breed. It is up to the PDCA and its members to determine if indeed the head has been over emphasized at the expense of the body.

At what point will the new standard mention the personality of the Pug? We know that he is a natural showman, who craves the attention of all he meets. But what of the caring, intelligent nature inside? This, too needs to be addressed. When the standard is brought into line with the AKC's standardization, it will at least fill in some of the omissions Pug breeders have dealt with for over 100 years. This kind of clarification would go a long way toward helping judges and breeders understand the standard. And then, maybe, the rest of the Pug's body will catch up with his head.

SECTION III
The Basis of Heredity

- *Basic Genetics*
- *Analyzing a Pedigree*

CHAPTER 6

Basic Genetics

Consistent breeding of show-quality dogs should be considered an art. To some breeders it comes naturally, others have to learn this art. Still others will never achieve success in this vital and important facet of pure bred dogs.

To some breeders "having an eye for a dog" is second nature. Breeders lacking this natural talent can become self-taught provided they have the intelligence and motivation to discern between the good and poor examples set before them.

Consistent breeding of show-quality specimens depends on important factors besides the natural or acquired talents of the breeder. The breeding stock itself is of prime importance and should be the very best the breeder can obtain. Many breeders still operate under the illusion that second best will produce as well as the choice specimen, pedigrees being equal. This will hold true in isolated instances, of course, but it will not hold true consistently.

Another important element contributing to the success or failure of any given breeding program is that of chance. Everything else being equal, sex distribution, puppy mortality, timing, transmission of the best factors (or the poorest), etc., all depends to a great extent on chance.

There is no shortcut to breed improvement—no miraculous or secret formula which can put Mother Nature out of business and place the breeder in full control. There are, however, many do's and don'ts which can be used as a formula of sorts to minimize the chances of failure and to encourage the chances of success. These do's and don'ts are axioms of our breed, yet there are breeders who ignore and bypass them.

The first step in your breeding program is to decide what is ideal. Until a breeder knows what kind of specimen he wants, he is stopped cold and can neither select the best nor discard the worst. This is where the breeder's capabilities and talents come into play. For this is the basis of selective breeding, and the backbone of any breeding program.

Characteristics such as height and coat color are known as inherited traits. They are traits which an offspring "inherits" or receives from his parents. Every living thing has an inheritance, or "heredity." Inherited traits are passed along from generation to generation. As a result of heredity, each generation is linked to older generations and to past generations. For example, a dog may resemble his parents with respect to height, head shape, and coat color. His grandsire or great grandsire may have also possessed the same identifying features.

A whole science known as genetics has grown up around the study of heredity. Specifically, the science of genetics is the study of how the reproduction process determines the characteristics of an offspring and how these characteristics are distributed.

According to Anthony Smith, writing in *The Human Pedigree*:

Gregor Mendel, a 19th-century monk living in Czechoslovakia, is credited as the founder of genetics. Basically, Mendel's work had proved that traits can be passed from one generation to the next, both with mathematical precision and in separate packets. Before this time, it had been assumed that inheritance was always the result of being colored water of a weaker hue. Mendel foresaw genes, the differing units of inheritance (that are named, incidentally, after the Greek for race). Genes remain distinct entities. They do not blend, like that of colored water. They produce, to continue the analogy, either plain water, or colored water or a mixture between the two. Moreover, assuming no other genes are involved to complicate the story, they continue to create three kinds of product in generation after generation. The packets remained distinct.

The mathematics also has a pleasing simplicity at least in the early stages. The human blue-eye/brown-eye situation is a good elementary example. There are genes for brown and genes for blue, everybody receives one of each from each parent. To receive two browns is to be brown-eyed. To receive two blues is to be blue-eyed. To receive one of each is also to be brown-eyed because the brown has the effect of masking the relative transparency of the blue.

This also signifies that brown is dominant over blue and will always cover over the recessive blue color. Blue will only be expressed when it, as a recessive, is inherited from both parents.

The clarity of Mendel's vision certainly helped science. It was assumed that all of inheritance was equally clear cut, with a ratio of 3:1, or his equally famous ratio of 9:3:1 (involving two characteristics) explaining all of our genetic fortunes. So they do (in a sense) but the real situation is *much* more complex. Only a *few* aspects of inheritance are controlled by a single pair of genes. Only a few more are controlled by two pairs. A feature like height, for example, or coat color may be organized by twenty or so pair of genes. Each pair is working in a Mendelian manner, but the cumulative effect of all of them working together is a bewilderment. The mathematics still have the same precision, but it is only for mathematicians, not for the rest of us. As for a feature like intelligence, with the brain differentiated to fill a tremendous range of different tasks, its inheritance cannot be thought of in a simple ratio of any kind.

There are literally thousands and thousands of paired genes within each animal. There are enough of them, and enough possible variations, to ensure that each specimen is unique. Never in history has there been a duplicate of any specimen. Never in all of future history will there be another one just like it again. Each dog is a combination that is entirely individual and yet its genes are common to the population it lives in. There is nothing unique about the genes themselves.

Piggybacking now upon Mendel's work and that of later scientists, let us look at how breeders can use this knowledge of genetics and breed better dogs.

Each dog contains a pair of genes in each of its cells for each trait (characteristic) that it inherits. One of the genes is contributed by the sire and the other by the dam. Determining coat color in Pugs is basically based upon four sets of genes, each representing different color characteristics. The first gene determines if a dog is a solid color (only seen in blacks), or if the black color is strictly limited in the area of coat covered (as seen in fawns). The second gene is the gene for the black color of Pugs. Its recessive partner is the gene for liver-colored dogs. As we have never seen a liver-colored Pug, the Pug as a breed carries the true gene for black. The third gene affecting coat color in Pugs is a gene that modifies the amount of red and yellow in the brown coat. It is the gene that produces the different shades of fawn, from apricot to silver. Fourth of the color-modifying genes is the gene for spotting.

The gene for the black color is carried in all Pugs, and as such is always a factor in breeding. All Pugs would be black, except for the modifying gene that inhibits the amount of black on the Pug. A true black Pug has no gene that modifies the amount of black on the dog, so a true black carries two genes for solid coloration. A true fawn Pug is just the opposite; it carries two genes that restrict the amount of black on the dog, and no genes to make the color solid. All of the first generation offspring of these two dogs will be black. One parent contributed the "factor" for solid coloration, while the other parent passed along the "factor" for restricted, or fawn, color. When crossing the two pure colors, black dogs will always result, because the gene for solid coloration is *dominant* over the one that restricts.

The recessive characteristic, for fawn, is the hidden or masked one that does not apear in the first generation hybrid offspring. A dog can show a recessive trait only when both factors passed on from the parents are recessive. The dominant trait will appear when one or both genes are dominant.

When a dog is dominant for a trait it is called homozygous for that trait. When it carries recessive genes for a trait i.e., "bug eyes," it is called heterozygous.

To clarify the matter a bit, let's see what happens when an all fawn hybrid specimen is crossed with another just like it. Every hybrid can pass on to each of its offspring either the fawn or black characteristics. Therefore, each color has a 50/50 chance of being transmitted to the offspring. These hybrids have a dominant solid black gene and a recessive, restricted-black (fawn) gene. Let's symbolize them as A-dominant, a-recessive. Since the combination is random, the ways in which these can be combined in a hybrid×hybrid cross are shown in Figure III-1. As shown, it is possible to predict not only the possible combinations of factors, but also the probability for each of the combinations.

Chance plays a part in both the biological and physical worlds. By "chance," it is meant events that happen at random. Mendel was aware of this and knew something of the laws of probability. He used these in explaining his results. This law says: "Be wary of interpreting the occurrence of a single random event." However, it goes on to postulate that if large numbers of occurrences of the same event take place at random, there is a kind of order in the result, in spite of the uncertainty of the occurrence of a single event.

Moving from the inheritance of a single trait to the inheritance of two traits simultaneously, life gets a bit more complex. Start by breeding a homozygous (pure) fawn dog that is short (also homozygous) to a tall black specimen that is also homozygous for its traits. Naturally enough, the breeding produces tall black offspring, since those traits are dominant. They look exactly like the black parent. Now, take these hybrid (heterozygous) offspring which are hybrid-tall, hybrid-black and mate them with like specimens. The resultant types can be quite interesting. There might be four different types produced. There could be a tall black type and a short one, as well as a tall fawn and a short one. These types are new combinations of the two traits.

Continuing in this vein, and for all other traits as well, the distribution ratio turns out to be just about 9:3:3:1. This means for every nine tall, black dogs in a hybrid×hybrid mating, there should be three tall, fawn dogs, three small, black dogs, and one short, fawn specimen. A quick glance shows 12 tall dogs to four short ones, and 12 blacks to four fawns. Both aspects demonstate the 3:1 ratio already established for the inheritance of a single trait in which segregation occurs.

For example, Mendel and later researchers also uncovered the fact that tallness is independent of color. This is called the "law of independent assortment" and is supported by numerous experiments. The probability of two or more related events is calculated by multiplying the individual probabilities. Thus, if the probability of one event occurring is ¼, and the probability of a simultaneous event is also ¼, then the probability of the two occurring together is ¼×¼, or $\frac{1}{16}$. That is, one in every 16.

In breeding for color in dogs, we find that the majority of factors which determine coat color appear to be "single factors," inherited according to Mendel's laws. However, many of these color factors are influenced by other genes which have the ability to modify the expression of the "key" gene in numerous ways and thus account for considerable variation in the finished product. As an example, while a dog may possess the "key genes" which have the ability to create the black mask and apricot color, independent modifying genes may alter its appearance by restricting or allowing full expression of the pigment in its coat, so that it looks smutty rather than clear.

Though the color of a dog's coat may be determined by a single gene or by a pair of genes, the skeletal structure of a dog is determined by the interactin of a large number of genes. It should be easy to understand why something as highly complex as the structure of a Pug's head or body is controlled by the actions of multiple hereditary factors.

Movement is a good example. No one gene labeled "gait" has the ability to determine whether an individual puppy will move properly or improperly. Rather, there are countless genes, working in concert, which determine these facts.

What factors enable an individual dog to move in a way which has been designated as correct for its particular breed? Every breed has a characteristic gait, which is determined by its structure; not the structure of the legs, or the feet, or the hips, or the shoulders, but the structure of all the parts working in concert for this breed. Thus, the Chow Chow moves with short steps and stilted action, the Pekingese and Bulldog "roll" along, the Miniature Pinscher has its hackney gait and the German Shepherd Dog covers ground rapidly with far-reaching steps and a

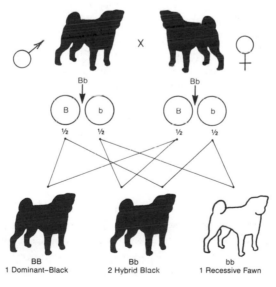

Figure III-1

smooth action. These differences in gait are the result of differences in structure—the manner in which all the body parts are assembled in an individual.

Whether a stifle is straight or short, or whether a foreface is deeply chiseled or built up is not determined, in all probability, by hereditary factors alone. When breeders seek to determine the manner in which any part of an animal's skeletal structure is inherited, they are not dealing with single-factor inheritance, but with multiple-factor inheritance.

Any attempt to explain multiple-factor inheritance fully would prove to be a real puzzle, for most dog breeders have no formal training in advanced genetics. However, the following facts may serve to give a better understanding of this complex subject:

1. What is seen and described as a single character (a leg, a foot, a tail, etc.) is often affected and influenced in its development by a large number of different and unrelated genes which are capable of independent assortment.
2. It is extremely difficult to sort out the various genes which influence a particular characteristic and to determine the specific effect each has on that characteristic. In other words, just how important is a given gene in the development of a particular characteristic?
3. Some genes have a direct, complete influence on the development of a character (dominant genes). Some have only a partial effect, being neutralized to some extent by the action of the opposing member of the pair of which it is one (incompletely dominant genes). Some genes are completely masked and have no effect unless such genes comprise both members of a given pair (recessive genes).
4. The combination of multiple gene effects together with environmental influences, is the rule rather than the exception in such characteristics as body length, height, weight, head and muzzle development, tooth characteristics, foot size and shape, muscle and bone development, and such recognized faults as loose shoulders, flat ribs, cowhocks, weak pasterns and splay feet. As an example, body size depends upon some genes that affect all the tissue and upon others that influence only certain regions, such as the legs, neck, head or tail. In addition, diet, exercise and other environmental influences determine the degree to which genes are able to stimulate and produce growth of the different tissues, organs and body parts.

There are some 130 breeds eligible for registration with the American Kennel Club. None of the breeds is "pure bred" in the true genetic sense of the word. All of them are subject to variations of form and type which may account for considerable differences in appearance between specimens of the same breed. Unlike certain strains of laboratory mice, which have been standardized by inbreeding and selection, and which are like peas in a pod, no breed of dog exists which duplicates its own kind without variation.

Major differences between breeds are probably due to independent genes which may be found in one breed and not in another. Therefore, the manner in which the multiple hereditary factors responsible for the construction of a Greyhound's body are inherited, may differ from the manner in which countless genes which build a Chihuahua's body are inherited. To understand the manner in which complex parts such as the body, legs, head, and other structural parts are inherited, the following will be necessary:

1. Observations of a large number of animals, resulting in careful and accurate records of the differences in structure which exist within the breed.
2. Accurately recording breeding tests between the animals of contrasting structural types, and recording observations of their resultant offspring. This may well require the crossing of breeds at one or more genetic research laboratories (as was done in the controlled experiments done by Dr. C.C. Little at the Jackson Memorial Laboratory of Bar Harbor, Maine). In this way, extreme types can be compared and the inheritance of marked differences in structure can be studied.
3. The making available of these records to scientists who are qualified to analyze them. The task of breeding and raising a large enough number of animals representing different breeds, the recording of observations of their structural types and the types of their offspring is beyond the finances and ability of any one person or any one institution. However, such data could be collected by breeders at no additional expense and a small amount of additional work. Each breeder's records could be sent to a central laboratory for analysis and any resulting conclusions could, in turn, be made available to breeders.

What kind of questions pertaining to inheritance in dogs can geneticists answer right now? Information pertaining to a great variety of subjects is available, including: color differences found in the coat, eyes, and skin of most breeds of dog; differences in the length, quantity, texture and distribution of hair; various reproductive problems such as fertility, fecundity, the production of stillborn or non-viable young, and such conditions as monorchidism; various abnormalities of the eye; malformations resulting from arrested development such as harelip, cleft palate, cleft abdomen, etc.; such diseases as hemophilia and night blindness; differences in ear, eye, nose, jaw, foot and tail characteristics; differences in head size and shape; and numerous physiological differences resulting in characteristic patterns of behavior.

Many of the characteristics in the above list are influenced by multiple genes and/or are affected in varying degrees by environmental factors. Therefore, the available information pertaining to most of these subjects is incomplete; though in some breeds and for some characteristics it is surprisingly extensive. New information is being added daily, as geneticists all over the world make their contributions available.

Many breeders have practiced linebreeding (grandfather to granddaughter, etc.) but have only skirted around the edges of inbreeding (brother to sister, father to daughter, and mother to son matings) shying away from carrying it to its full potential. As a means of finding out which animals have the best genes, inbreeding deserves more use than it has received. Not only does it uncover recessives more surely than any other method, but also, it increases the relationship between the inbred animal and its parents and other relatives so that the animal's pedigree and the merits of the family to which it belongs become more dependable as indicators of its own genes.

Considerable inbreeding is necessary if family selection is to be very effective. The gene is the unit of inheritance, but, for our purposes, the animal is the smallest unit which can be chosen or rejected for breeding purposes. To breed exclusively to one or two of the best specimens available would tend to fix their qualities, both good and bad. In fact, that is the essence of what happens under extreme inbreeding. Moreover, the breeder will make at least a few mistakes in estimating which animals have the very best inheritance. Hence, in a practical program, the breeder will hesitate to use even a very good stud too extensively.

The breeder also is far from having final authority, to decide how many offspring each of his bitches will produce. Some of his basic stock may die or prove to be sterile or will be prevented by a wide variety of factors from having as many get as the breeder wants. Bitches from which he wants a top stud dog may persist in producing only females for several litters. Consequently, he must work with what he has because he did not get what he wanted from more desirable specimens.

The ideal plan for the most rapid improvement of the breed may differ from the plan of the individual breeder chiefly in that he dare not risk quite so much inbreeding deterioration. If the object were to improve the breed with little regard for immediate show prospects, then it would be a different story. This is an important point and deserves more attention.

Inbreeding refers to the mating of two closely-related individuals. Most breeders practice inbreeding to a limited extent, even though they may call it "close line breeding." Actually, the breeding of half brother × half sister, as well as niece × uncle or nephew × aunt is a limited form of inbreeding. For purposes of this discussion, however, inbreeding will refer to the mating of full brother × full sister, father × daughter, and son × mother. Most breeders probably consider these three categories as representative of true inbreeding.

It is not the purpose of this chapter to advocate or condemn the practice of inbreeding, but rather to ascertain what it can and cannot accomplish. It will also be the objective to present known facts and dispel some common fallacies.

It would certainly be interesting to know exactly what percentage of inbreeding takes place in various breeds and what results are obtained. Speaking in generalities, it would probably be safe to say that only one or two percent of all champions finishing within the past ten years were the products of inbreeding. On this basis, it would be reasonable to conclude that the practice of close inbreeding on these terms is relatively rare.

In the breeding of domestic animals, such as cattle, chickens, etc., as well as plant breeding, inbreeding is regarded as a most valuable tool to fix a desired type and purify a strain. This raises the question as to why inbreeding has not gained more widespread acceptance among dog breeders. By combining inbreeding with the selection of those individuals most nearly ideal in appearance and temperament, the desired stability of the stock is quickly obtained.

Breeding the offspring of the father × daughter or son × mother mating back to a parent is called "backcrossing." To illustrate this, suppose an outstanding male specimen is produced and the breeder's thought is to obtain more of the same type: the male is bred back to his dam, and the breeder retains the best bitch puppies in the resulting litter. By breeding these back to the excellent male (backcrossing), there is a good chance that some of the puppies produced as a result of this backcross will greatly resemble the outstanding sire. In backcrossing to a superior male, one may find some inbreeding degeneration in the offspring, but this is improbable according to Dr. Ojvind Winge in his book, *Inheritance in Dogs*.

The mating of brothers × sisters is far more likely to produce inbreeding degeneration. This is because a brother × sister mating is the most intense form of inbreeding. Studies show that those breeders who have attempted to cross full brothers and sisters, for the purpose of fixing good characteristics in their stock, give very contradictory reports of their results. It has been found that the mating of brother × sister results in somewhat decreased vitality and robustness in the offspring.

It may happen that abnormal or stillborn individuals are segregated out in the litter if special genes are carried in the stock. Everything depends upon the hereditary nature of the animals concerned. Inbreeding degeneration is of such a peculiar nature that it may be totally abolished by a single crossing with unrelated or distantly related animals. However, if it had made its appearance, the breeder should know it was present in the hereditary make-up of his stock.

Most of the studies on inbreeding are in agreement with one another. The decline in vigor, including the extinction of certain lines, follows largely the regrouping and fixing (making alike) of *recessive* genes which are, on the whole, injurious to the breed. However, along with the fixing of such recessives, there is also a fixing of gene pairs which are beneficial and desirable. It is a matter of chance as to what combination gene pairs a family finally comes to possess, except that selection is always at work weeding out combinations that are not well adapted to the conditions of life. There is a common belief that inbreeding causes the production of monstrosities and defects. Seemingly reliable evidence indicates that inbreeding itself has no specific connection with the production of monstrosities. Inbreeding seems merely to have brought to light genetic traits in the original stock. Inbreeding does not *create* problems or virtues, it *uncovers* them.

One of the most interesting and extensive investigations of inbreeding in animals was done by the U.S. Department of Agriculture. Thirty-five healthy and vigorous females were selected from general breeding stock and mated with a like number of similarly selected males. The matings were numbered and the offspring of each mating were kept separate and mated exclusively brother × sister. Only the best two of each generation were selected to carry on the succeeding generations.

Two striking results followed this close inbreeding. First, each family became more like itself. While this was going on, there was a gradual elimination of sub-branches. Second, there was a decline in vigor during the first nine years, covering about 12 generations. This decline applied to weight, fertility and vitality in the young.

During the second nine years of inbreeding, there was no further decline in vigor of the inbred animals as a group. This stability was taken to mean that after 12 generations, the families had become essentially pure-bred—that is, no longer different with respect to many genes.

What does all this mean in relation to breeding good dogs? From the foregoing data, several conclusions come to mind. Inbreeding coupled with selection can be utilized to "fix" traits in breeding stock at a rapid rate. These traits may be good or they may be undesirable, depending entirely upon the individual's hereditary nature. Inbreeding creates nothing new—it merely intensifies what is already present. If the hereditary nature of an individual already contains undesirable traits, these will naturally be manifested when the recessive genes become grouped and fixed. This applies to the desirable traits as well.

The term "genotype" refers to the complete genetic make-up of an individual, in contrast to the outward appearance of the individual, which is called "phenotype." In selecting puppies to retain for breeding stock, breeders must rely on phenotype because they have no way of knowing an unproven individual's genotype. Inbreeding can reduce geno-type and phenotype to one common denominator.

Suppose that an outstanding specimen appears as the product of inbreeding. What would this mean in terms of breeding? It would mean that this specimen has a greater chance of passing on his visible traits rather than possible hidden ones. Prepotent dogs and bitches are usually those that are pure for many of their outstanding characteristics. Since such a limited amount of inbreeding has been carried on in most breeds, prepotent specimens have become pure for certain traits more or less by chance, for they have appeared in most breeds as products of outcross-ing, as well as by line breeding. Since line breeding, and especially close line breeding, is a limited form of inbreeding, the same good and bad points apply to line breeding, but in a much more modified degree. The practice of inbreeding appears to be extremely limited in dogs, so one must assume that breeders are willing to trade slower progress for a lower element of risk with respect to degeneration.

Now to review present conclusions insofar as a breeding program is concerned. Assume that you have selected a given bitch to be either line bred or outcrossed and the proper stud dog which compliments her has been chosen. The breeding has been made, the puppies are tenderly watched over, and have begun to grow up. Hopefully, it will be a good breeding and the results will yield several good prospects, all carrying the dam's good traits but showing great improvement in the areas where she needed help. But what if it doesn't turn out this way? What if the breeding results in general disappointment with none of the puppies showing much improvement? You might well ask how this can possibly happen when all the proper aspects were taken into consideration in planning this breeding.

Remember the concept of "dominance"? Test breeding is the only true way of determining whether a dog or bitch is especially dominant. Here again, line breeding comes into play, for the closely line-bred dog or bitch has a *much* better chance of being dominant by virtue of a concentrated bloodline than the dog or bitch that is not line bred. When selecting a stud to compliment your bitch, it is important to take into consideration the qualities of his parents as well. For example, suppose a stud is sought to improve the bitch in head. Obviously, a dog with a beautiful head is chosen, but it is also important that his parents had beautiful heads. Then the stud can be considered "homozygous" for this trait. If the dog selected does not have parents with beautiful heads, or only one parent has a beautiful head, he is said to be "heterozygous" for this characteristic and his chances of reproducing it are diminished. Dominant dogs and bitches are homozygous for more of their traits, while less dominant dogs and bitches are primarily heterozygous in their genetic make-up.

The great majority of dogs and bitches are probably dominant for some of their traits and not especially dominant for others. It is up to the breeder to attempt to match the proper combination of dominant traits, which is why the dog and bitch should compliment each other— that being the best practical way of attempting to come up with the right combinations. There are some dogs and bitches that are completely non-dominant in their genetic make-up when bred to a dominant partner, so good things result provided that their partner is of top quality. In this fashion, a number of dogs and bitches in a breed have "produced" top-quality offspring when they themselves were of lesser quality. When a non-dominant bitch is bred to a non-dominant stud, the resulting litter is bound to be a disappointment. When a dominant bitch is bred to a dominant stud it is possible that the resulting litter will be a failure. This explains why some "dream breedings" result in puppies which do not approach the quality of either parent.

There are some dominant sires which pass on their ability to produce to their sons which, in turn, pass on their producing ability to their sons, etc. Likewise, there are dominant bitches which pass on their producing ability to their daughters, granddaughters, great grandaughters, etc. Thus, some lines are noted for their outstanding producing sires and/or bitches. Such a line is a true "producing bloodline." A producing bitch, usually with a heritage of producing bitches behind her, bred to a proven stud dog will usually come through with those sought-after champions. To this, only one additional qualification need be added— that the breeder exercise some degree of intelligence.

Much discussion between breeders has centered on the subject of which parent contributes the most, the sire or the dam. As we have seen, each contribute 50% of their genetic heritage; but by so doing, their respective factors of dominance and recessiveness are brought into play. Thus, in reality, there is not an equal contribution. If there were, there would be no outstanding producers.

The producing bitch is a very special entity unto herself. Those fortunate enough to own or to have owned one will surely attest to this. When a bitch has produced champion offspring she is singled out for recognition, and well she should be. Depending upon his popularity, the stud dog's production is unlimited; this is not true in the case of the bitch. Many stud dogs, in achieving a producing record, have sired hundreds and hundreds of puppies. The average bitch will produce between 20 and 30 offspring in her lifetime, which drastically limits her chances of producing champions in any great numbers. Taking this limitation into account, it becomes quite obvious that those bitches which produce quality in any amount must possess an attribute different from the average. That attribute is dominance.

The producing bitch may or may not contribute the qualities she herself possesses. Her puppies will, however, bear a resemblence to one another and to subsequent puppies she will produce, regardless of the sire. Whether closely line bred or outcrossed, whether bred to a sire of note or to a comparative unknown, the consistency of quality and type will be apparent in the offspring.

There is no foolproof way to determine in advance those bitches destined to become "producers." The odds will have it, though, that their dams were producers and their granddams and even their great-granddams. Chances are, they will come from a line noted for the pro-ducing ability of its bitches.

Occasionally a bitch will come along with little or no producing heritage close behind her, yet she will be a standout in producing ability. It can only be assumed that such a specimen inherited a genetic make-up "different" from that of her immediate ancestors, or else the potential was always there, but remained untapped until some enterprising breeder parlayed it to advantage. There are known instances when specific bitches will produce only with one particular dog and not with others. In such cases, the desired results are achieved through an ideal "blend-ing" rather than by virtue of dominance. It might be well to mention the fact that some bitches are extremely negative. Such a bitch bred to a prepotent sire will necessarily produce only as a result of the stud's dominance.

The availability of a true producing bitch is necessarily limited. Whereas all are free to breed to the outstanding sires of the breed, few have access to the producing bitches. Their offspring can and should command top prices; demand always exceeds supply. Their bitch pup-pies especially are highly valued, for it is primarily through them that continuity is achieved.

The producing bitch imparts something extra special to her offsp-ring. Though all but impossible to define, this "something extra" is determined genetically, as well as the more obvious physical traits which are handed down. She is also a good mother, conscientious but not fanatical, calm, and possessing an even temperament.

In summary a basic knowledge of genetics will allow the breeding of better specimens and thus improve the breed. It is not possible to be a successful breeder by hit and miss breedings. Hoping that Dame Fortune will smile on you is trusting to chance; not scientific principles. Utilizing the contents of this chapter and other parts of this section will enable a conscientious breeder to score and score well in the winners circle.

CHAPTER 7

Analyzing A Pedigree

Anyone who has ever purchased a purebred dog should have received a pedigree. It contains a list of names that usually go back to the fifth generation. Most newcomers have pored over their first pedigrees with great intensity, trying to sort out the infrequent "Ch." preceding a dog's name. In addition, most pedigrees also list the breeder's name, the date of birth, and the American Kennel Club registration number.

Unfortunately, most pedigrees, even those with many champions listed, have little meaning. More useful would be a pedigree that lists the color of each dog, perhaps its measurements and the number of champions it has produced. A picture of each dog in the first three generations would add frosting to the cake. To most owners, the list of names has little significance other than to highlight the champions of renown scattered here and there through an otherwise nondescript pedigree.

As a list of the dog's forebearers, the pedigree can be used by the wise breeder as a predictor of what kind of offspring the dog/bitch will throw. In effect, pedigree analysis is supposed to be able to help predict the next generation based upon previous ones.

That this is possible is true only in part. A good pedigree confirms what a dog's type and proven ability to produce good stock have already proclaimed. The proof of the dog/bitch is in the puppies. The role of the ancestors is but a prelude to what is contained in the puppy's chromosomes.

It is a proven fact that an offspring of two parents who are themselves of high quality and are recognized producers of stock of consistent excellence, are likely to produce well.

Remember, at all times, quality begets quality. A good example of the breeders' art is illustrated in the all-time top producing sire, Ch. Wolf's Li'l Joe. Bred by Esther and Gus Wolf, he was a champion at nine months of age. Retired at the age of six with six Best in Show wins, an accomplishment in itself, he then went on to produce 73 champion get. And the quality of his get and grandchildren is also spectacular. For example, one of Joe's champion offspring was a bitch who became Ch. Robertson's Fanci Babe, ROM. She was a true Gore girl who produced five champions of her own. Bred to two early Sheffield bitches (Ch.

Sheffield's Sure Fire and Ch. Sheffield's Sally Sunshine), he produced 10 champions that carried the Sheffield name, as well as seven others. Other bitches who produced numerous quality get from Li'l Joe included Ch. Funny Fahey and Ch. Fiesta's Fahey (who together produced four famous Fahey Pugs, including Ch. Farmer Joe Fahey), Ch. Kauffee Royal Gemini, Wiseman's Biza D'Orza (Ch. Wise Lore's Jomaha, Ch. Wise Lore's Showdown Sherman, and Ch. Wise Lore's U Otta Kno Who) and Dougan's Darling Dreamer (dam of five champions from Li'l Joe).

CH. CAMEO'S SUPER STUFF

In 1981, at Westminster Kennel Club, Ch. Dhandy's Favorite Woodchuck went Best in Show, the only Pug to have done so. Woodchuck was a great-grandson on both his sire and dam's lines of Li'l Joe.

PEDIGREE OF: CH. WOLF'S LI'L JOE

CH. PHILWIL ABBOT
INT. CH. PHILWIL CHERUB OF GLENVA
CH. PHILWIL CANDY
CH. SHORT SNORT OF EVEN SO
CH. HARLOO PHILIP (Imp)
CH PINE ECHO'S SEE SEE
CH. PHILWIL GARNET (Imp)
CH. CHEERIO OF EVEN SO
INT. CH. PHILWIL CHERUB OF GLENVA
CH. BLONDO HILL HAPPY BIRTHDAY
CH. MELCROFT MAID O'MIST
Dilly Dally of Even So
INT. CH. KOBBY KNOLL HIMSELF
Floradora of Even So
CH. PINE ECHO'S VING LING

CH. WOLF'S LI'L JOE

INT. CH. PHILWIL CHERUB OF GLENVA
CH. SHORT SNORT OF EVEN SO
CH. PINE ECHO'S SEE SEE
CH. WOLF'S LI'L SHORT SNORT, CDX
CH. BLONDO HILL TOM FOOL
Wolf's Lulu Belle
Missie Toy
CH. WOLF'S KAUFFEE ROYAL ROSE, CD
Sammy
CH. FURST'S JACK
Adair's Tiffany
CH. FURST'S PRINCESS
Hazelbridge Hercules
Furst's Sunday Girl
Petsie

Ch. Sheffield's Stuff 'N Nonsense is a dramatic example of linebreeding on the male side. Stuffy is another of the breed's all-time top producers with 65 champion get. He has two Best In Show winning offspring, and traces much of his heritage back through careful linebreeding on his father's lineage.

Samet Paul of Paramin, Stuffy's sire, was a highly influential dog, with such offspring as the Bernalee trio of Champions: Bernalee Mars, and Bernalee Saturn, both excellent sires, and Bernalee Venus, a top producing bitch. That he had an influence on Sheffield lines is an understatement, with 12 Sheffield Champion get. Besides Stuff'N Nonsense, Samet Paul also sired Ch. Sheffield's Sneaky Pete and Ch. Sheffield's Country Cousin.

Stuffy's dam, Ch. Sheffield's Sweeter Than Wine, is a successful cross of Sheffield and Li'l Joe lines. Her dam, Ch. Sheffield's Sure Fire, is the top producing dam of Pug champions. The remarkable thing about Stuffy's record of producing Champion get is that it seemed to matter very little what bloodlines he was bred to. He was a prepotent sire. His famous winning offspring have come from kennels all over the country, including Nazrep, Marlos, Menehune, Hallagan, Bonjor, Rosened, Bornfree, and most recently, Manalapan and Porter. There is little doubt that Ch. Sheffield's Stuff'N Nonsense will have a lasting effect upon the Pug breed for many generations.

PEDIGREE OF: CH. SHEFFIELD'S STUFF'N NONSENSE

Phiddler of Paramin
Auwil Heron of Paramin
Pincushion of Paramin
Phirefly of Paramin
ENG. CH. PICKADOR OF PARAMIN
Phillipa of Paramin
ENG. CH. PHANTASIA OF PARAMIN
CH. SAMET PAUL OF PARAMIN, ROM (Imp.)
ENG. CH. PARAMIN FARMFORD FLAREPATH
ENG. CH. PARAMIN DILLYPIN PANTALOON
Dillypin Desiree
Paramin Paulette
ENG. CH. ADORAM DILLYPIN DAMON
ENG. CH. DILLYPIN DELIGHTFUL DOREEN OF DOBRAY
ENG. CH. DOBRAY FRIVOLITY OF GAIFONS
CH. SHEFFIELD'S STUFF'N NONSENSE, ROM
CH. SHORT SNORT OF EVEN SO
CH. CHEERIO OF EVEN SO
Dilly Dally of Even So
CH. WOLF'S LI'L JOE
CH. WOLF'S LI'L SHORT SNORT, CDX
CH. WOLF'S KAUFFEE ROYAL ROSE, CD
Furst's Princess
CH. SHEFFIELD'S SWEETER THAN WINE
CH. WALL'S WARRIOR OF PARAMIN
AM. CAN. CH. SHEFFIELD'S SUNDAY PUNCH
CH. SERENADE OF SHEFFIELD
AM. CAN. CH. SHEFFIELD'S SURE-FIRE
CH. PARAMIN FARMFORD FLAREPATH
CH. SHEFFIELD'S LUCY LOCKET SHOGO
CH. SHEFFIELD'S SUNNY PEACH

A very strongly line-bred bitch is Ch. Darden's Mee Tu. Mee Tu is the product of many generations of Gore and Darden breeding. Her offspring include Ch. Darden's B. A. Winner, who was Best of Winners at the Greater Atlanta Pug Club in 1988.

The only anomaly within this pedigree is the addition of English and Ivanwold blood through Ch. Ivanwold High Tor. That breeding was a true outcross of bloodlines. It is important to remember that in any pedigree, the appearance of the names "Nunnally" and "Robertson" are still to be considered "Gore" blood.

PEDIGREE OF: CH. DARDEN'S MEE TU

Gore's Easy Mark
CH. ROBERTSON'S PINTO
CH. REINITZ BABE DOLL OF GORE
CH. ROBERTSON'S TALK TO ME JOHN
Adair's Lyndon B. Of Gore
Robertson's Milo
Gore's You Bet
CH. DARDEN'S LITTLE JOHN OF GORE
CH. ROBERTSON'S BOURBON PRINCE
CH. GORE'S UP 'N ADAM, ROM
CH. ROBERTSON'S GOLDELLE
CH. GORE'S UP 'N FANCI BEBE
AM. CAN. CH. WOLF'S LI'L JOE
CH. ROBERTSON'S FANCI BABE, ROM
CH. REINITZ BABE DOLL OF GORE

CH. DARDEN'S MEE TU

CH. ROBERTSON'S BUC-O-NUNNALLY
CH. ROBERTSON'S BOURBON PRINCE
Nunnally's Derby Doll
CH. GORE'S UP 'N ADAM, ROM
CH. IVANWOLD HIGH TOR
CH. ROBERTSON'S GOLDELLE
CH. REINITZ BABE DOLL OF GORE
Darden's Gee Whiz of Southland, ROM
CH. ROBERTSON'S BUC-O-NUNNALLY
CH. ROBERTSON'S BOURBON PRINCE
Nunnally's Derby Doll
CH. SOUTHLAND'S DIXIE OF CROWELL
AM. CAN. CH. WOLF'S LI'L JOE
Carol's Sassy Caper of Crowell
Haigwood Fifi De Romega

An excellent example of line breeding in a black bitch is Silvertown Onyx, bred by Polly Lamarine, and owned by Doris Aldrich. "Amy" was a product of black and fawn breeding, but her record as a producer speaks for itself. Bred to the famous Ch. Hazelbridge Black Eros, an imported black, she produced Ch. Kendorics Silvertown Nugget and Ch. Silvertown Jasper. Bred to Tosh's Angus of Thorn, she produced Ch. Kendoric's Great Alexeev, a magnificent black sire, and Ch. Kendoric's Peter Pellette. Ch. Kendoric Ravencroft Miranda, a bitch, was also out of Amy ex Tosh's Angus of Thorn.

An examination of the pedigree reveals a strong tie to Ch. Otto of Rydens, an English import, and Ch. Sabbaday Echo, a product of many generations of close breeding himself.

PEDIGREE OF: SILVERTOWN ONYX

CH. VIKIRI LITTLE BLACK SAMBO (B)
Cappoquin Khubla Khan (B)
Wheatland's Minnie Pearl
AM. CAN. CH. PUG PEN'S CAPTAIN MIDNIGHT (B)
Hercourt's Satchmo
Pug Pen's Smudge Pot (B)
Hercourt's Gina
AM. CAN. CH. SABBADAY CAPTAIN'S KIDD (B)
CH. OTTO OF RYDENS (B. Imp)
CH. SABBADAY OPUS (F)
Allen's Susie Q (F)
Sabbaday Silver Lace (F)
CH. SABBADAY SUMMIT OF NORTH'BORO (F)
CH. SABBADAY SILVER LINING (F)
Sabbaday Stand Pat (F)

SILVERTOWN ONYX

CH. OTTO OF RYDENS (B. Imp)
CH. SABBADAY OPUS (F)
Allen's Susie Q (F)
AM. BER CH. SABBADAY BONANZA (F)
CH. SABBADAY ECHO
Sabbaday Firecracker
Three Cedars Butter Side Up
AM. CAN. CH. SABBADAY FAVOR
CH. SABBADAY BLUE CHIP
AM. CAN. CH. SABBADAY BY REQUEST
Sabbaday Star Fire
Sabbaday Amanda
CH. SABBADAY ECHO
Sabbaday Angel-Face
Sabbaday Jane Fahey

In order to be a good breeder, one must use the pedigree as a basic record. A good breeder uses records to identify outstanding bloodlines, possessing the ability of a dog to pass its traits on to its progeny. Such bloodlines, coupled with descriptive data obtained through first-hand accounts or other VERY reliable sources, should constitute the information to be considered in planning a mating. In Europe, many breeders ask for the critiques done in the show ring on the dogs they plan to use for breeding. This gives them added objective information from which to make their breeding judgments.

Experienced breeders are able to read meaning into a well-prepared pedigree, because they can draw upon their personal knowledge of the dogs, the breeders, and the "type" presented by any certain kennel. Most pedigrees are little more than an incomplete jumble of names arranged in chronological order, linking one generation to the next. A record of a producing bitch should include records of the pups produced from each sire she has been bred to. Information about the pups' wins should be included, where there are any, or any defects that may have been thrown, such as a mismarked puppy. While not perfect, this method could give a better background on the dogs in any pedigree. However, breeding of some famous dogs were made on a strength-to-weakness basis, as well.

The story goes that a breeder (in another breed) sent his nice bitch to a heavily campaigned and advertised stud dog. Now this dog was a sometimes breeder. If he didn't like the bitch, too bad. On this occasion he didn't take to the bitch and so ignored her. When the handler called the owner of the bitch to inform him, the owner said to breed her to any available stud since she would be out of season by the time he got her home and bred to another dog. This was done. From this chance mating came the top winning and producing dog in that breed's history. That such matings produce top specimens is more a tribute to Lady Luck than to the breeder's art.

There are wide differences existing in the gene structure of dogs, even from the same litters, and only a few of any breeding can be outstanding as producers. Thus, the existence of famous names in a pedigree is not enough. It is no assurance whatever that the pedigree is a good one.

Good breeders follow the maxim of "Every generation a good one." This means that each individual in a pedigree was a producer and that the line came down in a fixed series of progressions. It is not enough to have famous sires or dams spotted throughout the pedigree. It is necessary that their offspring were also producers so the qualities of those famous dogs can be brought down to succeeding generations.

Each ancestor contributes to the heredity pool in its own unique way. Some improve upon the genes they receive while others degrade those qualities. A good bloodline is one in which each individual specimen has contributed to the "goodness" of the gene pool. Certain individual animals dramatically improve upon those characteristics and it is these animals that should be perpetuated.

An outstanding pedigree shows an unbroken line of production in a form that a breeder can recognize immediately. Unfortunately, many a good pedigree has been turned into a poor one when one of the animals involved turns out to be an inferior producer (especially one close up) or a producer of serious faults. Unless each specimen is in turn followed by superior producers, it may reach a dead end for that line.

To have only a few good individuals in a pedigree is not enough. One has to appreciate that these individuals moved the breed toward the ideal. However, the ones to which they were bred may have carried genes detrimental to the breed, and, as a result, the influence of the noted producer may have been nullified.

While it is difficult for a modern breeder to assess the capability of any given dog or bitch in a pedigree to produce specific characteristics; he can be assured by an unbroken string of top producers that the gene pool is tending toward the overall ideal of the breed.

Livestock breeders have for many years recognized the necessity of maintaining an unbroken record of each line of ancestry. Voluminous computerized records are kept by the dairy cattle industry. Painstaking care is shown in selecting herd sires and keeping track of the milk and butterfat production of their offspring. The industry's ability to select proper specimens through computer analysis puts dog breeding to shame. Of course the payoff in dollars is so great that this type of record keeping can be justified.

A great producing sire or dam produces a much higher average of good dogs among its progeny than does its less outstanding sons or daughters. When the great producing sire and the great producing dam are mated together, the average quality of the progeny is brought to its highest level. Even in this extremely favorable mating, however, the sampling nature of Mendelian inheritance and the range of natural variations would ensure that some of the offspring would be above and some below the average of the parents. In this case, "the drag of the race" would provide an entirely practical guarantee that the great majority of the offspring would be inferior to their great producing parents, as producers. Only the occasional one would be superior or even their equal.

With a pedigree that contains little but names, the older, more experienced breeder has an advantage, for he has undoubtedly seen many of the specimens listed. To the novice, pedigrees are to a large extent a mystery—a genealogical puzzle. The experienced breeder fills in, from his own knowledge, whatever he knows of the weighted averages of individuality and producing powers of each of the parents, the direct ancestors, and many collateral relatives. This is truly reading a pedigree, a gift of knowledge and insight which few breeders of any breed ever obtain.

The case of the newcomer is not so hopeless as it may seem, however. Before the usual pedigree can ever begin to become a reliable part of the basis of breeding, it is necessary to find out how superior or inferior each of the different ancestors was as a producer.

As pointed out earlier, progeny from superior sires and dams are more likely to be superior producers than the progeny of animals selected on the basis of individual merit and pedigree. However, it is sad to report that vast numbers breed to the winner of the day without regard for the genetic make-up of the dog. Perhaps that's why the average staying power of a breeder is only five years. It's like the Las Vegas syndrome—hit it big now or forget it.

Progeny testing is invaluable, for it reveals the true genetic make-up of the sires and dams. It is the heredity concealed in the genes of an individual which determines its value as a producer. All methods of arriving at the true nature of this heredity are merely estimates or approximations, except the actual testing in which this true nature definitely is revealed in the progeny itself.

The most accurate index of the breeding worth of sires and dams is the average quality of their offspring as a whole. In the absence of an ability to gauge this average accurately, the index lies in a random sample of the offspring rather than in the production of one super individual with the qualities of the other offspring unknown. As a consequence, a bloodline or a single mating which is known to produce a high average of good individuals must be considered a better bet. It offers more substantial assurances that a champion will be forthcoming in the next litter, than one which has produced one champion but a lower average quality in all of the other offspring.

Experience has shown that the great mass of every breed fails to produce the required degree of excellence and is lost insofar as the perpetuation of the breed is concerned. The same principle applies to each line of ancestry and to the offspring of even the greatest sires and dams, no matter how carefully the selections are made. It is common knowledge that the most *prepotent* sires of every breed have sired puppies which were inferior producers or even carried serious genetic faults. Thus it may be said that the purity of the line, even in the best appearing pedigrees, is no purity at all unless the progeny test can definitely be applied to each of the ancestors.

It is equally apparent that the mere appearance of famous individuals in a pedigree is not a sufficient guarantee that the line now retains any of those individual's good qualities, which may have been dissipated in their own or any succeeding generation by one or more inferior producers. To provide a reliable tool for the breeder bent on producing winners, the pedigree must show only lines of ancestors which are known to have a strong degree of purity for the sought after qualities.

Decidedly more data is needed in most pedigrees. Until such data can be supplied, the short pedigree going directly to the superior producers is the best pedigree. Genetic research has shown that by far the greatest hereditary influence is exerted by the parents themselves, and that hereditary influence decreases rapidly in each more remote generation. Until tested, the most desirable breeding animal is one directly descended from known superior producers. Each intermediate generation of ancestors of undetermined or unknown breeding powers greatly lessens the probabilities of producing superior puppies.

The following are the Executive Editor's *Cardinal Principles of Breeding*:

1. Breed only to a dog that is old enough to have a history of producing top-flight stock.
2. Stay close within your own bloodline.
3. Be sure the breeding stock you use has an unbroken producing line.
4. Do not breed to the current winner unless it meets the above stated standards.

SECTION IV

Becoming a Breeder

- *The Stud Dog*
- *The Bitch and Her Puppies*
- *Nutrition for Puppies and Adults*
- *Problems of Early Puppyhood*
- *Choosing the Best Puppies*

CHAPTER 8

The Stud Dog

The dog you select to stand at stud should have certain things going for him. First, he should be masculine in appearance and, to at least your appraisal, conform closely to the breed standard. A major mistake made by breeders is to keep a dog that is overdone in some features in the hope he can overcome a bitch with deficiencies in these areas. It doesn't work that way! Breeding an oversize dog to a small bitch in the hope of getting average size puppies is a futile effort. The hallmark of a good breeder, one who understands basic genetics, is breeding to dogs who conform to the standard. Extremes should be avoided like the plague. They only add complications to a breeding program down the road.

Second, it is extremely important that the stud dog come from an unbroken line of producers on both his sire's and dam's side. By unbroken it is meant that at least his sire, grandfather and great grandfather should have produced ten or more champions each. If his sire is still young he may not have hit that mark, but from reading the magazines and seeing his offspring an intelligent breeder can tell if he is going to make it. This unbroken line helps to ensure that he is likely to be homozygous for his good traits. An unbroken producing bitch line is frosting on the cake. It's usually more difficult to find because bitches have fewer offspring. So, when a dog is found that has unbroken producing lines for three generations on his sire's and dam's side, there is an excellent chance of having a prepotent stud.

Third, is appearance. Let's face it, if the male is not constructed right or if his color is not quite right, he is not going to be a great show dog. While the dog doesn't have to be a great show winner to attract the bitches, it helps. Believe me, it helps. Of course there are outstanding examples of non-titled dogs being excellent studs. However, they are few and far between.

There is more to breeding than just dropping a bitch in season into the stud dog's pen and hoping for the best.

First off, let's talk about a subject that never seems to be addressed in the literature about stud dogs, the psyche of the dog. Young stud dogs need to be brought along slowly. If he is a show dog to begin with, he is most likely outgoing and the "gung ho" type. If he is not, please do not think about using him at stud. Behavior traits such as shyness and lack of aggressiveness are transmitted to the next generation just as beautiful necks or slipped stifles are.

He should be taught to get along with other male dogs. Do *not* put him in with an older male too early on. If you do, there is a good likelihood that he will be intimidated and it may harm his prospects of being a good stud. Good stud dogs have to be aggressive in the breeding box. Dogs who have been intimidated early seldom shape up. However, running, playing and even puppy fighting with littermates or slightly older puppies doesn't seem to have a detrimental effect.

The young male, until he is old enough to stand up for himself, should be quartered first with puppies his own age and then introduced to older bitches as kennel mates. It's not a good idea to keep him in a pen by himself. Socialization is extremely important. Time for play as a puppy and a companion to keep him from boredom helps his growth and development.

His quarters and food should present no special problems. Serious breeders all feed their dogs a nourishing and balanced diet. Study after study in colleges of veterinary medicine and by nutritionists at major dog food companies, have shown that the major brands of dry dog food come as close to meeting the total needs of the dog as any elaborately concocted breeder's formula. Each of you has probably learned to add three drops of this and two teaspoons of that, but honestly, a good dry food does the trick. Many breeders spice up the basic diet with their own version of goodies, including table scraps, to break up the monotony or to stimulate a finicky eater. However, for the most part, this is more cosmetic than nutritional. If it makes you feel better, feed him those extra goodies. Supplements will be discussed in the chapter on Nutrition For Puppies and Adults. Do not get him fat and out of condition. That could do terrible things to his libido.

A very important aspect of being the owner of a stud dog is to make sure he can produce puppies. Therefore, at around 11–12 months of age it's a good idea to trundle him off to the vet's for a check on his sperm count. This will tell you if he is producing enough viable sperm cells to make sure he can fertilize eggs in the ovum of a bitch. Sometimes it is found that while a stud produces spermatozoa, they are not active. The chances of this dog being able to fertilize an egg is markedly reduced. While this problem is usually found in older dogs, it happens often enough in young animals to be of concern. Thus the sperm count exam is important, and should be done yearly.

Since we are dealing with the breeding of a warm-blooded mammal, there is need to be concerned with his general health. Sexual contact with a variety of bitches exposes the dog to a wide variety of minor infections and some major ones. Some, if not promptly identified and treated, can lead to sterility—and there goes the farm! Other non-sexual infections and illnesses, such as urinary infections, stones, etc., can also reduce a dog's ability to sire puppies. Since it is not desirable for any of these things to happen stud dog owners need to watch their young Romeos like a hawk.

It's a good idea to have your vet check all incoming bitches. While checking them for obvious signs of infection, especially brucellosis, he can also run a smear to see when they are ready to breed. The dog should also be checked frequently to see if there is any type of discharge from his penis. A dog at regular stud should not have a discharge. Usually he will lick himself frequently to keep the area clean. After breeding it is also a good idea to rinse off the area with a clean saline solution. Your vet may also advise flushing out the penile area after breeding using a special solution.

The testicles and penis are the male organs of reproduction. Testicles are housed in a sac called the scrotum. The AKC will not allow dogs who are cryptorchids (neither testicle descended) nor monorchids (a dog that has only one testicle descended) to be shown.

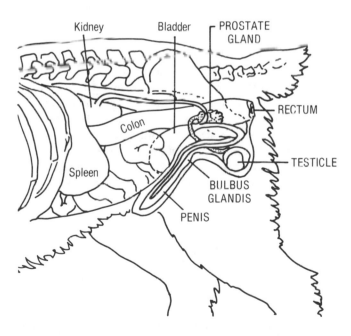

Figure IV-1. Left side of dog showing genital organs and related parts.

The male's testicles are outside the body because the internal heat of the body would curtail the production of sperm. There is a special muscle that keeps them close to the body for warmth in cold weather and relaxes and lets them down to get air cooled in hot weather.

In the male fetus the gonads, or sex organs, develop in the abdominal cavity—migrating during gestation toward their eventual position. Shortly before birth they hover over an opening in the muscular structure of the pubic area through which they will descend to reach the scrotal sac. This external position is vital to the fertility of the animal, for production of live sperm can only proceed at a temperature several degrees cooler than normal body temperature. The glandular tissue of the testes are nourished and supported by arteries, veins, nerves, connective tissue and duct work, collectively known as the spermatic cord. The scrotum acts as a thermostat. As noted above, there are many involuntary muscle fibers within it that are stimulated to contract with the environmental temperature pulling the testes closer to the body for warmth. Contraction also occurs as a result of any stimulus which might be interpreted by the dog as a threat of physical harm—sight of a strange dog, being picked up, etc. This contraction does not force the testicles back up into the abdominal cavity of the adult dog because the inguinal rings have tightened and will not allow them to be drawn back up. The tightening of the rings usually occurs at about ten months of age.

There are a number of reasons why a dog may be a monorchid or cryptorchid. For example the size of the opening through the muscles may be too small to allow for easy passage of the testes, or the spermatic cord may not be long enough for the testes to remain in the scrotum most of the time, and as the proportions of the inguinal ring and testes change in the growing puppy, the time comes when the testes may be trapped above the ring as they grow at different rates. Also, there exists a fibrous muscular band which attaches both to the testes and scrotal wall, gradually shortening and actually guiding the testes in their descent. Possibly this structure could be at fault.

The important thing about all of this is to help the prospective stud dog owner learn about the anatomy of the reproduction organs of the dog. From the foregoing, is it any wonder that many puppies are described as being down one day and up the next?

Next time you place that favorite male puppy up on the grooming table be wary when probing for all of his standard equipment. The scrotal muscles may contract and the still generous inguinal rings may allow the disappearance of the parts sought.

Great luck, a youngster has been found that has "IT" and it is decided to let the world share in the good fortune of owning him. It's a good idea to get him started on the right foot with a cooperative, experienced bitch, one of your own preferably. By introducing the young and inexperienced stud to a "woman of the world," his first experience will result in an easy and successful breeding. Like all males, his ego will soar as a result. This is important. He needs to have the feeling of accomplishment and success. A feisty, difficult bitch the first time around could very well frustrate the youngster and, as a result, he may not be too enthusiastic about future breedings. Remember, we want a confident and aggressive stud dog in the breeding box. There will be difficult bitches to come so it's best to bring him along slow and easy until he will be a match for these fearsome females.

When the bitch is ready to breed (as your stud gains experience he will not pay too much attention to her until she is really ready) both animals should be allowed to exercise and relieve themselves just before being brought together. It's also a good idea not to feed them before mating. Bring the bitch in first. The place should be quiet and away from noise and other dogs. Spend a few minutes petting her and telling her how wonderful she is. Then bring the dog in on a lead. Do not allow him to come lunging in and make a frustrated leap at her. This can cause her to panic and bite him out of fear.

After a few minutes of pirouetting around together—she throwing her vulva in his face and he, with his ears curled on top of his head, trying to lick fore and aft—take off the lead. Allow them to court for a few minutes. She should tell you she is ready by being coquettish and continually backing into the dog.

Now comes the important time for the future success of the young stud. The dog needs to learn the owner is there to help and should not back away from breeding the bitch just because someone is holding her.

Having planned ahead, there will be a large non-skid rug on the floor. Place the bitch on the rug, add a little vaseline around the vulva and face her rump toward the dog. Pat her on the fanny to encourage the dog to come ahead. Generally speaking, he will. As a rule he will lick her again around the vulva. Some dogs are truly considerate lovers, they will go around to the front and gently lick at the bitches eyes and ears. These are true gentlemen. However, this will get him nowhere, so again encourage him to come around to where the action is. If he is unsure of himself, lift the bitch's rear and dangle it in front of the dog's nose.

By now, encouraged and emboldened, the male will mount the bitch from the rear and begin to slowly probe for the opening to the vagina. Once he discovers it, he will begin to move more rapidly. This is a critical time. Some young dogs are so far off the target they never get near the right opening. It's time to gently reposition the bitch so he can have a better angle. This may occur any number of times. He may get frustrated and back off. Don't get excited, this is normal in a young dog. He may even get so excited and confused that he swings around and tries to breed her from the front. This approach never ends successfully.

If your stud is getting all hot and bothered and not having much success, take a break. Put the dog back by himself for a couple of hours. Don't let him wear himself out. This lack of success can make him lose interest. Pet him and tell him how great he is. At the end of that time, try again. The approach should be the same. If it happens a second time the bitch may not be ready. And if after 20 minutes of fruitless endeavor you do not have a tie, there is always tomorrow. Do not work the young dog to the pont of exhaustion. When the next day rolls around you can begin again, giving him maximum encouragement. Don't let him fool around again or he will learn bad habits and think that he had to perform these antics before breeding the bitch.

Get him back on track. Show him the business end again, and encourage him to proceed. By now you have noticed a red, bone-like proturberance sticking out from the penis sheath. This, of course, is the penis itself. As a dog continues to probe and finds the opening, he will begin to move frantically. As he moves in this fashion, a section just behind the pointed penis bone begins to swell. It is capable of great enlargement. This enlargement of the bulbous takes place due to its filling with blood, and it becomes some three times larger than the rest of the penis. In this way, the dog, once having made penetration, is "tied" to the bitch; it is entirely due to the male, the bitch having no part in the initial tying.

When a tie has occurred, the semen is pumped in spurts into the vagina. The bitch then helps to keep the penis enlarged as she begins to have a series of pulsating waves which cause a slight tightening and relaxing of the vagina. Some males will stay tied for up to 60 minutes and others as little as five. A five-minute successful tie is just as satisfactory as a longer one, because the semen has moved up through the uterus and fallopian tubes to the ovarian capsules by the end of five minutes.

Once the dog and bitch are successfully tied, the male characteristically tries to lift his rear leg over the bitch to keep the tie in a back-to-back position. Some dogs merely slide off the back of a bitch and maintain a tie facing in the same direction. One thing you can count on, they will not stay in one position for any length of time. If someone were to chart the moves of a dog and a bitch during a thirty minute tie, it would look like break dancing at its best. Because of this it may be a good idea to have two people involved at this point: one at the bitch's head and one at the male's.

Every now and then a fractious bitch will be sent for breeding. She can be frightened about being shipped, or just plain spooked by a variety of things. Certainly one doesn't want a stud to be bitten by a frightened bitch, nor to have one's own fingers lacerated (yes, even a frightened Pug may bite!). The easiest solution is to muzzle the bitch's jaws, but these are Pugs we're talking about! Usually an extra pair of firm hands will gently restrain the bitch from doing any harm to you or the stud. If absolutely necessary, a wire muzzle can protect you from snapping teeth.

After the tie has been broken, there sometimes will be a rush of fluid from the bitch. Don't worry about it, the sperm is well on its way up the fallopian tubes. Gently move the bitch to a quiet pen, apart from other dogs, and give her fresh water and an opportunity to relieve herself. The dog should be petted and told how well he has done. This is also a good time to flush out his sheath, and if you vet has recommended any medication, apply it now. Then, the dog, too, should be put in a separate quiet pen with fresh water. It is not a good idea to put him back with a group of male dogs. The opportunity for a serious fight is greatest at this time. The other dogs smell him and get quite upset that it wasn't their turn.

How often can the dog be used at stud? If the dog is in good condition he should be able to be used every day for a week. Some serious breeders who, when faced with many bitches to be bred to a popular stud, have used the dog in the morning and the evening for at least three days. If a dog is used regularly, he can be used from day-to-day for a long time. However, if a dog is seldom used, he should not be expected to be able to service day-after-day for any great length of time.

Nature is most generous with sperm. In one good mating a dog may discharge millions, and by and large, a copious amount of sperm is produced in dogs who are used regularly.

All this Olympian activity may be possible for a short time, but for good health and good management, three times a week in normal use seems about right for the average study. Of course, most breeders would give their eye teeth for such a popular dog. An individual bitch should be serviced twice—once every other day—for the best chance of conception.

For some breeders to breed to a stud of their choice is often difficult, especially in countries that have quarantine restricitons. In the U.S., the basic cost of shipping, the possibility of the dog being booked, the chance of making connections with a popular stud who is out on circuit being campaigned, etc., are some of the problems that can produce a great deal of frustration. The use of frozen sperm opens up many new possibilities. Owners of popular stud dogs should definitely look into it. At the time of this writing, there are five AKC-sanctioned collection stations. There should be many more in the near future.

Collecting sperm from dogs is not like collecting from cattle. One collection from the latter produces enough to inseminate over 100 cows. The largest amount collected, at one time, over the many years of research in dogs was 22 vials. Usually two to three vials are used to breed a bitch on two to three occasions while she is in season.

The estimated time to store enough semen to inseminate 30 bitches differs by age, health, and sperm quantity and quality. Estimate approximately a month for a young dog, approximately three months for a dog of eight or nine years of age or older. Collection is still time consuming.

It doesn't take one long to recognize that, in the early stages, those males of outstanding quality will make up the main reservoir of the sperm bank. It is suggested by the collection centers that collection be done at a young age—three to five years.

Limitations in quality and quantity due to old age lengthen the period necessary to store enough sperm for even a few bitches. In addition, the daily routine of a dog's life may limit freezability: The settling down in a new environment, changes in diet/water, minor health problems, etc. It is also not uncommon to get poor freeze results from a stud dog that has not been used for a month or longer. For the dog, once he settles down, the process of collection is a pleasant experience.

Up to now the discussion has touched only on the "easy" part of being a stud dog owner. Next is a look into the day-by-day tasks of the business. Trying to plan a schedule is virtually impossible. Even though some bitch owners say they plan to breed to your dog at the bitch's next season, that can be three to seven months away. Certainly knowing the exact week, let alone the day, is clearly impossible. The bitch's owner will call and say the bitch is on the way. (My God, I've got three unanticipated bitches here now!) Mother Nature does not keep an exact schedule. Unless the bitch's owner has actually sent a deposit to hold a stud service for June of 19__ (this is so rare it would come as a shock), a breeder can only approximate the arrival of his dog's fan club. That's why it is important to keep the stud in top condition . . . he may need to perform yeoman service on short notice.

Okay, now it's known the bitch will be arriving on Tiddlewink Airlines, flight #111, at 1:05 a.m., and has to be picked up at the airport. Those living in a metropolis where there are dog delivery services available that provide for both pickup and delivery are most fortunate. However, these services are expensive. Therefore, being a typical small breeder, it means trudging off to the airport giving up a good night's sleep in the process. When a bitch is shipped air freight or air express, the airlines seem to have a conspiracy as to how long to make you wait to pick up live cargo.

The plane arrives and gets unloaded. No dog! It seems they wait until all the baggage is unloaded to take off the livestock and then they transport them to the air freight building at the other end of the field. This means that 1:05 a.m. has now stretched to close to 3:00 a.m.

before they release the bitch. After letting her relieve herself, putting her back in the crate, driving home and then putting her safely in an isolation pen (hopefully you have planned ahead and provided a special quiet run) we're talking 5:00 a.m. before you get to sleep. Now that's fun!

A good stud dog owner will have found out that various dog food companies, and others, print standard stud contracts. These usually provide for payment in advance and a guaranteed return service if the bitch misses. Both of these stipulations are well advised. As well meaning as most breeders are, many stud fees are either late or not paid at all. Some breeders even wait until they are sure the bitch is pregnant before taking pen in hand. Be firm, no check, no service. This is an expensive hobby, you deserve to be paid for breeding, feeding, picking up and delivering the bitch to and from the airport. By the way, it is a good idea to call the owner collect when the bitch has arrived and also when the bitch is being returned.

What if the dog is either standing at stud at his handler's or being actively campaigned? This can get tricky. If the handler is taking care of the breeding, he expects to be paid for his services. So . . . expect very little from the stud fee unless the dog is so famous as a *prepotent* stud that the stud fees allow you to drive a Mercedes. Expect the handler to ask for 50% or more of the stud fee. Don't complain, they work hard for their money. When the dog is at home, all of the fee can go into the piggy bank. Of course, someone has to perform 100% of the work connected with it.

A real problem can occur when you try to get the in-season bitch together with an actively campaigned dog. Airline schedules and the phone become your steady companion. You arrange for the bitch to be shipped to Toonerville and to arrive at 3:30 in the afternoon. This looks like good planning, because there is a show in Slyville the same day and your handler has to drive through Toonerville on his way to Lizard Butte where the third show on the circuit is being held the following day.

Lucky you, your dog goes Best in Show at Slyville! After the pictures and the congratulations, your handler feeds his string of dogs, cleans up, packs his motorhome and looks at his watch, it's 6:45 p.m. He needs to get going for he has to be in Lizard Butte by 10:00 p.m. to hold his reserved overnight parking at the show grounds. He also needs to pick up that bitch at the Toonerville airport and then find a decent place to eat. He also must call and tell you that your dog went "all the way" that day, before you plow a furrow in the rug pacing around waiting for the news.

Now, are you ready for this? When he arrives at the airport he finds the air freight office is closed—not to open until 7:00 a.m. Don't laugh, it happens! Small airports don't stay open all night. So, what does the handler do? He's showing his client's Beagles at 8:00 a.m. the next morning! The purpose of this commentary is not to try to solve this particular problem, but to allow some insight into the problems of breeding to a dog being actively campaigned.

Now, for a most important item: How much should be charged for the dog's services? A good rule of thumb says that for a young unproven stud, charge 65%-75% of the average being charged. Don't include the Mr. Big's who have already sired 20 or more champions in your calculations. Their fees are elevated based upon accomplishment. You are charging a fee based upon hope and good bloodlines. After the dog has sired at least five champions boost his fee to the average being charged. If he should prove to be a *prepotent* stud and sires some 115 champion offspring, a price more commensurate with his siring abilities should be set. Don't be afraid to ask a price above the average. The average breeder, like the average buyer of goods, equates a good price with a good product.

There are four major things to consider when you decide to promote a stud dog: How often to advertise? How big should the advertisement be? How to use words and pictures to get people to do what you want them to do? And, where to place the advertising to get the best results?

A cardinal rule of advertising is repetition. It has been found that no matter how good the advertisement is, it won't sell unless it is repeated often. The more often an ad is seen, the more likely it will be remembered.

On average, both readership and responses increase as the size of the advertisement increases. However, a full page will not get twice as much attention as a half page. A half-page advertisement will usually be noticed by such a high percentage of readers that it would be impossible to double the readership. On the other hand, a single column ad—a couple of inches deep—will attract the attention of such a small percentage of readers that doubling its size is likely to double its readership. Advertising experts say that nearly everyone involved with print advertising would like their ad to be larger than it should be.

Get their attention. Try to prove that you have a better stud dog for their bitch than anyone else. The more physical the better. Push—better puppies, better puppy sales, etc., and you need to back it up with logic and proof. Cite examples. The magic formula could be stated, "to get what you *want*, do what I want." By citing all the famous and near famous breeders who have bred to your dog, you get them to identify— "if I do the same thing as those famous people did, I will be right in line with those big shots and get champions to boot." This type of identification advertising is highly successful, because it appeals to the need to belong to a group and it unifies people.

First promote his winning look to all-breed magazines and newspapers to catch the eye of both the all-rounders and specialty judges and to help his career along. Then, after his winning record is established, turn greater emphasis to the breed magazines to promote his offspring.

When promoting the dog both as a show dog and as a stud, you have a chicken-and-egg situation. The early advertisements should emphasize his winning record and his winning (producing) ancestors. Later, as the bitches come in, is the time to stress the numbers of bitches being bred to him. Finally, as he produces, trumpet the achievements of his offspring and the history of the producers behind him.

CHAPTER 9

The Bitch and Her Puppies

It has been said that a good bitch is worth her weight in gold. I don't know what gold is selling for today but it's a good bet a really good bitch is worth it. "Really good" doesn't necessarily mean one who will win Westminster. However, she should be a solid bitch who is good enough to finish—or come mighty close—and who comes from a top-producing bloodline. In the chapter, The Stud Dog, emphasis was placed on the continuous, unbroken line of champion ancestors. This holds true in bitches as well, although it is somewhat harder to obtain because of the limited number of puppies they produce when compared to the male.

To begin, assume you have been fortunate and have procured the best bitch that is affordable and she comes from producing bloodlines. Now all that has to be done is sit back and count the champions in each litter. Right? Wrong! There are many extraneous factors to deal with before that can even be a possibility.

It's best to start at the beginning. When thinking about breeding that good bitch, first make sure she is in good condition. Take her to the veterinarian to have her thoroughly checked out. This should include checking for heartworm and other parasites and to make sure she is not carrying a sexually-transmitted disease like brucellosis, which can cause sterility and abortions. All this should be done at least a couple of months before she is due in season.

If there are any problems they can be taken care of early. It is important that she be parasite free. Check for this once again just before she is to be bred. Parasites can be quite debilitating to the puppies. The bitch needs to be in tip-top shape.

Her diet should continue along normal lines with plenty of exercise and fresh water. Be sure she is lean and hard. A fat bitch spells trouble in the whelping box.

Once she has been bred, there is nothing special to do for the first few weeks. She should have good nourishment, fresh water and normal exercise. Be sure her diet is well balanced. Most of the good commercial dry foods provide this. After the third week increase her intake to twice what she has been eating. Feed her twice a day to make digestion easier.

After week seven has gone by, feed at the same level but spread it over three feedings. All this time she should be getting regular exercise. In the last three weeks cut out any hard-to-digest foods and walk her briskly on lead, but don't let her overextend herself physically. The week before she is due to whelp, modify her diet by making it more liquid—to assist her to eliminate easily. Within three days of whelping give her a teaspoon full of milk of magnesia daily.

The average whelping time is 63 days after conception. No two bitches are alike, and whelping can occur from the 59th day to the 65th day just as easily. Remember the Boy Scout motto—"Be Prepared!"

There are a number of things that can be done to prepare for the arrival of the puppies. First, prepare a comfortable, quiet place for the bitch to whelp. This is not time for a block party, so set-up to keep vistors out. Either make or buy a whelping box. This box should sit above the floor (a minimum of 2") to be out of drafts. It should have enough room for the dam to lie just outside an area where the puppies will snuggle but allow her some respite from them when she needs it. Of course, the bigger the bitch, the larger the box. It should have a lip to keep the puppies in. It should also have enough room for her to whelp the puppies without feeling crowded and allow you room to assist her if you need to. The whelping area should have a good supply of newspaper for sterilization reasons (newsprint is antiseptic) and to allow the bitch in labor to dig as she tries to nest. The floor itself should be covered with a rough surface like indoor/outdoor carpeting, to allow the puppies to gain traction while they are nursing. After a couple of weeks, cover this over with newspaper since the mother will probably no longer clean up after them and it can get messy.

It's also a good idea to have a "pig rail" (a protective barrier) around the inside flooring. This rail can be constructed from large broom handles. Its purpose is to protect the puppy that may crawl behind his mother and be trapped or crushed before she can see, smell or hear him. This is more prone to happen when there is a large litter. There should be an outside heating source (either under the flooring or just above) to make sure the puppies don't get chilled. Newborn puppies are unable to generate enough body heat to insulate themselves. It's imperative to supply that warmth externally. Listen for crying, this indicates something is wrong and it's often lack of warmth. Puppies will pile on one another to help keep warm. After about ten days their internal "furnace" can stoke up enough body heat to protect themselves. If the puppies are scattered around the box and not heaped together, the heat is too high.

There are some other supplies that are needed. Since the puppies usually don't come all at once, a place is needed to keep the puppies that have arrived in sight of the mother but out of the way as she whelps the next one. Most people use a small cardboard box with high sides. (Get a

Table IV-1. Sixty-Three Day Whelping Table

Date Bred	Puppies Due	Date Bred	Puppies Due	Date Bred	Puppies Due	Date Bred	Puppies Due	Date Bred	Puppies Due	Date Bred	Puppies Due	Date Bred	Puppies Due	Date Bred	Puppies Due	Date Bred	Puppies Due	Date Bred	Puppies Due	Date Bred	Puppies Due	Date Bred	Puppies Due
JANUARY	MARCH	FEBRUARY	APRIL	MARCH	MAY	APRIL	JUNE	MAY	JULY	JUNE	AUGUST	JULY	SEPTEMBER	AUGUST	OCTOBER	SEPTEMBER	NOVEMBER	OCTOBER	DECEMBER	NOVEMBER	JANUARY	DECEMBER	FEBRUARY
1	5	1	5	1	3	1	3	1	3	1	3	1	2	1	3	1	3	1	3	1	3	1	2
2	6	2	6	2	4	2	4	2	4	2	4	2	3	2	4	2	4	2	4	2	4	2	3
3	7	3	7	3	5	3	5	3	5	3	5	3	4	3	5	3	5	3	5	3	5	3	4
4	8	4	8	4	6	4	6	4	6	4	6	4	5	4	6	4	6	4	6	4	6	4	5
5	9	5	9	5	7	5	7	5	7	5	7	5	6	5	7	5	7	5	7	5	7	5	6
6	10	6	10	6	8	6	8	6	8	6	8	6	7	6	8	6	8	6	8	6	8	6	7
7	11	7	11	7	9	7	9	7	9	7	9	7	8	7	9	7	9	7	9	7	9	7	8
8	12	8	12	8	10	8	10	8	10	8	10	8	9	8	10	8	10	8	10	8	10	8	9
9	13	9	13	9	11	9	11	9	11	9	11	9	10	9	11	9	11	9	11	9	11	9	10
10	14	10	14	10	12	10	12	10	12	10	12	10	11	10	12	10	12	10	12	10	12	10	11
11	15	11	15	11	13	11	13	11	13	11	13	11	12	11	13	11	13	11	13	11	13	11	12
12	16	12	16	12	14	12	14	12	14	12	14	12	13	12	14	12	14	12	14	12	14	12	13
13	17	13	17	13	15	13	15	13	15	13	15	13	14	13	15	13	15	13	15	13	15	13	14
14	18	14	18	14	16	14	16	14	16	14	16	14	15	14	16	14	16	14	16	14	16	14	15
15	19	15	19	15	17	15	17	15	17	15	17	15	16	15	17	15	17	15	17	15	17	15	16
16	20	16	20	16	18	16	18	16	18	16	18	16	17	16	18	16	18	16	18	16	18	16	17
17	21	17	21	17	19	17	19	17	19	17	19	17	18	17	19	17	19	17	19	17	19	17	18
18	22	18	22	18	20	18	20	18	20	18	20	18	19	18	20	18	20	18	20	18	20	18	19
19	23	19	23	19	21	19	21	19	21	19	21	19	20	19	21	19	21	19	21	19	21	19	20
20	24	20	24	20	22	20	22	20	22	20	22	20	21	20	22	20	22	20	22	20	22	20	21
21	25	21	25	21	23	21	23	21	23	21	23	21	22	21	23	21	23	21	23	21	23	21	22
22	26	22	26	22	24	22	24	22	24	22	24	22	23	22	24	22	24	22	24	22	24	22	23
23	27	23	27	23	25	23	25	23	25	23	25	23	24	23	25	23	25	23	25	23	25	23	24
24	28	24	28	24	26	24	26	24	26	24	26	24	25	24	26	24	26	24	26	24	26	24	25
25	29	25	29	25	27	25	27	25	27	25	27	25	26	25	27	25	27	25	27	25	27	25	26
26	30	26	30	26	28	26	28	26	28	26	28	26	27	26	28	26	28	26	28	26	28	26	27
27	31	27	1 (May)	27	29	27	29	27	29	27	29	27	28	27	29	27	29	27	29	27	29	27	28
28	1 (Apr)	28	2	28	30	28	30	28	30	28	30	28	29	28	30	28	30	28	30	28	30	28	1 (Mar)
29	2			29	31	29	1 (Jul)	29	31	29	31	29	30	29	31	29	1 (Dec)	29	31	29	31	29	2
30	3			30	1 (Jun)	30	2	30	1 (Aug)	30	1 (Sep)	30	1 (Oct)	30	1 (Nov)	30	2	30	1 (Jan)	30	1 (Feb)	30	3
31	4			31	2			31	2			31	2	31	2			31	2			31	4

clean one from your supermarket.) At the bottom of this box put a heating pad or a hot water bottle. Cover it with a rough towel. Make sure it doesn't get too warm. After the dam has cleaned up each puppy, roughly licking it with her tongue and drying it off, she may wish to nurse it. Let her try. But most of the time Mother Nature is telling her to prepare for the next whelp. If the bitch starts to dig at the papers on the floor of the box, remove the puppy and place it in the cardboard box. You may wish to leave the box in the corner of the whelping box. However, if the bitch starts to whirl around while whelping, get the box out of there and up on some surface where it won't be knocked down. Be sure the bitch can see it at all times.

Clean, sharp scissors, alcohol and string should also be present. The scissors—which along with the string—should be sitting in the alcohol, are to cut the umbilical cord if necessary. Cut it at least 2″ from the puppy. Later, when the puppy is in the cardboard box, tie off the cord with the string. Disposable towels, washcloths, cotton swabs, toenail clipper, garbage pail and pans for warm and cold water are among the other supplies that you should have on hand.

Harking back to the "Be Prepared" motto, there should also be on hand a small syringe with a rubber bulb on it. These can be found in most drug stores and are called "aspirators." They are like the kind used for basting, only smaller. If you can't find the proper tool, use your basting syringe. The purpose of this device is to clear the puppies nostrils and lungs of excess fluid. Some puppies are born sputtering because fluid has accumulated in their nostrils or lungs during their trip through the birth canal. Try to suck the fluid from the nostrils first. Listen for a wheezing sound, this means there is still fluid. The puppy will also cough or choke. If all the fluid is still not out and the puppy is still sputtering, take the next step. Wrap the pup in the rough washcloth and—grasping it under the chest and hindquarters—raise it above head level and then swing it down between your legs to try and give centrifugal force a chance to expel the fluid. Hold the puppy face down during this maneuver. Be firm but gentle—never do this violently. Repeat two or three times. This should do the trick. The heat in the bottom of the cardboard box should dry out any excess fluid.

As the time of whelping approaches, the bitch will have been giving all sorts of signs. In the last ten days her shape begins to change as the puppies drop down lower. She now begins to look like a stuffed sausage. As the fateful day approaches, she will seem restless and be unable to settle down for any length of time. She acts as though she can't get comfortable. She will also want to keep you in her sight. She may or may not show an interest in the whelping box. Some bitches go to it, sniff around and walk away, while others lie in it and occasionally dig it up. Take her temperature on a regular basis as she grows more restless.

A reading of 101.5 is normal for a dog. Just before whelping she can take a sudden drop to about 98 degrees. Unless the temperature drops, it's pretty sure there will be no immediate action. Oh yes, just so there is no misunderstanding, this may not be a piece of cake. Most bitches whelp at night. There are exceptions to these rules—but, "Be Prepared." It's a good idea for someone to stay close by the whelping box to keep an eye on things. You can take turns as the time draws near.

The most important sign to look for after her temperature starts to drop is the breaking of the water sac. There will suddenly be a small pool of water around her. This is often referred to as "the water breaking." This means that real action is close at hand, at least in a matter of hours.

When her temperature goes down, alert the vet that a whelping is imminent and request that he stand by if any problems come up. Of course, being a well-prepared person, the vet was alerted at least a month ago that you might need his help. He was alerted, wasn't he!

If this is the bitch's first litter she may be a bit confused and frightened by all this. Pet her and tell her how wonderful she is. Get her over to the whelping box and make her comfortable. She may pace, she may dig or she may settle down. But, rest assured, she will probably do all three. She will also make everyone nervous. Allow things to proceed on their own. Don't panic! Let her go four or five hours *if she seems in no distress.* HOWEVER, if she goes into hard labor and has not delivered a puppy in a few hour's time, check with your vet. "Hard labor" means digging up papers, heavy panting, obvious straining followed by short rest periods. She may also issue large groans as she bears down. All this is normal if it is followed by the birth of a puppy.

As she bears down, sometimes standing in a defecating position, sometimes lying on her side, a blob will appear issuing from her vagina and with one big push, she will force it out. Usually she will reach back and break the sac, cut the umbilical cord with her teeth, and start to lick the puppy to stimulate a cry. If she does not do so immediately or if she seems confused you need to step in, cut the cord, and take the puppy out of the sac. Then clear its lungs and nose and give it back to its dam to stimulate.

Many dams will eat the afterbirth (the blueish/black blob attached to the sac the puppy came in). Let her eat a couple. It stimulates delivery of the next puppies. If she makes no move to do so, remove it and put it into a garbage pail. *Keep track of the afterbirths*—make sure they are all accounted for. A retained afterbirth can cause great harm to the bitch. In fact, once she has finished whelping, be sure to take her to the vet—to check her over and to make sure no afterbirths have been retained. The vet may give her a shot of pituitrin or a similar drug to induce the uterus to force out anything that's been retained.

Puppies may come one right after another or there can be hours between deliveries. Remember, as long as she does not seem in distress, any pattern can be considered normal. If labor persists for a prolonged time and no puppies are forthcoming, call the vet even though she has whelped one or more pupies already. You *may* have a problem. (For more detailed information on whelping, read *The Great American Dog Show Game*, by Alvin Grossman, published by Doral Publishing.)

The vet will probably advise bringing her to the clinic where he can examine her to determine her problem. In most cases, it is usually only a sluggish uterus and he will give her a shot to speed things along and send her home to whelp the rest of the puppies. On occasion, there is a problem and he might opt to do a Caesarean section—that is, take the rest of the puppies surgically. Usually he will perform this surgery immediately. Some bitches have a problem and cannot even push the puppies down into the birthing canal. The vet may take these puppies by C-section without having her try to go into serious labor. It's a good idea to have another small box, with a hot-water bottle in it, when you go to the vet so any puppies delivered there can be taken care of.

Mary Donnelly, writing in the March 1987 issue of *The Min Pin Monthly*, also says to take a crate along to bring the bitch home if she has to have a Caesarean.

If you feel the trip from the vet will take an hour or more, you may consider giving the puppies the opportunity to nurse before you leave the office. This will also help you see if you will have any problems introducing them to nursing. You can take a supply of formula with you in the event you have to feed or supplement them.

Once home, the dam should be your first concern. Position her on her side with her back flush against the side of the whelping box. Don't worry, she won't be going anywhere for several hours. With the pan of warm cleaning water, dip your disposable towel and clean any blood from her incision or vaginal area. Because she has had a C-section, she will bleed a bit more than she would from a normal birth. (In a normal birth, the bitch will have a blackish discharge at first turning to bright red shortly thereafter.) Those little pups won't take long learning to explore the dam so you must keep her clean until she can take over. If you will notice, her tongue is probably hanging from the side of her mouth. Take a bowl of clean water and dip a cloth in, squeeze most of the excess water back into the bowl and just moisten her tongue and mouth. Never put water into her mouth at this point. She could choke because her natural reflexes are on vacation because of the anesthetic.

Don't leave the puppies alone for too long a period. They will get cold and hungry. There are a number of things that need to be done promptly. Begin with the smallest ones. Use a toenail clipper and take the tips off their nails to preclude their causing problems with the stitches. Eliminate as much discomfort for the dam as possible. Once this is done, introduce the puppy to his dam. Let it sniff and try on its own to fit a teat to nurse. If the pup needs help, gently open its mouth and squeeze a bit of milk on the pup's tongue. (Even without a C-section some pups have to be shown how to nurse and others just dig right in.) If the puppy won't cooperate, go ahead and give it a bit of formula. Continue this process until all the puppies have had their toenails cut and have been fed.

It is important to remember *you* must do everything for the puppies. The bitch may be "out of it" anywhere from 6 to 12 hours . . . or more. This is normal. During the time she is helpless, someone must carefully watch her and care for the puppies at the same time. Hopefully there will be help and shifts can be rotated. If not, roll up your sleeves.

As soon as the puppies are fed and the bitch has been cleaned up again, help the pups to eliminate their waste. Dip a cotton ball in warm water, squeeze out most of the excess and gently rub it on their genitalia. This should produce urination. Do the same around the anal area for a bowel movement. (This doesn't always work for there is a "plug" in there that is a bit hard to intially dislodge.) If there is not initial success in getting a bowel movement, be patient and try tickling the anal area with a swab. If that doesn't work, don't be too alarmed for the dam will soon be awake and will take care of this.

Generally, most puppies are worn out by now and ready to curl up next to their dam and go to sleep . . . but you can count on one or two little brats to be obnoxious and climb on her or try to see what's on the other side of the box. Let them explore but try to convince them to stay in the heated area. The dam is not going to grab them and cuddle them, so you want to keep them warm. They expected life to be different and are finding out that their mother isn't doing her job. Go ahead and clean the bitch again while they explore and you cast longing eyes at the bed nearby. NO!! you can't go to sleep yet!

Try and moisten the bitch's mouth again. While taking care of business, be aware if the bitch feels cold to the touch. Once all the puppies have settled down for a nap, you can drape a light sheet over the dam and the puppies. (Do not attempt to do this with a dam who has not had a C-section.) Now it's possible to lay down. There is a specific way to lay down. (Why should this be easy?) Stretch out, but be sure you are close enough to the box so a hand can rest against the bitch. It is not advisable to fall asleep but since you are exhausted, it will happen anyway. The bitch will undoubtedly wait until you have just fallen asleep to wake up. (Just like she had her emergency C-section at 3:00 a.m.) Hopefully, you will feel her stir and awaken.

Just because she starts to stir does not mean she is anywhere close to being left alone. Do not not let her stand on her own right away. She is not in control. She may think she is but she could fall and injure herself and/or her puppies.

Usually the first time she stirs she will not need to relieve herself. She may, or may not, be interested in her litter. In most cases, she is going to be convinced to go back to sleep. Offer her a bit of water but not too much. Too much water at this time can cause nausea. Just about five good laps is all she needs. Be assured she needs cleaning again and the pups have been awakened and want to eat. So take care of this all over again.

Some dams will shake as they come awake. More often than not, this is caused by the anesthetic. This shaking can be slight or strong. In the event she shakes to the extent it could cause injury to the puppies, calm her by petting and covering the puppies a bit away from her. If at any time the shaking is too much, or there is a concern for any reason, call the veterinarian.

When the bitch really becomes restless she won't be talked into going back to sleep. Try to judge by the control she exhibits as to how stable she is. Take her outside when she becomes too restless. On her first trip, carry her. Place her in a safe area and be ready to assist her should she fall.

The rest of the recovery consists of your attention to the dam and the safety of her and her litter. If you are patient and see her through her "time of need," she will eventually ease you right out of a job.

Now, whether the puppies have arrived normally or by C-section, they are pursuing normal puppy behavior. Their primary concerns are keeping warm and being fed. A healthy dam will be able to take care of those needs. Be sure to keep a keen eye on both the dam and the puppies; watch for signs of distress . . . crying, being unable to settle down, and/or looking bloated—all portend trouble for the puppies. Call the vet. Watch the bitch to see if her discharge turns from a blackish color to bright red. See if she has milk and if the puppies can nurse from her. It is *extremely* important to stay vigilant for the next three weeks. It's a critical time.

There are times, however, when you may be faced with either losing the dam through complications from whelping or she cannot nurse her puppies due to a variety of reasons. YOU are now the mother and must deal with these orphaned puppies. Times like these test the mettle of any dog breeder. R.K. Mohrman, Director of the Pet Nutrition and Care Center at the Ralston Purina Company has some sage advice when you find yourself in this predicament.

Several critical problems must be addressed in caring for orphan puppies. Among these are chilling, dehydration and hypoglycemia. These problems are interrelated and may exist concurrently. Close observation and prompt attention if any of these problems develop are essential to survival. Of course, proper feeding of the orphan puppies is extremely important. A veterinarian should examine the puppies to determine if special therapy is needed.

Chilling

Chilling in newborn puppies (as described in the chapter Problems of Early Puppyhood) can lead to significant mortality. A puppy will dissipate far more body heat per pound of body weight than an adult dog. The normal newborn puppy depends on radiant heat from the bitch to help maintain its body temperature. In the absence of the bitch, various methods of providing heat can be used, such as: incubators, heating pads, heat lamps or hot water bottles.

Rectal temperatures in a newborn puppy range from 95 to 99°F (Fahrenheit) for the first week, 97 to 100°F for the second and third weeks, and reach the normal temperature of an adult dog (100.5 to

102.5°F) by the fourth week.

When the rectal temperature drops below 94°F, the accompanying metabolic alterations are life-threatning. Therefore, immediate action is necessary to provide the warmth the puppy needs to survive. A healthy newborn can survive chilling if warmed slowly.

During the first four days of its life, the orphan puppy should be maintained in an environmental temperature of 85 to 90°F. The temperature may gradually be decreased to 80°F by the seventh to tenth day and to 72°F by the end of the fourth week. If the litter is large, the temperature need not be as high. As puppies huddle together, their body heat provides additional warmth.

CAUTION: *Too rapid warming of a chilled puppy may result in its death.*

Dehydration

The lack of regular liquid intake or the exposure of the puppy to a low humidity environment can easily result in dehydration. The inefficiency of the digestion and metabolism of a chilled puppy may also lead to dehydration and other serious changes.

Experienced breeders can detect dehydration by the sense of touch. Two signs of dehydration are the loss of elasticity in the skin and dry and sticky mucous membranes in the mouth. If dehydration is severe or persistent, a veterinarian should be contacted immediately

An environmental relative humidity of 55 to 65 percent is adequate to prevent drying of the skin in a normal newborn puppy. However, a relative humidity of 85 to 90 percent is more effective in maintaining puppies if they are small and weak.

CAUTION: *The environmental temperature should not exceed 90°F when high humidity is provided. A temperature of 95°F coupled with relative humidity of 95 percent can lead to repiratory distress.*

Feeding

Total nutrition for the newborn orphans must be supplied by a bitch-milk replacer until the pups are about three weeks of age. At this age, the pups are ready to start nibbling moistened solid food.

Bitch-milk replacers are:
1. Commercial bitch-milk replacers, *e.g.* Esbilac, Vetalac, etc.
2. Emergency home-formulated bitch-milk replacer:
   1 cup milk
   1 tablespoon corn oil
   Salt (a pinch)
   1 drop high-quality oral multiple vitamins for dogs
   3 egg yolks (albumin)
   Blend mixture uniformly
3. Purina Puppy Chow brand dog food: 20 grams (2/3 oz. by weight) or 1/4-cup (8 oz. measure). Water: 80 grams (2-2/3 ounces by weight) or 1/4-cup (8 ounce measure). Blend into a soft gruel. Other formulas are to be found in the chapter Nutrition for Puppies and Adults.

Food Temperature

Since the newborn may have trouble generating enough heat to maintain its body temperature, the milk replacer should be warmed to 95-100°F for the best results. As the puppies grow older, the replacer can be fed at room temperature.

Feeding Methods

Spoon-feeding is slow and requires great patience. Each spoonful must be slowly "poured" into the puppy's mouth to prevent liquid from entering the lungs. The pup's head must not be elevated, or the lungs may fill with fluids. Newborn pups usually do not have a "gag" reflex to signal this.

Dropper-feeding accomplishes the same result as spoon-feeding but it is somewhat cleaner and generally speedier.

Baby bottles with premature infant-size nipples can be used for some puppies. Some doll-size bottles with high-quality rubber nipples are even better. Bottle-feeding is preferable to spoon or dropper-feeding but is less satisfactory than tube-feeding. Tube-feeding is the easiest, cleanest and most efficient way of hand-feeding.

The following equipment is needed for tube-feeding:

Syringe: 10 to 50 ml., preferably plastic

Tubing: No. 10 catheter or small, semi-rigid tube that can easily be passed into the puppy's stomach. (Consult your veterinarian.)

Adhesive tape: To mark the depth of the tube in the puppy's stomach.

Disinfectant: To flush tube and syringe after each feeding. (Be sure to rinse thoroughly after disinfecting.)

1. Mark the tube. The feeding tube should extend into the puppy's stomach but not far enough to cause either pressure or perforation. Measure the tube alongside the puppy's body on the outside. (Tube should extend almost to the far end of the ribcage.) Place tape on the tube to mark the correct distance of the insertion. As the puppy grows, the tape can be moved so the tube can be inserted further.
2. Fill the syringe and expell all the air.
3. Hold the puppy horizontally, with the head extended but not raised, so the tube will slide into the esophagus. This helps keep fluids from entering the lungs.
4. Moisten the tube with a few drops of milk replacer for lubrication. Insert the tube gently through the mouth, throat and esophagus into the stomach. If the puppy struggles, withdraw the tube and try again. Do not force it.
5. Gently inject syringe contents into the stomach. If a slight resistance is met, the stomach is probably full. Withdraw the tube.
6. Massage the genital and anal area with a moist cotton cloth to stimulate excretion. Stimulating the pups following each feeding teaches the pup to defecate.

Amount To Feed

Puppies being fed by spoon, dropper or bottle reject food when they are full. When tube-feeding, care must be taken not to overfeed, since fluid can be drawn into the pup's lungs. When adequate liquid has been injected into the pup the syringe plunger will become more difficult to push as resistance to flow increases.

In establishing the amount to feed a newborn puppy check the recommendations in the chapter on Nutrition in Puppies and Adults. Basically, a one pound puppy (when fed four times a day) should consume 21 cc per feeding.

Some puppies, during their first feedings, cannot handle the determined amount per feeding. More than the scheduled four feedings may be necessary for the appropriate caloric intake.

Monitor the pup's weight and continue to adjust the pup's intake proportionally throughout the use of milk replacer formula.

CAUTION: *Diarrhea is a common digestive disorder in very young puppies. Consult your veterinarian if diarrhea develops, as alterations in the feeding program may be necessary.*

Feeding Schedule

Three meals, equally spaced during a 24-hour period are ample for feeding puppies when adequate nutrients are provided. Four or more daily feedings may be necessary if the puppies are small. Tube- and hand-feeding can generally be ended by the third week and certainly by the fourth. By this time, the puppy can consume food, free-choice, from a dish.

Cleaning Puppies

As has been stated earlier in this chapter and elsewhere, the puppy's genital and anal areas must be stimulated after feeding to effect urination. Use a moist cloth or a piece of cotton to do this. This cleaning should continue for the first two weeks. If you do not do this, the puppy may suffer from constipation.

Bowl Feeding

By two-and-one-half to three weeks, the puppies can start to eat food from the dish along with the bitch-milk replacer.

A gruel can be made by thoroughly moistening dry puppy food with water to reach the consistency of a thick milkshake. The mixture must not be sloppy, or the puppies will not consume very much. As the consumption of supplemental food increases, the amount of water can be decreased.

By four weeks, orphaned puppies can consume enough moistened solid food to meet their needs.

It is better to avoid starting puppies on a meat-milk-baby food regimen. This creates extra work and can also create finicky eaters. Many times such foods will not meet the nutritional needs of growing puppies.

Size and Sex of a Litter

It is helpful to understand how the size and sex of a litter is determined. One of the most informative and entertaining articles I have read on the subject was written by Patricia Gail Burnham, a Greyhound breeder from Sacramento, California. Her article "Breeding, Litter Size and Gender" appeared in an issue of the *American Cocker Review* and I will attempt to paraphrase the information so that it is most applicable.

The number of puppies in a litter at whelping time is determined by several different factors. The order in which they occur, are:

1. The number of ova (gametes) produced by the dam;
2. The number of ova that are successfully fertilized and implanted in the uterus;
3. The prenatal mortality rate among the embryos while they are developing.

It is not possible to end up with more puppies than the number of ova that the bitch produces. As a bitch ages, the number of ova will often decrease. Bitches don't manufacture ova on demand the way a male dog can manufacture sperm. All the ova a bitch will ever have are stored in her ovaries.

In each season some of them will be shed (ovulated) into her uterus for a chance at fertilization. Elderly bitches quite commonly produce two or three puppy litters. Sometimes, just living hard can have the same effect on a bitch as old age.

If a bitch does produce a large number of ova, what happens next? The ova need to be fertilized. If they are not fertilized, or if they are fertilized and not implanted, they will perish. If a bitch ovulates over an extended period of time and she is bred late in her season, then the ova which were produced early may have died unfertilized before the sperm could reach them, and the result can be a small litter.

Sometimes there is a noticeable difference in birth weight. It is a good idea not to consider the small ones runts. They may have been conceived a few days later than their larger litter mates and may grow up to be average-sized adults.

All the puppies in a litter are never conceived simultaneously, since all the ova are not released at once. Ovulation takes place over an extended period, so at birth some of the puppies may be 59 days old while others may be 64 days old. A few days' difference in puppies of this age can create noticeable differences in size.

The mature size of a dog is determined by its heredity and its nutrition. Its size at birth is determined by the size of its dam, the number of puppies in the litter, and their individual dates of conception. The small puppies could just be more refined than the others and could always be smaller. Only time will tell.

The sire is always responsible for the sex of the offspring. The rule applies equally to people and dogs. While dams are often blamed for not producing males, they have nothing to do with the sex of their offspring. If the bitch determined the sex of the offspring, then all the puppies would be bitches, because the only chromosomes that a bitch can contribute to her offspring are those that she and every female has, homozygous (XX) sex chromosomes.

What's the difference between boys and girls? It's not sugar and spice and puppy dog's tails. It's the makeup of their sex chromosomes. All of the chromosome pairs are matched to each other with the exception of one pair. Dogs (and people) each have one pair of chromosomes that may or may not match. This is the chromosome pair that determines sex. Sex chromosomes may be either X chromosomes (which are named for their shape) or X chromosomes that are missing one leg, which makes them Y chromosomes (again named for their shape).

All females have two homozygous X chromosomes. They are XX genetically. All males are heterozygous (unmatched). They have one X and one Y chromosome to be XY genetically.

In each breeding, all ova contain an X chromosome, which is all a female can donate, while the sperm can contain either an X or a Y chromosome. If the X-carrying ovum is fertilized by an X-carrying sperm, then the result is female (XX). If the X-carrying ovum is fertilized by a Y-carrying sperm, then the result is a male (XY).

What influences whether an X- or a Y-carrying sperm reaches the ovum to fertilize it? The Y chromosome is smaller and lighter weight than the X chromosome. This enables the Y chromosome-carrying (male) sperm to swim faster than the heavier X-carrying (female) sperm. This gives the males an edge in the upstream sprint to reach the ovum that is waiting to be fertilized.

As a result, slightly more than 50% of the fertilized ova are male. More males are conceived than females. However, things even up, because males have a higher mortality rate than females, both in the womb and later.

What if ova are not ready and waiting when the sperm arrive? If sperm have to wait in the uterus or fallopian tubes for an ovum to arrive, then the odds change. Female sperm live longer than male ones. As the wait increases, the males die off and leave the female sperm waiting when the ovum arrives.

This is the reason that some breeders advise breeding as early as the bitch will stand to maximize the chance for female puppies. The idea is to breed—if she will allow it—before the bitch ovulates. This allows the male sperm time to die off and leaves the female sperm waiting when the ova arrive. Whether this has a basis in fact is not known.

What can influence the number of males and females in a litter other than the time of the breeding? The age of the sire can influence the gender of the puppies. As a stud dog ages, all his sperm slow down. Instead of a sprint, the race to fertilize the ova becomes an endurance race in which the female sperm's greater lifespan and hardiness can offset the male sperm's early speed advantage. When they are both slowed down, then the male sperm's higher mortality rate gives the female sperm the advantage.

With the information gleaned from this section on Becoming A Breeder, you should have the knowledge to breed good ones and to be a successful exhibitor. Now it's up to you to put into practice what you have learned. Good luck!

CHAPTER 10

Nutrition for Puppies and Adults

Nutrition of dogs can be maintained at a high level through the use of good commercial diets. It is not necessary for the owner to be an expert in nutrition, but some background in this science is helpful in understanding the problems that may be encountered in the normal care of your dog.

Dog food is generally prepared in one of two ways; dry and canned. Dry food is usually cooked cereal and meat blended together. The cereal grains need to be cooked or heated to improve digestibility. Fats are added to increase calories; vitamins and minerals are added as needed. Dry foods contain about 10% moisture.

A subject frequently discussed among "dog people" is the addition of supplements to commercially prepared dog foods. But supplements are usually unneccessary because major dog food manufacturers incorporate into their products all the protein, vitamins, minerals, and other nutrients dogs are known to need. The diet may be specific for a particular life stage such as adult maintenance or growth, or it may be shown as complete and balanced for all stages of life. When it is fed to normal dogs of any breed, no additional supplementation in the forms of vitamins, minerals, meats or other additives is needed.

Dry meals are usually pelleted, sprayed with oil and crumbled. Biscuit and kibbled foods are baked on sheets and then kibbled or broken into small bits. Expanded foods are mixed, cooked and forced through a die to make nuggets which are then expanded with steam, dried and coated with oil. Food to be expanded must be at least 40% carbohydrates or the expansion process will not work.

Soft-moist foods, which are considered dry foods, contain about 25% moisture. They can be stored in cellophane without refrigeration due to the added preservatives.

Canned foods come in four types:
1. "Ration" types are usually the cheapest and are a mix of cereals, meat products, fats, etc. to make a complete diet containing 50–70% water.
2. All animal tissue may be beef, chicken, horsemeat, etc. Generally this type is not balanced although some may add supplements. These are

sometimes used to improve palatability of dry foods.

3. "Chunk" style has meat by-products ground and extruded into pellets or chunks. Some of the cheaper ones have vegetable matter mixed in. A gravy or juice is added.
4. "Stews" are meat or chunks mixed with vegetables.

Nutritional Requirements

The exact nutritional requirements of any dog are complicated by the wide variation in size, hair coat, activity, etc. Diets can be suggested based on body weight, but the final determination must be based on how the individual responds to the diet. Gain or loss in weight, change in activity, etc. must be observed and some adjustments made.

WHEN TO SUPPLEMENT. There are generally two exceptions to the rule that supplementation is not necessary when dogs receive a complete and balanced commercial diet. These instances are: (1) to correct a specific deficiency due to the dog's inability to utilize the normal level of a particular nutrient, and (2) to stimulate food intake, particularly during periods of hard work or heavy lactation. This includes hard-working dogs such as bird dogs or sled dogs and bitches with large litters that require a high level of milk production. The addition of 10% to 20% meat or meat by-products to the diet will normally increase food acceptance and as a result will increase food intake. At this level of supplementation, the nutritional balance of the commercial product would not be affected.

WATER. Fresh and clean water should be available at all times. The amount of water needed is dependent upon the type of food provided (dry, canned, semi-soft, etc.), but generally a dog gets 25% of its total water requirements from drinking.

PROTEIN. Ten of the approximately twenty amino acids that make up protein are essential for the dog. The dog must receive adequate amounts of these ten proteins for good nutrition. The natural sources containing these ten are milk, eggs, meat and soybeans. Sources such as gelatin, flour and wheat are incomplete.

Also important is the ratio of nitrogen retained to the amount of nitrogen taken into the body. In this respect, eggs, muscle meat and organ meat are all good. Some legumes such as soybeans are only fair. Most other vegetative proteins are poor. As dogs get older, this vegetative type of food tends to overwork the kidneys. This is especially important with chronic kidney disease in old dogs. More dog food companies produce products for each stage in a dogs life—from puppyhood to old age and including special diets for lactating bitches.

Another important aspect of protein is digestibility. A good quality dry ration has about 75% digestibility, while canned foods are up to

95%. Some typical figures for digestibility are:

Horsemeat	91%	Meat scraps	75–86%
Fishmeal	99%	Soybean meal	86%
Liver meal	88%	Linseed meal	81%

The dog's utilization of protein is dependent upon both the biological value and the digestibility. The digestibility of protein in the dog is related to the temperature to which the protein is subjected during processing. Some dog foods that seem to have proper ingredients at the time they are mixed, can give disappointing results. This may well be due to the processing at high temperatures or heating for long periods of time.

It is generally recommended that the dietary crude protein for adult dogs be 18 to 25% on a dry basis. For example, if a canned food is 12% protein and has a 50% moisture content then it is really 24% protein on a "dry basis." If the protein is of high quality, such as from milk, eggs, and meat, the total needed would be less than if it contains substantial amounts of the vegetative proteins.

FAT. Fats and oils have an important effect on palatability. A small increase in fat in a diet may greatly increase its acceptability to the dog. Fats supply essential fatty acids, particularly linolenic and arachidonic acids. Pork fat is an excellent source of these essential fatty acids. Other sources are animal fats, corn oil, olive oil, and raw linseed oil. A dietary deficiency of the essential fatty acids leads to defective growth, dry hair, scaly skin, and susceptibility to skin infections.

The absorption of vitamins A, D, E, and K is associated with the absorption of fats. Rancid fat destroys vitamins A and E. Extended use of rancid fats can cause hair loss, rash, loss of appetite, constipation progressing to diarrhea and even death. Commercial dog foods must therefore use an antioxidant to retard rancidity.

The principal danger of excess fat in the diet is that it contains more energy than is needed and leads to storage of fat and obesity.

CARBOHYDRATES. Requirements for carbohydrates in the dog are not known. The dog can utilize as much as 65 to 70% in his diet. Since this is the cheapest source of energy, it composes the major part of commercial foods. Carbohydrates are well utilized if properly prepared. Potatoes, oats and corn are poorly utilized unless cooked. High levels of uncooked starch can cause diarrhea. Milk can upset some dogs as some do not have the lactase enzyme needed to digest lactose, the milk sugar. Fresh cow's milk is 50% lactose. In some dogs, a ration with as much as 10% dried skim milk may cause diarrhea.

FIBER. Fiber is also a part of the carbohydrate portion of the ration. It is only slightly digested. Some fibers absorb water and produce a more voluminous stool. This can help stimulate intestinal action, especially in old or inactive animals. Fiber aids in the prevention of constipation and other intestinal problems. Most foods have 1 to 8% fiber. Reducing diets may have as much as 32% fiber. Sources of fiber are cellulose, bran, beet pulp, and string beans.

GROSS ENERGY. Dogs expend energy in every form of body activity. This energy comes from food or from destruction of body sources. Carbohydrates and fats provide the main source of energy for dogs. Caloric requirements are greater per pound of body weight for small dogs than for large dogs. From Table IV-2, determine the number of calories per pound of body weight a puppy requires for his age. For example, a ten-week old puppy weighing 10 lbs. would require 650 calories per day. At twelve weeks and weighing 15 lbs. he would need 840 calories daily. Divide the number of calories contained in one pound of feed into the number of calories required by the puppy on a daily basis to determine how much to offer the puppy initially. Using the example: At ten weeks, he requires 650 calories per day. Divide this by 690 (the number of calories in one pound of a popular dry puppy food) and the answer is approximately 1.0 lbs.

There are various theories on how often to feed a dog. The *Gaines Basic Guide To Canine Nutrition* establishes this schedule: Up to 5 months feed 3 times daily; from 5 to 12 months feed twice daily; over 12 months feed twice daily for the rest of the dog's life.

Divide the amount of food needed each day into the appropriate number of feedings to determine the amount of food to give the puppy at each feeding. For example: For a twelve-week old pup, the appropriate number of feedings per day is three. Divide the puppy's 1 lb of food into 3 servings of 1/3 lb. each.

Russel V. Brown writing in the February 1987 issue of *The Basenji*, points out "While caloric needs vary with age and activity, a rule of thumb is that for dogs of 5 to 65 lbs. the need is $S(33-1/4 X) = kcal/$ day. In this case "X" is the body weight in pounds. A 20-lb. dog would work out as $20(33-20/4) = 20(28) = 560$ kcals per day. For dogs over 65 lbs., the formula is $18X = kcal/day$. The following adjustments are recommended:

    a. Age adjustments
       1. add 10% for dogs 1 year of age
       2. add 30% for dogs 6 months of age
       3. add 60% for dogs 3 months of age

    b. Activity variable
       1. add 25% for moderate activity
       2. add 60% for heavy activity (hunting or coursing)

Daily Caloric Needs of Puppies

Weeks	1	2	3	4	5	10	15	20	25	30	40	50	60	70
5	100	200	300	400	500	1000	1500							
6	90	180	270	360	450	900	1350							
7	80	160	240	320	400	800	1200							
8	75	150	225	300	375	750	1125	1500						
9	70	140	210	280	350	700	1050	1400						
10		130	195	260	325	650	975	1300	1625					
11			180	240	300	600	900	1200	1500	1680				
12				224	280	550	840	1128	1400	1560				
13				208	260	520	780	1040	1300	1440	1920			
14					240	480	720	960	1200	1350	1800			
15						450	675	900	1125	1260	1680	2100		
16						420	630	840	1050	1170	1560	1950		
17							585	780	975	1080	1440	1800	2160	
18								720	900	990	1320	1650	1980	
19									825	900	1280	1500	1800	2100

To determine the number of calories needed by a particular puppy, find the dog's weight in the top row of numbers and move downward until you come to the line corresponding to the dog's age. The figure in the spot where the two lines intersect is the number of calories that puppy needs during a 24-hour period.

Table IV-2. Daily Caloric Needs of Puppies

c. Pregnancy and lactation
  1. from conception to whelping—increase 20%
  2. at whelping—increase 25%
  3. 2nd week of lactation—increase 50%
  4. 3rd week of lactation—increase 75%
  5. 4th week of lactation—increase 100%

Authors Note: "Kcal" is the scientific term for what laymen call calorie."

Some find that the portion-control methods such as the feeding schedule listed above is inconvenient. They opt for the self-feeding method which is also called the free-choice method. Free choice ensures that the puppy's food consumption correlates with his rate of growth. The idea behind free-choice feeding is that it provides reasonable assurance that the puppy is obtaining all he needs for growth, even though these needs are essentially changing.

Free-choice advocates believe that dogs generally know quite accurately what their needs are and eat accordingly. (This is generally true.) Free-choice works especially well for the pup who dawdles over his food for hours. A slight variation on the free-choice scheme is to feed the pup all he can eat in a specified time period, usually 20 minutes. The pup would be fed for those time periods a certain number of times a day. This timed method may not be suitable for the slow or picky eater (or the glutton) for that matter. Studies have indicated that free-choice eaters tend to turn out heavier by some 23% and that these weight differences were principally in body fat.

Other controlled studies have proven that overfeeding can cause skelatal problems. When overfed, puppies may develop hip dysplasia (a disintegration of the ball and socket joint) more often, earlier, and more severely, than littermates who were fed less. Breeds larger in size are particularly vulnerable to these skeletal defects.

If in doubt on how much to feed, slight underfeeding is preferable to overfeeding. Studies have shown no serious effects from slight underfeeding. On the contrary, when obesity develops through overfeeding, the number of fat cells increase in the puppy. Facts prove that the chance of a dog being obese as an adult has its roots in overfeeding as a puppy.

Regardless of the feeding method used, food should be served lukewarm or at room temperature. If the food is prepared with an ingredient that can spoil quickly, such as meat or milk, be sure to serve fresh food only.

Estimating Caloric Content

In determining how much to feed a dog, use the following:

a. Dry food usually contains about 1360 calories per pound.

b. Canned food can be estimated at 475 calories per pound.

MINERALS. Calcium and phosphorus are needed in a ratio of 1.2 parts calcium to 1 part phosphorous. A deficiency causes rickets and other less serious diseases. Young and old dogs need additional calcium. Common sources are bone meal, skim milk, and alfalfa leaf meal. Sources of phosphorous are bone meal and meat scraps. Vitamin D is necessary for proper utilization of the calcium and phosphorous.

Magnesium is needed for bones and teeth—bone meal is a good source. Sodium chloride should be in the diet as 1% salt. Sulphur and potassium are needed, and are usually in the foods dogs eat. Iron's best sources are liver and eggs. A strict vegetarian diet will cause iron deficiency. Trace minerals (copper, cobalt, manganese, zinc, and iodine) are contained in milk, liver and egg yolks for copper, in fish scraps for iodine and most other foods contain the rest.

VITAMINS. Vitamin A is important to vision, bone growth and skin health. Deficiency may cause lack of appetite, poor growth, excessive shedding, lowered resistance to disease and infection etc. Severe deficiency can cause deafness in dogs. On the other hand, too much is harmful and can cause birth defects, anorexia, weight loss and bone problems.

Vitamin D deficiencies are most often found in large breeds. Deficiencies cause rickets in the young and softening of the bones in adults, and irregular teeth development or eruption. Sources of vitamin D are sunlight, irradiated yeast, fish liver oils and egg yolks. Too much vitamin D can cause anorexia, calcification, and other problems.

Vitamin E deficiency may involve reproductive and lactation problems. It may be involved in muscular dystrophy. Natural sources are corn oil, wheat germ oil, fish and egg yolk. It seems to be of some value topically in wound healing.

Vitamin K is involved in blood clotting. It is found in egg yolk, liver and alfalfa. Most dogs can synthesize enough in the intestines.

Thiamine deficiency causes anorexia, weight loss, dehydration, paralysis, and convulsions. Over-heating during the processing of dog food destroys thiamine. It is also commonly destroyed if dry food is stored in a hot location, such as a feed store without adequate cooling facilities. Best natural sources are raw liver, wheat germ and brewer's yeast. High-carbohydrate diets (particularly bread and potatoes) increase the need for thiamine. Fats may decrease the need.

Riboflavin, niacin and pyridoxine are all B vitamins found in liver, wheat germ, leafy vegatables, yeast and milk. Riboflavin deficiency can cause dry scaly skin, muscular weakness, abnormal redness of hindlegs and chest due to capillary congestion, anemia, and sudden death. Niacin deficiency can lead to pellagia or black tongue disease with oral ulcers. Pyridoxine deficiency can also cause anemia.

Choline deficiency causes fatty liver. Best sources are liver, yeast and soybean oil.

Biotin deficiency causes posterior paralysis and seborrhea. Raw egg whites contain a substance that ties up biotin. A diet of all raw egg whites should not be fed. Natural sources are liver and yeast.

B-12 is important in blood formation. Dogs used in heavy work need a good supply. Dogs produce B-12 in their intestines and when given foods that have enough B-12, can function adequately. Large doses of antibiotics may stop this synthesis. Best sources are liver, milk, cheese, eggs and meat.

Vitamin C (ascorbic acid) deficiency may cause delayed wound healing and scurvy-type lesions of the mouth and gums, loose teeth, bloody diarrhea, and tender joints. Generally the bacteria in the gut produce sufficient C. However, intestinal problems can effect the amount produced.

Table IV-3. Milk from the Lactating Bitch

	Bitch	Evaporated Milk	Cow
Fat	8.3%	6.6%	4.0%
Protein	7.5%	5.8%	3.5%
Lactose	3.7%	8.2%	4.9%
Calories	1.2	1.15	0.68

The 7.5% protein in bitches milk is equivalent to 30% dry dog food, but is probably all digestible. Dry dog food protein is only about 80% digestible unless it comes from a meat or fish source. A pup must consume twice as much cow's milk to get the protein of bitches' milk, but would then get three times as much lactose sugar which it has difficulty digesting. As a result, pups frequently have diarrhea on cow's milk. Non-fat dry milk is even worse for without the fat the percentage of lactose is even greater. (For more information on feeding the bitch, see chapter on The Bitch and Her Puppies.)

Weaning Puppies

It's a good idea to feed puppies a diet of 115 calories for each pound of their body weight three to four times a day. Begin to wean them at four to seven weeks of age. Seven to ten days should see the puppies no longer dependent on their mother. Often the dam will begin to wean the puppies on her own. During the weaning process, take the dam away during the day for gradually longer periods of time. Feed them three times a day. Puppies often gulp a lot of air when learning to eat solid foods. Slow them down by spreading out the food in a large pan. Chopped meat and small kibble may be better than finely ground meal because it passes through the intestines more slowly, causing fewer digestive problems.

Feeding Older Puppies

The first step in any puppy's feeding program is to weigh him. From birth through six months the breeder should weigh and record each pup's growth weekly.

The next step is to determine the diet to be fed. This depends, in a large measure, on the stage of growth the puppy has reached. Young puppies require twice as much energy per unit of body weight as an adult dog. But feeding the rapidly-growing puppy twice as much food of the adult variety is not the answer. The diet must include a protein with high net protein utilization value. This is because the puppy's digestive tract is immature and cannot fully digest and utilize the energy and nutrients which adult foods include. The total need for all nutrients is double for a puppy, and the nutrients must be in an easily digestible form.

When acquiring a puppy from a breeder be sure to find out the details of his feeding program. The breeder should provide you with the type of food the pup is used to, the feeding times and the amount of food to be fed. Whether you agree with the program or not, duplicate it for several days until the pup is accustomed to his new surroundings.

After the puppy is settled, don't hesitate to change food or feeding methods if there is a need to do so. Using the information above, use good judgment in selecting the commercial dog food best suited to his size and needs. Make the change in his diet gradual so as not to cause diarrhea. Dry food is the most popular because it is normally most convenient, feed efficient, and economical.

Be sure to choose a high quality dog food. Not only will it be better for the dog's health but it will also require less food to meet his nutritional needs. Don't be misled by how much the puppy eats, it's the performance of the food that counts. A lower quality food is also less digestible and will result in the puppy eating more to compensate; the increased food eaten will further reduce the digestibility of the food.

Don't try to save money by feeding maintenance, or low-quality foods. The pup can't possibly eat all he would need to meet his requirements for growth. The puppy will end up with a pot-bellied appearance, slower growth, poor muscle and bone development and less resistance to disease and parasites.

Regardless of the form of commercial dog food used, Donald R.

Collins, DVM, author of *The Collins Guide To Dog Nutrition*, believes every growing puppy should have liver in his diet. Liver is a good source of most of the good things an animal needs. It can be fed chopped, raw, or slightly braised. To avoid giving the puppy diarrhea, feed small amounts at first and gradually increase to no more than 10% of his total diet.

Catering to a dog's nutritional needs is one thing; catering to his nutritional desires is yet another. Do not permit a puppy to dictate his food preferences.This reverses the positions of authority and can cause training problems as well. It could also create nutritional deficiencies.

The goal should be that by the time a pup has reached maturity, his digestive system should be capable of handling all the foods he will eat during his adult life. This programs should help him to reach the average (as stipulated in the breed standard) height and weight. A great deal of time, effort, and money will—no doubt—be invested in this young prospective puppy. Many hopes and dreams may be fulfilled through him; help him to fulfill those aspirations by providing him with the best possible feeding program.

And when he reaches adulthood, continue feeding him a well-balanced nutritious diet. The payback is a healthy, handsome dog.

Material for the content of this chapter is drawn from three main sources: (1) "Nutrition and Feeding of Basenjis," by Russel V. Brown which appeared in the February 1987 issue of *The Basenji*; (2) "Feeding Your Puppy," by Ann Bierman which appeared in the March 1987 issue of *Golden Retriever Review*; and, (3) "Supplementation—May Be Hazardous to Your Pet's Health" by R.K. Mohrman published in the March/April 1980 issue of the *Great Dane Reporter*.

CHAPTER **11**

Problems of Early Puppyhood

Breeding and raising puppies is a complex process. There are many factors that decide how puppies will turn out. Will they survive the embryonic stage only to fall victim to the myriad diseases of puppyhood? Often a puppy has no control over its own destiny. The health of the dam, the presence of parasites, the cleanliness of the environment and the quality of care his dam and breeders give to him, are all controlling factors in whether he survives. Whether or not a puppy develops along normal lines either before or after birth depends entirely on its environment and the hereditary characteristics and tendencies which have been handed down by its parents. Puppies which are fed inadequate, unbalanced diets not only fail to grow properly but also develop nutritional diseases and structural distortions such as anemia, rickets, etc. The diet provided his dam and that provided for the growing puppy constitutes part of his environment. If the diet is unsuitable, the puppy's environment is unfavorable for proper development.

Nursing

Bruce R. Wittels, DVM, writing in the January/February 1985 issue of the *Great Dane Reporter* states:

The ability to nurse is the most important factor in determining whether a newborn pup will survive the first few hours and days of life. Nursing ability depends upon the maturity of the litter, body temperature and adequate lung function. If a bitch is underfed or improperly nourished before and during pregnancy, the likelihood of premature whelping is greatly increased. This leads to underdevelopment of the lungs and therefore failure of the lungs to fully oxygenate the blood. This limited respiratory capacity causes a decreased nursing time due to more time needed for breathing. With a premature whelping there is a lack of subcutaneous fat on the newborn and as a result a decreased body temperature and chilling. Because of this, energy is expended to keep the body as warm as possible and less energy is available for nursing. Diminished nursing ability is directly caused by chilling with lack of energy secondary. Therefore, it is important not to let the litter become chilled no matter what the cause.

There are other diseases, cited later in this chapter, other than malnutrition of the bitch, that affect the nursing ability of the newly born.

It is very important that the pups suckle within the first few hours. The ingestion of nutrients gives them energy and strength since they are no longer being nourished by the placenta. Colostrum is only present in the mammary glands for four to six hours and nursing during this time provides maternal immunity to many viral and bacterial diseases. The puppy acquires some maternal immunity via the placenta during pregnancy, but the most important acquistion is by the ingestion of colostrum. If a pup isn't nursing, it must be placed on a nipple and encouraged to do so. It may be necessary to milk the bitch and force feed the pup. If all efforts are unsuccessful, put the pup on antibiotics, watch it closely, and keep it confined until it can be started on a series of adult vaccines.

Most people know that at six weeks of age their dogs need to be vaccinated, but apparently what isn't known is which vaccines are given. Almost all puppies seen in my practice that have previously been vaccinated have been given an adult vaccine at six weeks of age; i.e. distemper, hepatitis, leptospirosis, and parvovirus combination—this is not proper. If the bitch had previously been vaccinated, this vaccine has no beneficial effect and can do possible harm.

Colostrum contains many antibodies called immunoglobulins which function to destroy bacteria and viral infections to which a pup is exposed. These immunoglobulins last for approximately eight to ten weeks. If an adult vaccine is used at six weeks of age they act as foreign viruses and are destroyed by the antibodies of maternal immunity. This vaccine can be injurious to the animal if it is simultaneously being infected with the real disease entity. The specific immunoglobulins are then divided between destroying the real infection and the vaccine. If the viral strength is more than that of the antibodies, the body will succumb to the disease.

Many immunologists believe that six-week old dogs should be vaccinated with a human measles vaccine and a killed parvovirus vaccine. Human measles vaccine boosts the maternal immunity against canine distemper and does not challenge it. A killed parvovirus vaccine is used due to the lack of transmission of adequate antibodies from the bitch to properly protect the pups for more than six weeks. This vaccination will often help to stimulate the pups own immune system to produce antibodies against this potentially deadly virus.

Puppies should nurse for three to four weeks. During this nursing period the major emphasis is on nutrition of the mother, as well as all of the dietary needs of the litter which are derived from her. With a very large litter or if the dam is not producing enough milk, the diet should be supplemented with such milk replacements as Esbilac or Unilac. Generally, a pup should be gaining weight daily, at the rate of approximately one gram for each pound of body weight expected at maturity. However, attempts to over-supplement in order to reach this goal are highly inadvisable. The following table, abstracted from *Lab Report 2, #4 Neonatal Puppy Mortality* was prepared by the Cornell Research Laboratory, Veterinary Virus Research Institute, New York.

Weight Gain

Two-fold increase at 8–10 days
(1 gm. of expected adult weight/day)

Body Temperature

Week 1–2; 94–99°F
Week 2–4; 97–100°F

Water Requirements

2–3 oz./lb./day (newborn puppies)

Caloric Requirements

60–100 kcal/lb./day
(newborn puppies can become hypoglycemic if not fed every day)

Parasites

An unfavorable environment may seriously hinder normal development before birth as well as afterward. The prenatal environment provided for the growing embryo may be unsuitable because the mother has been improperly fed and cared for during pregnancy or because she is infested with worms. Even though nature will rob the mother to feed the unformed young, the puppies may be so lacking in vitality as the result of malnutrition that they are either born dead or die shortly after birth. Newborn puppies which are suffering from malnutrition are not necessarily skinny puppies. They may be well formed and appear to be healthy, but like adult dogs that have waxed fat from an unbalanced diet and lack of exercise, they may be anemic and so weak that they are unable to cope with the difficulties encountered during birth and unable to adjust themselves successfully to the new environment. Puppies which are born with worms acquired from their dam, may not show signs of illness until they are three or four weeks of age, when they may sicken and die very quickly. There are a number of worm infestations that a breeder needs to be concerned about. Table IV-4 illustrates the wide variety of internal parasites and the probability of infestation at any age by percent. People have misconceptions about internal parasites. Some think you can immunize dogs against them. Others apparently think that when parasites are removed that is the end of them. Yet others have the idea that when a dog reaches a year of age he is no longer susceptible to them. By studying the table you will see that there is no time in a dog's life when he is immune to parasites, but in certain cases—such as coccidiosis—he is more likely to be infected when he is quite young. Because information concerning the proper care of the bitch (see chapter on The Bitch and Her Puppies) during pregnancy and

Table IV-4. Estimated Probability of Intestinal Parasite Infestation at Any Age by Percent*

Age	Roundworms	Hookworms	Whipworms	Tapeworms Flea-Host	Rabbit-Host	Rivolta	Coccidiosis Bigemina	Felis
0–3 weeks	40	20	0	3	0	0	0	8
4–11 weeks	50	20	5	9	1	9	1	7
12–23 weeks	42	20	10	10	1	6	1	5
24–51 weeks	27	20	25	14	1	3	2	3
1 year	17	20	28	14	3	2	3	3
2 years	16	20	30	14	5	2	1	2
3 years	15	20	30	14	4	2	1	1
4 years	14	20	30	14	4	2	1	1
5 years	13	20	30	14	3	2	0	1
6 years	12	20	30	14	2	2	0	1
7 years	11	20	30	14	1	1	0	0
8 years	10	20	30	14	0	1	0	0
9 years	9	20	30	14	0	1	0	0
10–15 years	8	20	30	14	0	1	0	0

*Based on a study of 4,000 fecal examinations of Connecticut dogs.

From The Cocker Spaniel, by Leon F. Whitney, DVM, Practical Science Publishing Co.

the prevention of worm infestations is readily available today, malnutrition and parasites need not be major causes of puppy losses.

Injuries

Injuries recieved either before or after birth may result in the death of one or more puppies in a litter, in spite of the fact that every precaution may have been taken to prevent such injuries. In the case of a large litter (but even in a small or average size litter), the embryos may be crowded together too closely to allow for proper development, resulting in distortions or in the premature birth of small, weak puppies.

Carelessness on the part of a nervous or inexperienced bitch undoubtedly accounts for the loss of many puppies which are born alive and which appear to be strong and healthy at birth. Even the best of mothers may occasionaly sit or lie on a puppy, crushing or smothering it.

Pre-Natal Problems

The bitch's endocrine system—which is responsible for the secretions of such important glands as the thyroid, pituitary, adrenal and reproductive glands—may fail to work properly during pregnancy because of disease or hereditary factors, resulting in the arrested development or malformation of the embryos or in the premature birth of the litter. Abnormal functioning of the endocrine system may also cause various mating and whelping difficulties, such as dystocia (painful or delayed delivery), and lack of un adequate milk supply, which may account for puppy losses. If an inadequate amount of endocrine secretions (hormones) is produced within the unborn puppy itself, its development may be temporarily or permanently stopped at any stage. If development is arrested in the early stages, the partly-formed embryo or embyros affected may be aborted or reabsorbed by the bitch, or they may lie dormant in a "petrified" state awaiting the termination of gestation. If development is arrested in latter stages, the embryo may be born alive but malformed.

Many so-called "freaks" are the result of arrested development during the embryonic stage, resulting in such malformations as harelip, cleft palate, cleft abdomen, cleft skull, etc. All of the malformations are the result of the parts of the embryo failing to unite properly during development. If this failure is complete, any part of the embryo may be disunited by a deep cleft which may affect one side of the body more than the other, or it may affect both sides equally. If the growth of the embryo is retarded in a very late stage of development, only a slight cleft or other malformation may mar its perfection.

An analysis of litter records done by the Roscoe B. Jackson Memorial Laboratory indicates a higher percentage of puppies are stillborn or die shortly before birth in the first litter than in the second, third, fourth, and fifth litters. In a study of 337 litters, the percentage of dead puppies in the first litter was 5.7 percent, while in the fourth litter the percentage was 2.0 percent and in the fifth litter 2.8 percent. Because the cause of death could not be determined accurately in most cases, it is assumed that inexperience on the part of the bitch in whelping and caring for her first litter is partly responsible for the higher death rate. After the fifth litter, however, the death rate increased considerably, the percentage of dead puppies in the sixth litter averaging 18.7 percent. However, the steady decrease in incidence of death until the fourth or fifth litters indicates intra-uterine conditions in older bitches are more likely to be unfavorable for the production of normal young.

Fading Puppies

Fading puppy syndrome is often confused with toxic milk syndrome. It is estimated that 28% of all puppies die in the first week after birth. Some of these puppies suffer from lethal congenital defects, maternal neglect or accidents, such as being crushed in a whelping box. A large proportion of them, however, die from what is defined as the "fading puppy syndrome." The syndrome is part of a specific disease entity but perhaps the true "fading puppy" is the individual who: (1) was born malnourished because its dam did not receive adequate nutrition during gestation; (2) is too weak to nurse effectively; (3) is not receiving an adequate supply of milk; (4) is in an environment that is not sufficiently warm; or, (5) a combination of these factors. Unless supplementary feeding is started within a few hours of birth, with frequent weight checks to monitor progress, and unless adequate heat is provided, these puppies become chilled, weak, and ultimately "fade" and die.

Newborn puppies differ physiologically from adult dogs in several important ways. It is necessary to understand these differences to realize why puppies succumb rapidly to stress and to appreciate the importance of proper environment and care. They have body temperatures of 94 to 97°F for the first two weeks of life as compared to the adult dog's normal temperature of 100 to 101.5°F. They do not have a shivering reflex until about six days of age and thus cannot maintain body heat. Their heart beats and respiratory rates are faster than the adult dog. Newborns must be kept in an environmental temperature of 85 to 90°F for the first week of life; the temperature is gradually decreased to 70°F by the time the puppies are weaning age. They should gain 1 to 1½ grams daily for each pound of anticipated adult weight and should double birth rate in eight to ten days.

Neonatal Septicemia

Neonatal septicemia affects puppies from one to four days of age. It

---

is caused by a staphylococcus infection in the vaginal tract of the bitch, transmitted to the puppy at birth. An unclean environment should not be overlooked as a precipitating factor in the disease.

Infected puppies have swollen abdomens with bluish discoloration on the flanks. They cry, are hypothermic, dehydrated and refuse to nurse. Death occurs 12 to 18 hours after bloating and crying unless antibiotic treatment is started immediately. Supportive therapy (heat, glucose and water) as described under Puppy Septicemia also must be administered.

Prevention involves a pre-breeding veterinary examination with antibiotic therapy if necessary to counteract infection. Since an unsanitary environment is frequently involved in neonatal (and puppy) septicemia, kenneling should be clean and so should everything to which the newborn puppies are exposed. This includes your hands and the scissors used to cut the umbilical cords. The cords should be dipped in or swabbed with iodine.

Puppy Septicemia

Puppy septicemia is the leading cause of death by disease in infant puppies, occurring from four to forty days of age. It happens typically in vigorous puppies that were born normally and are efficient nursers. Illness is sudden. First one puppy starts to cry. It has abdominal distension, diarrhea and may have rapid respiration. Then it refuses to nurse, becomes dehydrated and loses weight rapidly. Death usually follows 18 hours after onset of symptoms. Another puppy becomes sick, then another and another. Septicemia can demolish most or all of a litter within five to six days.

It is caused by bacteria of the streptococcus, staphylococcus, escherichia or pseudomonas types and frequently is associated with a metritis or mastitis (inflamation of the womb or of the breasts) infection in the bitch. Metritis is a uterine infection that may be acute or chronic. In the acute phase, the bitch becomes ill soon after the litter is whelped; depressed with an abnormal vaginal discharge and a temperature which may rise to 104°F. Chronic metritis may not cause overt symptoms in the bitch and, in fact, may not be evidenced until she whelps stillborn puppies or puppies that succumb to infection shortly after birth. Mastitis is painful and fever producing for the bitch. It can transmit bacterial infection to the litter.

Sick puppies are chilled, have low blood sugar, and are dehydrated. Immediate concerns are to counteract these conditions. Otherwise, the puppies will die too quickly for further therapy to be effective. They must be taken from the bitch and the following actions taken:

For Chilling: Slow warming. The sick puppy's body temperature has usually fallen to 78 to 94°F. It must be placed in an environmental temperature—incubator, heat lamp or heat pad—of 85 to 90°F until the body temperature has risen to normal for the infant puppy. Circulation must be stimulated by frequently turning and massaging the puppy during the slow warming process. Only the surfaces of the puppy's body will be warmed if this is not done. Temperature of the newborn puppy can be taken with an infant's rectal thermometer. Hold the puppy up by the base of the tail and insert the thermometer one-half inch into the rectum. Enviromental temperature can be monitored with an inside thermometer on the floor of the whelping box or incubator. Relative humidity should be 55 to 60 percent; this can be accomplished by using a home humidifier in the room in which the whelping box is placed.

For Low Blood Sugar (Hypoglycemia): Glucose therapy. The sick puppy's blood sugar must be increased rapidly and the administration of glucose solution, which is absorbed directly into the stomach, is the best way of doing this. Give the puppy 5 to 15% glucose in water, orally, 1 to 2 cc. (milliliters) every half hour. As the puppy's condition improves, gradually increase the dosage to 4 to 6 cc. These puppies should not be given formula; it may not be absorbed and thus may cause intestinal blockage.

For Dehydration: Water, given orally. The glucose and water therapy described above should be sufficient. If the puppy's condition is extremely serious, the veterinarian may think it advisable to administer subcutaneous hydrating solutions.

Other therapy, recommended by the veterinarian, may be to give antibiotics in some cases. Gamma globulin serum is considered effective. The owner may also be asked to give the puppies commercial formula or a few drops of *very fresh* liver juice every few hours after they have started to rally; this is strength enhancing.

As was learned in a preceding chapter, prevention starts with a prebreeding veterinary examination of the bitch. Bacterial culture and sensitivity testing should be performed on specimens removed from the vagina. These tests should be mandatory when a bitch has a history of uterine infection, stillborn puppies or puppies that die soon after birth from bacterial infection. Appropriate antibiotic therapy should take place before breeding if the bitch tests positive. It may be advisable to have another course of antibiotics 48 hours before whelping and immediately after whelping. In no case should this be done haphazardly; antibiotics should be given only when necessary and under veterinary supervision.

Every effort should be made to have all the puppies take colostrum, the "first milk" produced by the bitch for 24 hours after whelping. This protects the puppy from disease for the first weeks of its life. Lack of colostrom seems to be among the precipitating factors of puppy septicemia.

The bitch should be in a state of nutritional good health, fed ample quantities of good-quality commercial dog food product recommended complete for gestation and lactation. A feeding alternative is a complete and balanced puppy food product. Its high caloric density and protein content are advantageous for the gestating or lactating bitch. Liver, one-half ounce per thirty pounds, is considered an excellent food supplement for the gestating bitch, contributing to the strength and vigor of the newborn litter.

Kenneling should be clean and well ventilated with appropriate temperature and humidity. Unsanitary quarters will predispose the litter to disease.

Canine Herpes Virus (Puppy Viremia)

This is another leading cause of death in young puppies, transmitted at whelping as puppies pass through the vagina of a recently infected bitch. Puppies can also be infected by littermates or infected adult dogs. The disease is usually fatal if contracted by puppies during the first three weeks of life. Older puppies with herpes virus usually have mild upper respiratory infections from which recovery is uneventful. Susceptibility of infant puppies is thought to be caused by their low body temperature. The canine herpes virus has been shown to multiply optimally at temperatures of 94 to 97°F, that of the neonatal puppy. It grows poorly at the body temperature of the adult dog.

Affected puppies have soft, green odorless bowel movements; this is the first symptom. They may vomit or retch, have shallow respiration which becomes gasping as the disease progresses, and they refuse to nurse. They cry pitifully and continuously.

Keeping puppies in a high environmental temperature for 24 hours is the only effective treatment; but even this is problematical. For three hours the temperature must be 100 degrees. The puppies need fluid to be given orally every 15 minutes, to prevent dehydration. Then the temperature can be reduced to 90° for the remainder of the 24-hour period. If the puppies survive, the chances are better than average that they will live. Treatment is not advised if a puppy already has started to cry; this indicates that hemorrhaging has started and survival is doubtful. If it should live, chronic kidney disease may develop during the first year of life.

In kennels where herpes virus is a recurrent problem, a preventive method is giving gamma globulin serum as an immunizing agent to neonatal puppies from dogs recovered from the disease. Since canine herpes virus is spread by direct contact with infected dogs, urine and other body secretions, overcrowding in kennels is a factor in disease transmission.

Toxic Milk Syndrome

Bacterial toxins in the bitch's milk, caused by incomplete emptying of the uterus, produce toxic effects in very young puppies, (up to two weeks of age). Sick puppies cry, bloat, have diarrhea and red swollen protruding rectums.

They must be taken from the bitch, placed in a warm environment and given 5 to 15% glucose in water orally until the bloating has sub-sided. The bitch should be treated with appropriate medication to cleanse the uterus and antibiotics to prevent infection. The puppies can be put back with her as soon as treatment has started. They should be given a simulated bitch's milk product during the interval between glu-cose and water therapy and being returned to the bitch.

Hemorrhagic Syndrome

Puppies have minimal production of a plasma protein called pro-thrombin during their first two or three days of life. Prothrombin is produced in the liver and, in conjunction with vitamin K_1, controls the clotting function of the blood. Without sufficient prothrombin, a hemorrhagic tendency can develop.

Affected puppies die within the first two or three days. They are lethargic, weak and decline rapidly in condition. Signs of hemorrhage may be lesions on the lips or tongue. Surviving puppies in the litter should receive vitamin K_1. Most complete and balanced dog foods have sufficient vitamin K for growth and maintenance of normal dogs.

Canine Parvovirus

Canine parvovirus has been recognized only since 1978 when epi-demics were reported throughout the world. In 1979, the virus became a formidable disease in the United States. At this time, random studies revealed that between 20 and 50% of dogs tested had significantly high antibody titers suggestive of previous parvovirus infection. By the summer of 1980, new cases seemed to occur primarily among puppies under six months of age and in family pets that had not encountered the virus previously. Recent information indicates that while the over-all mortality of those dogs infected with canine parvovirus is less than 1%, the mortality among clinically-ill dogs may be as great as 10-50%. These figures vary greatly among certain populations, since the severity of the disease appears to be influenced by such factors as crowding, age, and coinciding parasitic, protozoan infections. The incidence of the disease can be expected to decline as more dogs become resistant to the virus following infection or vaccination.

Canine parvovirus manifests itself in two distinct forms: enteritis and myocarditis. This chapter will concern itself only with the myocarditis form since it principally attacks puppies.

The myocarditis form occurs only in puppies born to a female that has no antibodies to parvovirus (one that has not had either the infection or current vaccination) and becomes infected with the virus during the first few days after giving birth. Lesions develop slowly in the puppies' heart muscle and heart failure is apparent several weeks later. The mortality rates in affected litters usually exceed 50%. Fortunately, the prevalence of the myocardial form already seems to be decreasing. The disease is due to the fact that many breeding bitches have been infected previously and thus have circulating antibodies which are transferred to the puppies through the placenta and in the colostrum. This maternal antibody protects the newborns during their first five weeks when they are the most susceptible to the myocardial form of parvovirus.

Parvoviruses are especially hard to inactivate because they are resistant to heat, detergents, and alcohol. They have been known to remain active in dog feces, the primary source of infection, for more than three months at room temperature. A dilute (1:30) bleach solution is recommended for disinfection, because it will inactivate the virus. Since sanitation alone is not adequate to completely halt the spread of parvovirus, vaccination is the most effective method for control.

Brucellosis

Brucella Canis is relatively newly found and just recently recognized. Infections frequently become chronic. It occurs explosively and spreads rapidly among dog populations. The all-prevailing nature of this disease under kennel conditions has been documented. One study found 86% of adult dogs became infected and 41 of 118 females aborted.

Although all breeds of dogs are susceptible and the disease is widespread in the U.S., reported incidence rates vary from one through six percent, depending upon the area samples (there seems to be a higher concentration in the south) and the type of diagnostic test employed.

Manifestations of B. Canis are similar to each of the other species of Brucella.

In the bitches:
1. Infected females may abort their litter without previous illness (typically in the final two weeks of gestation).
2. Pups born to infected mothers may be extremely weak; all or part of the litter may be still born.

3. Following an abortion there is usually a discharge from the vagina lasting for several weeks.
4. Early embryonic deaths with termination of the pregnancy may occur, suggesting to the owner that the bitch failed to conceive.

Once the disease has been established in the male, the organisms are primarily transmitted venerally.

Other Causes

When confronted with neonatal puppy deaths, the breeder also should consider the possibility of other infectious canine diseases: distemper, leptospirosis, canine infectious hepatitis and the "newest" disease coronavirus.

Most puppy deaths are preventible. With: (1) selection of sound breeding stock; (2) a healthy, well-nourished bitch; (3) clean kenneling; (4) adequate heat for the bitch and the litter; (5) careful supervision of puppies' early weight gains; and, (6) prompt veterinary assistance should puppies start to "fade," cry, or have any of the early symptoms of puppy diseases.

CHAPTER 12

Choosing the Best Puppies

Heredity and environment both play a major role in the development of a puppy. Understanding how a particular bloodline "works" can help a breeder immeasurably. By keeping careful records of each litter, a breeder should be able to more or less predict the outcome of each puppy in a given litter. And optimizing the puppies' environment should allow the puppies to reach their maximum growth potential.

Of course, no system is foolproof. Puppies which start off looking like real winners may end up as pet quality. Also, a puppy could seem like pet quality, be sold at a pet price, and end up succeeding in the show ring. It's impossible to be 100 percent absolute each and every time. But the information in this chapter should help reduce the number of bad judgment calls, and should help you—the breeder—develop puppies to their maximum potential and select the best show quality puppies in each litter.

Keeping Records

Keeping records of each litter provides the breeder with an invaluable tool. It allows the breeder to learn from the past, to predict the development of each puppy with a measure of confidence, and to relax a little during the "plaining out" and awkward phases (more about this later).

The more information available on past litters, the better. More information allows the breeder to predict more accurately the outcome of a particular puppy. It also makes apparent patterns of development peculiar to a given bloodline. For instance, the "plaining out" phase for bloodline X may start at three months and end at eight months. So if a puppy still looks "iffy" at seven months, the breeder need not worry too much. However, if he still has a case of the "uglies" at ten months, he's got to go.

Development is always easier to predict if the breeder is dealing within one family. When new bloodlines are added to the genetic maze, development and outcome will probably be different from earlier results. Even experienced breeders can expect unpredictable results and a few trying times when outcrossing.

This does not mean that results are always predictable even if the bloodline is not changed. Individual differences always play a major role in the genetic makeup of puppies. And no system, no matter how extensive and accurate, can guarantee similar results every time. But by keeping good records, breeders are able to stack the deck in their favor.

What kind of records should be kept? The measurements that are most useful are weight, height (floor-to-withers, floor-to-elbow, elbow-to-withers), and length (withers-to-tailset, point of shoulder-to-tailset). The measurements should be taken at birth, two weeks, four weeks, and then every four weeks until maturity is reached. This may be up to four years in Pugs. Notes on head and wrinkle development, heaviness of bone, ear type and taping required, and personality should also be recorded.

With enough "statistical" information the breeder should be able to answer the following types of questions with some accuracy:

1. At what age will this puppy attain full size?
2. At what age will this puppy attain ultimate development?
3. Will ultimate size and development be reached at the same time?
4. Can ultimate size be predicted by size at birth?
5. Do puppies in bloodline X develop at a uniform rate or do they go through growth spurts?
6. When will the growth spurts most likely occur?
7. When is the awkward stage for this bloodline?
8. Will one part of the body develop sooner than another part?
9. If more than one bloodline is bred at the kennel, what are the differences between them?

Being able to answer questions such as these can help the breeder predict the development of each puppy and to select the best show-quality puppies from the litter. *Caution—remember that just because a puppy is the best in its litter does not automatically make it a showdog.*

Puppy Development

Puppies are so cute and cuddly when they are born, each one is a winner in its own way. One may have a promising head, another may have great wrinkles, and a third a wonderful disposition. Your personal favorite may be the shy, gentle one in the corner. One thing is certain, most of these puppies will go through the awkward "plaining out" stage. Slowly, their lovely drop ears will lift and "fly" in the breeze. Their bodies will lose all signs of cuddliness as they take on an adolescent appearance becoming gangly "teenagers." But have patience! Most puppies emerge unscathed from this stage, and redisplay most of their original promise. *Caution—a poor puppy going into this phase will most likely emerge still a poor puppy.*

Not all puppies go through this phase. Some puppies are born beautiful and maintain beauty, balance, and proportion throughout their first year. These puppies, called "flyers," outshine their gangly siblings. These puppies are few and far between. In some cases, their litter mates also become outstanding dogs. When one of these comes along, beware of possible late-life development that can cause a champion to fall apart.

A good rule of thumb for beginning breeders is to pick the show quality puppies at nine weeks of age, before the onset of the "plaining out" phase. They usually reflect their adult potential more accurately then, rather than later during the awkward phase. More experienced breeders can draw from past information to determine the appropriate timing for selecting show-quality puppies from their bloodlines. Remember, when purchasing a puppy under nine weeks of age, you are buying potential; only after six months can you be fairly sure of getting a Pug that will possibly become a champion and one that can stand up under today's tough competition.

Some points to look for when purchasing that puppy include an over-all compactness or a boxy outline. You want a nice, round body—but beware of a pot belly, which could indicate worms. Next, look at bone and head, as Pugs are a head-oriented breed if there ever was one! A good-sized head, with a very flat profile and slight show of future wrinkles, should be looked for. Hold the pup overhead so that it has to look down at you. This shows the pattern and wrinkles that will come in. Look at the under-jaw: it should be wide, never pinched. In other words, the puppy should present the idea of a big mouth to you. Often, a wide tongue will come out of the future wide jaw and muzzle. Most Pug babies with a narrow and too-long tongue develop a pinched muzzle. If, at nine weeks, the puppy already has the full over-nose wrinkle, you are in luck. This feature, while not a requirement, defnitely enhances the best of Pug expressions and gives a short, flat profile to the face. Unfortunately, the over-nose roll does not usually become plain until the pup is 10 or 11 weeks old, and is often confused with the "bee-sting." There IS a difference. Most new Pug pups have the "bee-sting," that is, the big puff right over the nose, but this may or may not develop into the nice over-nose roll. Some lucky pups actually have both the bee-sting and the over-nose roll, making it easy to differentiate.

Besides wrinkle and jaw, look at the shape of the head (no apple heads here, please!) and ears. Often, ears look to be too large until the growth of the head and skull structure catches up with them. This usually occurs after the plaining out period. Of course, you want the fine black ear that stops at the outside corner of the eye, but this is a feature than often gets overlooked. The idea of color leads me to a warning: do not be swayed too much by the color of fawn the dog is. Remember, a fawn is a fawn is a fawn. They can be dark or light, apricot or silver, but whatever it is it should be a clear color, without smuttiness (black hairs within the coat). A future deep-apricot Pug is going to look quite dark at nine weeks of age (remember those black puppies?), while the light fawns of the future will be quite light as puppies. BUT, this does not mean that one is going to be any prettier at maturity than the other. The wrinkles will probably appear to be very dark, but they, too, lighten with age. Conversely, most ears will darken as the puppy grows up.

If the toenails are white or very light in a puppy they usually stay that way. Black nails often lighten with old age, but white nails will be obvious at any stage.

It is impossible to predict the exact timing of a puppy's awkward stage. It can start as early as eight weeks, but usually will not start until the puppy is three or four months old. Most puppies are out of the awkward stage by the time they are eight months old, but a puppy could come out of it at six or seven months. Generally, the timing is similar within the same bloodline. From past litter records, a breeder could determine that progeny of bloodline X usually enter the awkward stage between three and seven months of age, or about the time that the baby teeth are being lost. Then, when the next litter is born, the breeder can expect the same general timing. This helps reduce the amount of anxiety felt by the breeder. He may mentally "lock the puppy away" until it is seven months old and then pull it out for re-evaluation.

The rapid growth during this time can cause many puppies to develop an awkward, uncoordinated body. To make matters worse, different parts of the body can develop at different times. One puppy's legs may develop before its chest, giving it an "up-on-leg," pipestem look. It may walk around on stilts for months before finally filling in. Another pup may develop its forechest early. This may cause it to look low-to-the-ground and dumpy until its legs catch up.

Usually the body parts even out by the time maturity is reached, but not always. Many dreams of Best in Show have been shattered by a puppy whose body just never caught up with its head. Take it all in stride, and learn from experience which dogs to pin your hopes on. Depend on overall balance rather than a few great parts.

Environment

A puppy's genetic potential is determined at conception. But beneficial environmental factors the breeder provides help the puppy reach its full potential. Having a doting mother, avoiding illness, eating nutritious food in the right amount, and proper grooming and handling all help the puppy develop into a healthy, happy dog.

Not all good bitches make good mothers. If a bitch is lacking in maternal instinct, a lot of tender loving care is required on the part of the breeder. You will need to pick the puppy up, fondle it gently in your lap, and stroke and speak to it. This must be done at least twice a day. Nothing is as cute as a baby pup who needs to nuzzle up to a warm, comforting body. Never handle the puppy roughly. Use two hands when picking it up and putting it back with its littermates. Gentleness is most important; your goal is to have the pup trust you.

If a puppy gets off to a poor start, either through poor eating habits or illness, it will probably catch up with the rest of the pack eventually. It may continue growing after its littermates have reached maturity in order to make up for earlier lost time. An older puppy which has been similarly set back through illness will usually end up being about the same size as its littermates. Sometimes a breeder will write these puppies off as non-candidates for show dogs before they reach their full size. This can be a heartbreaking mistake.

Another mistake commonly made is to discard the too thin or too chubby puppy. If a puppy doesn't have enough meat on it, the breeder should seek to determine the reason. There may be something in its genetic makeup which does not allow it to utilize properly all the nutrients. On the other hand, sometimes a puppy is simply a poor eater. If it's an ingrained part of its personality there may be nothing the breeder can do to help it fill out. Read the chapters on "The Bitch and Her Puppies" and "Nutrition for Puppies and Adults" for more information on this vexing matter.

Chubby puppies tend to look the most awkward during the "plaining out" phase. Their extra weight exaggerates their faults. Before being evaluated by the breeder, this type of puppy should be put on a diet. Watch their weight closely, for extreme and prolonged obesity can lead to permanent structural defects.

Even if all the above guidelines are followed, even if the puppy has the benefit of the most experienced breeder, it still needs that magical spark to be a winner. This elusive spark of personality adds life and spunk to an otherwise empty, albeit lovely, animal. Without spark, the dog may never be able to handle itself with confidence in the ring. A winning dog is flashy and knows it. He prances into the ring and says "look at me, aren't I something!" And sure enough, he IS something. A duplicate of that dog, minus the personality, could become the all-time runner up.

Personality can be developed to a degree. Gently, and I do mean gently, playing with a puppy can help the puppy see that humans are okay. Never lunge at a puppy or hold it improperly. Both hands should support the puppy underneath at the chest and at the rear legs. Never frighten it or be rough. Puppies, like human babies, thrive on love and tenderness. As they grow older, you should take them with you to different places. You must prove to these pups that they can trust you and your judgment about people and places that are strange to them. Providing that emotional food will help the puppy gain confidence and, hopefully, that "spark" of personality.

When grading out the puppies at eight weeks, do not judge them only on a posed or show stance. First of all, it's possible to set a puppy, to get it to look the way you think it should look. All you achieve when you do this is to deceive yourself. Look for a short back. Check for wrinkle and flat face. Look at the front honestly, for sign of bad elbows, or a fiddle front. Check for a strong rear without any evidence of hocking in or out. Do not seek extremes. Put the pup down on the ground. It's important to see how it handles its feet and the shifting of weight at it moves about. Any puppy that is well coordinated is up on its toes and cuts and turns easily—that's the one to consider seriously. A posed dog does not give you the view that you need to evaluate the puppy fully. Down on the ground, on its own, the puppy that acts like it is king and goes all out, while still handling itself well is the one to watch.

Pug Heaven

SECTION V

The Versatile Pug

- *As a Show Dog*
- *As an Obedience Dog*

13

As A Show Dog

The Pug has always been a winner. His head has been his showpiece. But there is much more to the Pug than his head. The judges assess the total dog. With only a few minutes to spend on each specimen the judge hasn't got the time to spend with a dog who is not posing and showing every minute and asking for that win.

It is vital to your dog's career to have him trained to perform in the show ring. In fact, it's vital to your career as a breeder/exhibitor to have your dog shown at its best. Oftentimes the difference between winning and losing is how well your dog acts in the ring.

The show ring is the place where breeding decisions of the future are made. If your dog is not showing at its best, it may never find itself in the pedigrees of future immortals of the breed.

Training your dog properly can make the difference between a winner and an also ran. To insure you get words of wisdom about training I am going to quote one of the greatest handler/trainers of modern show dogs, Frank Sabella. Frank is now an AKC licensed judge. In his book (written with Shirlee Kalstone) *The Art of Handling Show Dogs*, published by B & E Publications, he covers all the bases in the early training of a show dog.

Introduction

Show training is so important that it becomes a part of the puppy's life. Training for the show ring should begin as soon as you purchase your puppy or from the time it is weaned, if you were its breeder. Especially with a baby puppy, your main objective is to begin establishing a pleasant, loving relationship which will become the basis of more formal training in the future.

Dogs are required to do two things in the conformation ring: to be set up or posed (and to hold that pose for an indefinite length of time during the judge's examination) and to gait (individually and in a group). While show training is not difficult, it does require time, patience, sensitivity and consistency on the part of the trainer.

Many people make the mistake of waiting for a puppy to grow up and then begin to train it. We don't mean to imply that some successful dogs did not start this way but, without a doubt, dogs that have the right kind of basic training as puppies are always the ones that stand in the ring with head and tail up, full of assurance. Just the repetition of correctly posing and leading the puppy will teach it to walk confidently on lead and to feel comfortable while being handled—and that's really what early training is for—to ensure that your puppy will grow into an adult that is confident and self assured in the show ring!

At what age should you begin training your puppy? Each dog is an individual and should be treated as such, so there are no "set" age limits as to when to begin basic or advanced show training. Generally, when you start basic training depends not only on your patience, sensitivity and consistency, but also on the puppy's capabilities and desire to accept being posed and lead trained.

Very young puppies are highly motivated by and responsive to their owners but, like babies, they have short concentration periods. Even though intelligence develops rapidly in a puppy, early training should always be started on a "fun" basis. Don't be in a hurry to start formal training too early; the first part of a puppy's life should be fun time and every dog should be allowed to enjoy its puppyhood.

Early Socialization Important

As the owner or breeder of a young puppy, you alone are responsible for its early socialization and training. Socialization can be described as the way in which a dog develops a relationship with its dam, littermates, other animals and man. Just as a youngster must receive a formal education and also learn to become a responsible member of society, so must you provide the best environment for your dog's potential to be brought out and developed completely. A young puppy is very impressionable and the socialization and training it receives at an early age sets the tone for its lifetime characteristics. If a puppy receives the proper socialization, is treated with sensitivity, patience and consistency, if it learns to be loved and respected, then it will always be happiest when pleasing you.

Earlier in this chapter, we mentioned that with a young puppy you want to begin basic training by establishing a happy and loving rapport between you and the dog. Pat and handle the puppy frequently, speaking reassuringly and using praise often. Let the puppy become accustomed to being petted and handled by strangers. A well-socialized puppy loves to make new friends and this kind of interaction between puppy and humans or other animals will be a prerequiste for the basic show training to follow. Hopefully, by the time the puppy is about 7 to 8 weeks old, it has learned a little about life. If it has been properly socialized, it is light-hearted and untroubled, because it has learned that it is loved and respected. Now it must be taught certain basics which lead eventually to more formal training for the show ring.

Here are some suggestions to consider before you begin basic training:

1. First training sessions should be given in familiar surroundings, preferably at home, and without noises or other distractions.
2. Make the first training periods short, not more than 10 minutes in length. As the sessions progress successfully, gradually lengthen each training period, but never more than 30 minutes in any single session.

3. If the puppy is restless or won't concentrate, postpone the lesson and try again the following day. Be sure, too, that you are not tired or impatient for the training sessions should always be relaxed and enjoyable for both of you.
4. Be consistent during the lessons. Use a firm tone of voice when giving commands. Some of the first words your puppy will learn in posing and lead training are "Come," "Stand," "Stay," and "No." Be sure you use the same word for the same command each time.
5. Remember that a young puppy is inexperienced, so be gentle and patient. Don't rush your puppy; give it time to understand what you expect and to learn how to respond.
6. Don't be too insistent at first. Puppies learn by repetition, correction and praise. Don't punish a puppy if it seems confused; instead, correct it until it does what you want, then offer plenty of praise. It is important that your puppy understand each training step thoroughly before going on to the next.
7. Always end each training session on a pleasant note and once again, give plenty of praise and perhaps reward the puppy with its favorite treat. A puppy can learn almost anything if given love and understanding.

Table Training

A grooming table should be one of your first investments, for it will be an indispensable help in establishing habit patterns. Most professional handlers, experienced exhibitors and breeders table train puppies at an early age because, aside from the convenience of having the animal at their working height, there is also an invaluable psychological advantage to table training (Figure V-1). Even though the puppy is off the ground and experiencing a new situation, it is given confidence by the presence of its owner and submits to any handling or grooming, thereby establishing a rapport between the puppy and trainer.

It is easier to control a young puppy by teaching it to pose on a table . . . and recently, it is common to see judges using tables in the ring to examine other small breeds. On larger breeds, even though adult dogs are posed on the ground, early table training will be invaluable for teaching ground posing later on.

The majority of coated breeds require some type of regular grooming in addition to preparation at the show before going into the ring. Even smooth-coated breeds need regular care. Early grooming training on the table will teach the dog to learn to relax. Later on, when the coat grows longer or the dog needs special attention, it will not object if it has to spend longer periods on the table and will rest and feel totally secure while being worked on. As a part of the training you should practice posing the dog at the end of each grooming session.

The table you select should be sturdy and covered with a non-slip rubber top. There are many different types of grooming tables: portable (which fold up and are easy to carry along to matches and shows), adjustable (which move up or down) or a combination crate with grooming table top (these often have drawers between the crate and top to hold equipment). Some tables are equipped with a post and loop collar, which can be slipped around a dog's neck to hold the head up

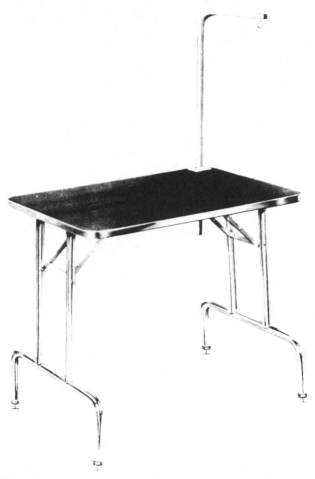

Figure V-1. A grooming table is of indispensable help in training young puppies. The portable type illustrated here is covered with a non-slip surface and has an adjustable post and loop which can be removed when not in use. Portable tables are easy to fold up, making them convenient to transport to and from matches and shows.

and keep it from moving or jumping off the table. If you do use a loop to give the puppy more confidence, never use one with any type of choking action. Never leave a young puppy alone with its head in a loop or standing by itself on a table unless you are sure it will stay.

Posing

You can start posing your puppy on a table as early as 6 weeks. In the beginnning just stand the puppy on the table and get it used to being off the ground. Once this has been accomplished, then start positioning the legs in a show pose. Next, begin training it to be handled—feel its body, look at its teeth and let other people do the same. Experiencing all this at an early age will give the puppy confidence and make it used to being handled by strangers, which will be invaluable later on for the puppy's show career. If you persevere in the beginning you will discover that your puppy will never forget this basic training and later it will be much easier to work with.

When lifting the puppy for the first time, care should be taken not to frighten it. Don't come down too quickly on the puppy or attempt to lift it by grasping the back of the neck or picking it up by the front legs. Instead, kneel down to the puppy's level and let it come to you. Speak assuringly and pat the puppy if you can. Then using both hands to lift the puppy's front and rear, pick it up and place it on the table. Do be aware that a puppy might try to wiggle out of your arms so make sure you have a secure grip on the dog as you lift it and after you set it down on the table.

Be sure the table surface is not slippery and use the following method to pose the puppy:

Figure V-2—Grasp the puppy with your left hand between the back legs and your right hand under the chest, at the same time giving the command 'stand' or 'stay'. When you pose the dog in the ring, in the majority of times this is the way it will be facing the judge. If the puppy fusses and does not want to stand, keep your hands in the same position and slightly lift the front feet off the table and put them down, then lift the rear legs off the table and put them down, doing both movements in a slight rocking motion. Repeat this several times to distract the puppy and get it to settle down.

Figure V-2.

Figure V-3—Move your right hand from under the chest and place it on the neck as shown, with the weight of the head resting on the top part of your hand. Don't grasp the neck too heavily; use a light touch, just enough so that you can control the puppy from moving to either side or out of your hand.

Figure V-4—If you have a small dog with an excellent front, simply grasp the puppy under the neck, raise it off its front legs, then drop it back onto the table.

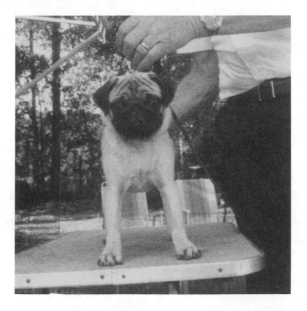

After your puppy learns how to stand properly, start posing it for longer periods of time. When the puppy can pose without fussing, the next step is to enlist the help of friends by having them go through the motions of lightly examining the dog—checking its bite and feeling the body—doing the things a judge will do in the ring. If you are training a male, in the ring the judge will check to see if both testicles are in place, so do remember to train your puppy to accept this procedure at an early age.

As the posing sessions progress, you can begin practicing the more subtle aspects of show posing, i.e., setting up the puppy in a variety of situations and on different ground surfaces, especially grass.

Lead Training

Of all the steps necessary to prepare a puppy for the show ring, probably lead training is the most important because there have been many potentially fine show dogs ruined by improper lead training. So many exhibitors wait until the last minute to lead break a dog then expect it all to happen in one try. Then they become impatient and treat the dog roughly and the puppy's reaction to all this is fear. Do remember that extreme patience is necessary because introduction to a collar and a lead can be a frightening experience for a young puppy.

Most canine behavior experts agree that at 6 weeks, a dog can have a small soft collar put around its neck. The younger the puppy becomes accustomed to wearing a collar around its neck, the easier it will be to lead train it later on. Begin by placing the collar around the puppy's neck for short periods of time and only while someone is in attendance. The first few times the puppy wears the collar, it may roll on the ground or try several other things to get the collar off, so never allow a baby puppy to be unsupervised. Make the first lesson short, not more than 5 to 10 minutes, then remove the collar, play with the puppy and praise it for being such a good dog.

After a period of about a week (or when the puppy is relaxed about wearing the collar) snap a lightweight lead onto the collar and let the puppy drag the lead freely about the floor. Allow the puppy to walk wherever it wants to go. If it starts to follow you, fine; but the first time the lead is attached, don't pick it up and jerk and pull the puppy in any way. After a few times of allowing the puppy to drag the lead around the floor, pick up the lead in your hand and let the puppy take you for a walk. Speak gently and walk wherever the puppy wants to go. Once again, don't pull or tug on the lead in an attempt to make the puppy follow you until it is completely accustomed to wearing the collar and lead.

When this has been accomplished, the next lesson is to try to walk the puppy on lead. The first time you try this, don't be surprised if your puppy pulls back or rolls over on the floor. Don't panic, just learn to be patient and speak gently. Put the snap adjustment under the puppy's neck at first so it won't be tempted to look over its shoulder or try to bite the lead. Squat down and call the puppy's name and the word "come" in your most inviting voice, to get the dog to move forward to you. If it balks or sits, try coaxing it to come forward for its favorite tidbit. You may have to give a slight forward pull to the lead to start the puppy toward you but remember, a slight pull does not mean a neck-breaking jolt for you can injure the neck and the puppy will associate the resulting pain with an unpleasant experience. If this is done several times without thinking, it can develop into a deep seated fear of the lead.

When the puppy comes to you, pat and praise it; then walk ahead with the lead in your hand and repeat this action to make the puppy move forward again. It should only take a short while until the puppy follows you. Eventually, the puppy will learn that if it obeys and follows you, there will be no pulling or jerking of the lead and that it will receive plenty of praise.

Once again, we caution that because a puppy's attention span is short, try to make each session brief, 10 minutes at most, then remove the lead, praise and play with the puppy. The main idea at this stage of training is to make the first lessons a "train and play" time that the puppy looks forward to and not something it dreads. After a few lessons, you'll find your puppy can be lead trained rather quickly and what is more important, that it enjoys the experience.

At this point, we want to offer some advice about early training. Always try to train the puppy to move on a loose lead to help develop its natural carriage. In the show ring you will be asked by many judges to move your dog on a loose lead and you will be prepared if you accustom your puppy to do it at an early age. When a puppy is taught to gait only on a tight lead, it gets used to leaning into the lead and without that pressure, feels completely lost. There is nothing harder to break than a dog that is used to leaning into the lead for support. Dogs that are trained on a tight lead also lose their natural head carriage and they often learn many other bad habits including sidewinding. In the ring, it is not uncommon to see exhibitors string up their dogs so tightly that the front feet hardly touch the ground. There is a trend to show certain breeds on a tight lead to make a more positive topline.

However, if a knowledgeable judge wants to discover whether the dog's topline is natural or man-made, he will ask that the dog be moved on a loose lead and, if that fault is present, it will be exposed.

While the puppy is being lead trained, don't train it to be hand posed at the same time. At first, these should be two seperate procedures. Animals learn by repetition and, if each time you stop leading the dog and then get down and set it up, the dog will anticipate this action and will become discouraged from learning to stand naturally and pose itself without being set up by hand. So many exhibitors hand pose their puppies after each gaiting session and when this happens, a puppy soon gets the idea that every time it stops on lead, someone will bend down to hold its head and tail. In the ring, after you have individually gaited your dog, many judges will ask you to let the dog stand on its own. If your puppy hasn't learned to stand naturally at the end of its lead, it won't be able to do so in the ring.

As the gaiting sessions progress, teach the puppy to move on your left side (eventually the dog should learn to move on your right side as well as your left). Encourage the puppy to stand naturally at the end of the lead each time it stops. To help get the puppy to stand alert, try attracting its attention with a squeaky toy, a ball or by offering its favorite tidbit. Doing this will start to teach the puppy the fundamentals of baiting.

After a while you will be ready to begin more advanced training. Replace the training collar with a one-piece show lead or, on large breeds, switch from the training collar to a choke chain or a more substantial type of collar for better control. (As the dog grows older, remember that any collar or chain should be worn only during practice sessions and then removed to prevent the hair from wearing away around the neck.) Before starting advanced training, be sure that the lead is correctly positioned around the dog's neck. It should be high under the chin and behind the ears to keep the dog under control at all times. This position will also help to train the puppy to keep its head up because for the first few weeks, a puppy may need a gentle reminder under its chin to learn to keep its head up.

Next you should begin advanced training by teaching the dog to move down and back in a straight line. Once the dog does this well, then try moving it in a circle. As a prerequisite to executing the individual patterns, practice doing figure-eights because this will teach the dog how to turn smoothly. Then you can begin the other movement patterns that will be used in the show ring—the "L," the "T," and the "Triangle." Vary the movement patterns in each session and remember not to overtrain. Always end each session on a pleasant note and give the dog lots of praise.

As your puppy matures, it should learn to gait on grass, concrete floors and other surfaces including rubber mats (these are used at indoor shows). Once the lessons go well at home, take the puppy out and get it used to walking on a lead and being posed in new and different surroundings. Parking lots of supermarkets and department stores are excellent for this as there are usually lots of people and all kinds of distractions. For the first few outings, be patient and give the puppy plenty of time to adjust and respond to strange surroundings. Occasionally, because of a pup's insecurities, it may revert back to not being well trained for the first few outings.

The greatest pitfall for most young dogs seems to be going to indoor shows because the lighting is strange and the echoes inside a building can sometimes distract a young dog. The inside of a department store or shopping mall can help you to overcome this problem. Always try to anticipate experiences that might distract and frighten a puppy at a show and try to solve them while the puppy is young. If you live in a rural area and none of these suggestions apply to you, take the puppy to matches as often as you can for this is the best place to gain experience with the least amount of tension.

You must work with your dog to determine its best speed in gaiting. Each dog is an individual and looks best when moving at a certain speed and if you want to show your dog to its best advantage, you should determine that correct speed. Have a friend move your dog at varying speeds in front of a knowledgeable person to learn the right speed for your puppy. Then practice the movement patterns at that speed until the dog can do them smoothly. No dog can move at its best speed if the handler moves improperly, so you should take long strides when gaiting the dog. A common error of the novice is to move the dog too slowly.

Short, stilted steps look clumsy and prevent the dog from moving smoothly. If you do not move fast enough yourself or with free and easy strides, you will prevent your dog from executing its most efficient movement. If you are showing a small breed take normal walking steps. For the medium or large breeds, move at a fast walk or run.

We should end the puppy lead training section with some advice about two common problems: sitting and sidling.

Sitting

When stopping, if you find that your puppy constantly sits, keep moving forward a few steps while attracting its attention at the same time with a piece of food or a toy, until the puppy understands that it must stand when it stops. If that does not work, bring the puppy forward a few steps, stop, then put your toe under its stomach to prevent it from sitting.

Another solution is to ask a friend to stand holding a long piece of rope or a show lead which encircles the dog's stomach. When you bring your puppy forward and it starts to sit, have your friend brace up its rear, but do not make this correction with a jerking motion. Breeds that sit when stopped are difficult to train to stand at the end of the leash with tail up (if that is desired in the breed). To remedy this, after you have trained the dog to stand when it has stopped, reach gently from a standing position and put up the tail, stroking underneath the tail until the puppy gets the idea of what you want it to do.

Sidewinding

A common characteristic during lead training is when a dog has a tendency to sidle. This can be caused by:

A. *The dog pulling away from you.* Solution: When the dog starts this habit on the lead or shows indications of doing so when moving individually, train the dog to move on your opposite side. In other words, if you are going away or coming back with the dog on your left side and it sidles, switch to going and coming with the dog on your right.

B. *A dog that has a tendency to look up at its handler while being gaited.* Solution: Never show a dog a toy or food while you are gaiting it as this can cause the dog to look up which may cause sidling. You can also try the alternate side method mentioned in (A) above.

C. *A dog is too short in back.* Solution: If you move at a faster speed, it will go sideways to be able to move at a faster speed. The best way to deal with this problem is to get someone to move the dog at different speeds so you are able to decide at what speed the dog levels off. Another solution to sidling is to put two show leads on a dog and have one person walk on either side of the puppy so that the puppy walks straight in the center. If after a few tries you feel this method is working, the best way to keep the problem from recurring is by constantly alternating the sides each time you take the dog up and back. Gaiting next to a fence or a wall so that the dog can only move straight ahead is another solution to sidling.

Temperament

Temperament plays a major role in puppy training. While most dogs need consistent training to learn what is required of them in the show ring, some dogs are "naturals" at showing. They are outgoing and love being the center of attention and always seem to show themselves off to the best advantage. While these extroverted dogs are exceptions, they always train quickly and easily.

If you experience a temperament problem ("sound" shyness or hand shyness for instance), try to determine what is causing the problem and especially whether you might be the cause of it, as poor temperament can be the result of environment as well as from breeding. In the event you have purchased an older puppy that exhibits temperament problems, consider obedience training for that is a good way for an animal to learn regimentation and to get out among people. Obedience training has been used successfully on dogs that were kennel raised without adequate human socialization at the proper time.

Another part of training your puppy for the show ring has nothing to do with the ring itself, but a means of making going to the show a lot easier on you and the dog. This part of the training has to do with getting the puppy "crate trained." At an early age the puppy should be introduced to the crate that will be his home away from home. One of the best approaches is to put the crate down on the floor near where the puppy has his water bowl. Leave the door open. Put a favorite tidbit inside and let the puppy size it up. Most puppies will be somewhat leery of this new object. However, the puppy—by its very nature—is a curious animal and so will begin to approach it, at first giving it a wide berth. Now this process may take hours as the puppy, often unsure of what this thing is will leave the room for awhile before screwing up its courage and coming back. Gradually, it will approach closer and closer until finally it will be within inches of the crate. Typically, this is when the puppy stops short and reaches out its neck and head while keeping the body ready for flight if this "thing" should prove to be unfriendly. If nothing jumps out of the crate the puppy will feel safe to try to go further and eventually get the tidbit. However, staying inside, oh no, not me!

With this first success you know you have him hooked. Leave the crate down and pay no attention to it or the puppy. A couple of times during the day, place a tidbit in the crate. You will find it gone sometime later. After a few days of this game and you are sure the puppy (and not the cat!) is eating the tidbits, place a favorite toy in the crate. Let this game go on for a couple of days as well. Your next step is to gently pick up the puppy and place it in the crate with a tidbit inside and gently close the door. Be sure the puppy can see you as you go about your daily chores. He will most likely fuss about being confined. Talk to him, tell him what a great fellow he is and—if necessary—give him another tidbit. He should be confined for only about 10 minutes the first time. When you let him out, praise him lavishly for being a good dog. Over the next weeks you can extend the time slowly until the puppy comes to accept a few hours confinement as natural.

Once you have gotten to this point you can begin to let him sleep in the crate. Be sure you get up early enough so he will be let out of the crate before he soils himself. It's a good idea to put in some rough toweling or carpeting. Later on you might want to use a wire bottom or papering.

Next, you want to take him for a car/van ride to accustom him to motion. One of the trips to a shopping center referred to above would be ideal. Don't make his first voyage out into the world too long, however. Many puppies get car sick rather easily so keep the trip short and talk reassuringly to the puppy the whole time you are on the road. If people pull up along side of you at stop lights and see you talking to yourself, don't be worried, just put your hand up to your ear and they will think you have a car phone.

14

As An Obedience Dog
by Amy Weiss

Clearing the Hurdle

It is with much enthusiasm that I urge you to enter the wonderful world of obedience with your dog. Lucky you...you have a responsive, intelligent and loyal breed and, as you enter into a training program with him, you will make him a joy to own and a pleasure to live with.

Whether your aim is to pursue an active obedience show career, or simply to have a more controllable and livable companion, obedience training can, and should, be a most positive experience for both of you. In this chapter, I am going to discuss the formal part of obedience training, going for obedience show awards and training your dog to be the best type of companion.

The first step will be to locate the best training classes you can possibly find. While I don't usually recommend serious training for a puppy under six months of age, I've seen great results with younger puppies entered in a so-called "kindergarten class." Here, the puppies are deliberately exposed to other puppies, sounds, smells, noises, etc., while learning gentle control from their owner. With the proper training methods and a good instructor, these early experiences can be invaluable. On the other end of the scale, it's just not true that "you can't teach an old dog new tricks."

Shop around for a good training class no matter what age your dog is. You might inquire of other breeders, contact the local kennel club or the local obedience club. Once you learn of a class, attend the first few times without your dog and observe the training methods used. A dog is a sensitive, willing worker and you want your training done with kindness, love and respect. Most of all you want to use lots of praise. If you pursue a training program in this manner your dog will respond to you and be a happy, tail-wagging worker.

Many trainers have found that using food as a reward *only* for an exercise done perfectly can be a great training incentive. While this method may be somewhat controversial, I have found it to be of the greatest incentive in training my dogs. Try to exercise thought and reasoning in your training. A dog thrives on gentleness and praise. Remember, his attitude toward this whole endeavor is learned only from you. A happy working, obedience-trained dog is a tribute to your training efforts and a wonderful advertisement for our breed. For those of you interested in showing your dog in obedience trials, the AKC Obedience Degrees are:

CD — Companion Dog
CDX — Companion Dog Excellent
UD — Utility Dog

TD — Tracking Dog
UDT — Utility Dog Tracker
UDTX — Utility Dog Tracker Excellent

To earn each of these degrees, your dog must score more than 50% of the available points in each exercise with a final score of 170 or more points (out of a possible 200) under three different judges, in at least three different shows. Obedience classes are divided into A and B classes. Let me break down the scoring for you.

The exercises and available points are as follows:

NOVICE (*To qualify for the CD Degree*):

Heel on Leash	40 points
Stand for Examination	30 points
Heel Free	40 points
Recall	30 points
Long Sit	30 points
Long Down	30 points

Novice A Class — The AKC Obedience Regulations state that the "A" Class shall be for dogs that have not won the title of CD and that a person who has previously handled or trained a dog that has won a CD may not be entered in this class. It's a true class for novices. No person may handle more than one dog in Novice A Class.

AM. CAN. CH. JAN'S HARMONICA MAN, C.D.

Novice B Class — This class is also for dogs that have not won their CD. However, dogs in this class may be handled by their owner or any other person. An exhibitor may handle more than one dog in this class. After you obtain your first CD on a dog, you must show all future entrants in this class. No dog may be entered in both Novice A and Novice B classes at any single trial.

OPEN *(To qualify for CDX Degree).* All exercises are done off the leash.

Heel Free .... 40 points
Drop on Recall .... 30 points
Retrieve on Flat .... 20 points
Retrieve over High Jump........... 30 points
Broad Jump .... 20 points
Long Sit *(handler out of sight)* .... 30 points
Long Down *(handler out of sight)* ..... 30 points

Open A Class — This class is for dogs that have won the CD title but have not as yet won their CDX Degree. Each dog must be handled by its owner or by a member of the immediate family.

KENDOVIC'S SORCERER, C.D.X. AND CADO'S CURE FOR THE BLUES

CH. JIGSAW PUZZLE OF THE PINES, C.D.

Open B Class — This class is for dogs that have won the title CD or CDX. A dog may continue to compete in this class even after it has won the UD title. Dogs in this class may be handled by the owner or any other person. No dog may be entered in both Open A and Open B classes at any one trial.

JAN'S LI'L GOLDEN NUGGET, C.D.X.

Heel Position

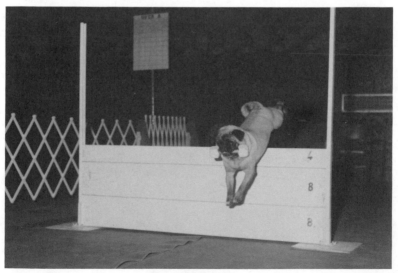

Over the Hurdle

UTILITY *(To qualify for Utility Degree)*

Signal Exercise . . . . 40 points
Scent Discrimination *(Article 1)* . . . . . . 30 points
Scent Discrimination *(Article 2)* . . . . . . 30 points
Directed Retrieve . . . . 30 points
Directed Jumping . . . . 40 points
Group Examination . . . . 30 points

Utility A and B Classes — A club may chose to divide the Utility class into "A" and "B" classes. When this is done the "A" class shall be for dogs which have won the title CDX and have not as yet won their UD title. The "B" class shall be for dogs that have won the title CDX and also UD (the latter may continue to compete in the Open B).

Down-Stay

TRACKING *(To qualify for TD Degree)*

The purpose of the Tracking Test (as set forth in the *AKC Obedience Regulations Book*) is to demonstrate the dog's ability to recognize and follow human scent and to use this skill in the service of mankind. Tracking, by its nature, is a vigorous noncompetitive outdoor sport. Tracking Tests should demonstrate willingness and enjoyment by the dog in his work, and should always represent the best in sportsmanship and camaraderie by the people involved. The regulations require that each track be designed to test dog and handler with a variety of terrain and scenting conditions. The dog is not asked to find the tracklayer, but he must overcome a series of typical scenting problems and locate objects dropped by the person whose track is being followed.

Doing a Retrieve

The Tracking Test must be performed with the dog wearing a harness to which is attached a leash between 30 and 40 feet long. The length of the track is to be not less than 440 yards nor more than 500 yards. The scent to be not less than one-half hour nor more than two hours old and that of a stranger who will leave an inconspicuous glove or wallet, dark in color, at the end of the track where it must be found and picked up by the dog. Tracking Tests require two judges for their conduct.

With each entry form for a dog that has not passed an AKC Tracking Test, there must be filed an original written statement, dated within six months of the date of the Test, signed by an AKC-approved tracking judge certifying that the dog is considered by him or her to be ready for such a test.

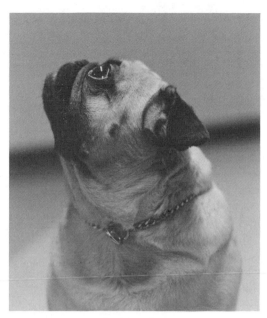

At Attention

TRACKING DOG EXCELLENT *(to qualify for the TDX Degree)*

The TDX Track shall not be less than 800 yards nor more than 1000 yards. The scent shall be not less than 3 hours nor more than 5 hours old and must be that of a stranger. Double cross tracks shall intersect the actual track at two widely separated points at right angles. The dog shall be challenged at several points on the track by changes in scent conditions. All types of terrain and cover, including gullies, woods and vegetation of any density may be used. Four personal articles shall be dropped on the track. Only the last article may be a glove or a wallet. The first article should be placed at the starting flag and be clearly visible to the handler. The 2nd, 3rd, and 4th articles should be dropped on the track at intervals and should not be visible to the handler from a distance of 20 feet.

It is said that "tracking is sport in the truest sense." The animal works for the sheer love of scenting. No dog can be forced to track. The tracking fraternity is known for its friendliness, its hospitality, and its encouragement to all participants. The thrill for the handler when the dog completes the test and locates the articles may be unsurpassed in any other AKC event.

It is possible for obedience dogs to attain championship status after they have achieved a Utility Degree. Obedience Trial Championship titles were approved by the AKC in 1977. Championship points will be recorded and any dog that has been awarded the title of Obedience Trial Champion may preface their name with O.T. Ch.

Requirements for the Obedience Trial Champion are as follows:

1. Must have won 100 points.
2. Must have a first place in Utility (at least 3 dogs competing).
3. Must have won a first place in Open B (at least 6 dogs).
4. Must have won a third first place under conditions 2 & 3 above.
5. Must have won these three first places under 3 different judges.

The points available are determined by the number of dogs competing both in Open B and Utility classes.

There are several non-regular classes offered for competition at some shows and trials. They include:

Graduate Novice	Versatility
Brace	Team
Veterans	

There are no degrees to be earned from competition in these classes. Scent Hurdle Demonstrations may be offered by any show-giving club, but they are not an AKC-recognized event. Obedience show classes are offered by dog training clubs, many all-breed clubs, and an increasing number of specialty breed clubs.

For more information, and in-depth explanations of each of the levels of obedience training and appropriate exercises, write to the American Kennel Club (51 Madison Avenue, New York, New York 10010) and ask for the *Obedience Regulations Book*. Single copies are free.

Now let's look at another reason for training your dog. There are many of you who won't want the formal competition of the obedience ring but want your dog to behave and be a good companion. For those of you who are interested in this aspect I would like to quote Curtis B. Hane writing in the March/April 1987 issue of the *Great Dane Reporter*.

Americans have always placed a high value on education. With students lining up for admission to colleges and graduate programs, schooling is again becoming big business. When it comes to their dogs, Americans are equally keen on education. Thus, the fields of obedience training, animal behavior modification, and counseling are also quickly becoming big business, offering countless services as complex as any university curriculum.

If you yourself are considering instruction for you and your dog, your choice must be an educated one. While some people harbor delusions of transforming the family pet into "Rex the Wonder Dog," your goals should be more realistic—teaching Spot not to pull your arms off when walked on a leash or competing in a local obedience trial. Perhaps

CH. JAN'S WILD PERSIMMON, C.D.

you are part of a smaller number who have a serious problem—a dog that bites, barks incessantly, or has the family in such a state of upheaval that permanent separation from the dog looms as the only solution (witness the need for many dog rescue organizations).

Whatever the problem, you may consider seeking the help of professionals in solving it. With some basic knowledge and a bit of consumer investigation, most people can find a program that suits the needs of both dog and owner.

Most dog training methods can be roughly divided into two groups: (1) obedience drills and exercises; and (2) behavioral counseling and training (to correct such problem behaviors as chewing, biting, and jumping up). This is an informal categorization, however, as many programs do not fit neatly into either group, offering aspects of both types of training. Therefore, choosing the right training program for your dog must be done carefully. You'll want to consider your own goals and financial resources and your dog's needs if you want the best chance for effective humane training.

There are four methods of dog training most commonly considered by dog owners: (1) the do-it-yourself method using one or more training manuals; (2) kennels or schools that board dogs for a predetermined length of time for training by in-house handlers; (3) the private trainer or counselor who provides individualized instruction (often in the pet owner's home); and (4) group classes for both dog and owner. Each method has its benefits and drawbacks.

Dog Training Manuals. It is possible with the aid of books to train your dog yourself. While this method can prove effective and economical, it also requires a little more care both in planning and in execution.

First, carefully read, cover to cover, at least two books before you begin the actual training. Many books cover only basic obedience exercises. With a bit of bookstore or library searching, however, you should be able to find at least one book that deals directly with the problem behavior(s) you are experiencing with your dog.

Second, keep in mind that a group class outside the home method has the advantage of introducing your dog to strange sounds and odors and especially, other dogs. Should you decide to train your dog yourself, avoid practicing soley in the familiar and isolated backyard. Once you have your dog under control, it is usually best to move training sessions to a public park or an isolated corner of a parking lot. This is the environment the two of you will ultimately face, so accustom your dog to its surroundings early.

Three good training books are *Playtraining Your Dog* by Patricia Gail Burnham (New York: St. Martin's Press, 1980); *The Dog Training Manual* by Kathryn Braund (Virginia: Denlinger Publishers, Ltd., 1984); *A Training Manual for Dog Owners* by the Monks of New Skete (Boston: Little, Brown and Company, 1978). These books deal with both obedience exercises and specific behavioral problems.

Kennels and Schools. Dog boarding facilities that house your dog for a period of time and promise to return to you an "obedient" dog are often merely profiting from an owner's laziness or insecurity. The handlers may employ inhumane methods and return dogs to untrained owners who dishearteningly watch their animals quickly revert to their previous poor behavior within a matter of days.

While not a recommended method, if you do intend—for whatever reason—to leave your dog in any facility for training by a professional handler, be certain to investigate carefully. These operations make a great many promises. Don't be innocently drawn in by a free school bus service, recorded telephone tips, elaborate graduation ceremonies, and other costly frills.

First, visit several kennels and evaluate what you see, smell, and hear.

Is there a noticeable odor? A well-run facility will be clean and neat. Do all fences and runs look and feel secure? Many dogs have escaped from poorly-designed runs. Listen for any sounds of shouting or confusion from the staff or tell tale signs of abuse or abusive equipment. Phyliss Wright, a former dog trainer, suggests a dog owner visit a facility at least twice before leaving a dog for training; three visits are not too many. Also, keep in mind that the "five-day quick train" method offered by many handlers is a myth. No reputable professional should offer or recommend such a program.

Second, it is essential that you insist upon follow-up sessions for you and your dog with the trainer. Any lessons the dog has learned will be wasted if the still uneducated owner returns to unsuccessful methods at home.

The Private Trainer. This method is perhaps the most effective means of correcting a dog's problem behavior. It is, for obvious reasons, also the most expensive, at $20 or more an hour. On the positive side, many private trainers are behaviorists who specialize in individualized programs emphasizing counseling for the owner and in-the-home instruction for dog and owner.

While most private trainers are reluctant to divulge their professional secrets, Mr. Bob Maida who operates a pet counseling and training facility in northern Virginia offers some tips he uses to stop destructive behavior:

1. Tie balloons on any area that your dog is chewing. When you see your dog near the area, walk over and casually pop the balloon.
2. Leave your radio on when you go out (no rock music—rock may make him aggressive) and turn on a light if it is or will be dark before you return.
3. When giving your dog verbal commands, change the inflection of your voice to a more powerful, no-nonsense tone.

Private instruction may be a worthwhile choice for all dogs but may be *essential* for some. Some dogs do not do well in a group setting, for example, aggressive dogs with meek owners. The disadvantage of a group setting, which often involves 15 or more dogs and owners is the amount of individual time that can be spent with each dog. Group classes sometimes cannot zero in on the person whose dog is having specific problems at home. By the very nature of such a class, instructors must come up with a universal method, a choreographed routine.

This individualized attention can be costly. Approximate prices can range anywhere from $50 for a two-hour session to over $350 for a complete program of behavioral counseling, in-the-home training, individualized lesson plans, and homework plans for the owner.

Two helpful books that explain dog counseling are *The Evans Guide for Counseling Dog Owners* by Job Michael Evans (New York: Howell

Book House, Inc., 1985) and *Understanding Your Dog* by Dr. Michael W. Fox (New York: Coward, McCann & Geoghegan, 1972).

   The Group Obedience Class. With the exception of books and manuals, the group class is certainly the most common method of dog training. However, when approached with the idea of training his dog in a group obedience class, the novice's first words may be: "But I want my puppy to stop jumping on visitors, not win a blue ribbon in a show!" True, most dog owners want to solve behavior problems and equally true, very few group instructors are behaviorists who have the time and expertise to address your specific needs. However, many dog trainers believe that obedience training in a group setting can both aid in the dog's socialization and establish a positive dog/owner relationship that carries over into behavior problem solving. When the dog misbehaves (for example, jumps up on a visitor) the dog can be told to "sit." If the classroom training has been successful, the dog will sit; thus the owner now has a means of communication through which he can make corrections.

   "Whatever a dog learns in class should be transferable to the home. The goal is for the dog and family to live in harmony," says Phyliss Wright. She emphasizes the importance of dog and owner simply spending time together: "Obedience training gives the dog an interaction with you, and the more interaction you have the closer you become as companions. Training sessions should be quality time between you and your dog." By taking an active role in your dog's training, the bond between owner and pet is strengthened.

   As mentioned earlier, when looking for an obedience class, be sure you observe at least one session before enrolling. An instructor who welcomes visitors is more likely to employ humane methods and enjoy working with both dogs and people. Carefully observe how the instructor handles dogs. Is a reward system used? Do not assume that all dog training instructors are, because of their daily involvement with animals, great lovers of dogs. As unfortunate as it may seem, some are in the business only for profit.

   If you have decided to enroll yourself and your dog in an obedience class, seek the recommendations of any acquaintances who have attended classes previously. If you have difficulty obtaining first-hand information, don't head for the Yellow Pages yet! Check first with one or more of the following resources: (1) your humane society; (2) your veterinarian; (3) the Better Business Bureau; and (4) your local consumer-protection agency.

   Group classes designed specifically for beginners usually emphasize the rudimentary obedience skills: heel on the leash, down, down-stay, heel-sit, sit-stay, and come when called. The knowledgeable instructor, however, will attempt to deal, whenever possible, with specific behavior

Sit-Stay

problems. Don't expect individual attention at every turn, but don't be afraid to ask questions and get involved. You will get out of the program only what you put into it.

The class will normally last from eight to ten weeks, one meeting per week. A knowledgeable instructor will stress at-home practice; set aside at least one-half hour (an hour if possible) for you and your dog to review the previous week's lesson. Also keep in mind that preliminary veterinary attention, particularly up-to-date vaccinations, is essential before exposing your dog to other animals.

Most good trainers endorse a training method with foundations in sound humane principles. They work to build a team . . . so the dog and owner have to work together, and they have to enjoy their work. Instruction should emphasize the practical benefits of training, always making a connection between class exercises and the home, yard and sidewalk. It's an excellent idea to explain to the class the purpose of the exercise.

As for the use of painful punishment devices, just about all the good teachers feel that anything that connects pain in the dog's mind with the owner should not be used. Positive reinforcement should be used. You don't punish your dog for getting on the sofa; you praise him for getting down. Praise and reprimand must be immediate: "Two seconds is too late. The dog will have forgotten already."

Let's look in on an advanced beginners program for adult dogs. This class is offered by a private training facility and held in the multipurpose room of a suburban YMCA.

Twenty dog/owner teams attend the Friday night class, the mid point in an eight-week series. Most arrive early to walk their dogs, to socialize, and to practice a few lessons before class. Terry, the instructor, stresses punctuality by closing the doors at the stroke of nine.

The class includes a wide variety of purebred and mixed-breed dogs and an equally diverse selection of owners, young and old, male and female. The owners attach training collars and long leads to their charges and take advantage of a short practice period, vying for space to put the finishing touches on that perfect heel. Terry, in a booming, no-nonsense voice, sets the class in motion, ordering the pairs to one side of the large and suddenly hushed room. Both dogs and owners are well trained in obeying verbal commands; the two-legged pupils obediently line up like happy recruits, their four-legged partners heeling at their sides.

The first lesson is "heel on a leash with turnaround," in which the dog must follow closely at its owners side while he walks several steps, quickly turns 180°, and then continues for several more steps. Most of the teams perform this exercise with relative ease, with two exceptions. Terry helps one team by simply correcting the attachment of the leather lead and collar and encouraging those having difficulty to intensify practice sessions at home.

Terry then moves quickly to the next exercise: the dog must stand for examination while the owner stands three feet in front holding the leash. Next, as an added temptation, the leash is dropped. The dog must stand perfectly still; any foot movement is corrected immediately. When this exercise is completed, Terry gives the signal to praise, and an echoing chorus of "Gooooooood Dog!" fills the room.

As a final drill for the evening, the dogs practice their "sit-stay," their passive poses belying their eagerness to run to their masters for some well-earned praise.

As the class winds down, Terry explains the homework for the week. Teams are to practice the "go to place" lesson, which teaches the dog to go on command to a physically defined place, such as a rug or dog bed and lie down. After a few student questions, the class ends.

A final word . . . as was said in the beginning of this chapter, the dog is first and foremost a companion animal. As such, its training should make dog and owner better companions through close interaction. Achieving this simple goal need not be a painful or inhumane process. Finding the training program that meets your needs requires some legwork, knowledge, and a large dose of common sense. With the right program, dedicated effort, and respect for your animal companion, the rewards for both of you can be impressive. Your bonds of companionship, respect, and understanding will be strengthened, and most importantly, the home you share will be more comfortable for both of you. □

SECTION VI

Famous People and Dogs Who Influenced The Breed

- *Outstanding Breeders and Kennels*
- *Dogs Who Influenced the Breed*

Celebrities attending the PDCA Specialty in 1958: (L-R) Ricardo Montalban, Lennie Hayton, Mrs. Montalbon, Richard Burton, Lena Horne, Duke of Windsor, Countess Kontozow Tolstoy, Mrs. Frothingham Wagstaff, Duchess of Windsor

CHAPTER 15

Outstanding Breeders and Kennels

FILOMENA DOHERTY — "Pugville"

The title of the "grande dame" of Pugs in the United States falls to Mrs. Filomena Doherty, former President of the Pug Dog Club of America and breeder of International Champion Pugville's Mighty Jim. But her beginning in dogs did not originate with Pugs. Instead, Mrs. Doherty started out with two Bulldogs. By her own admission she didn't know much about showing or breeding so she went to a show to watch and learn. Not long after that, both of her Bulldogs died of distemper — incurable in those days. Having seen Pugs at that first show, she then bought a "nice" male. The time soon came when she decided to buy a bitch for breeding. Mrs. Doherty went to a well-known kennel

CH. PUGVILLE'S MIGHTY JIM, the second pug to win the Toy Group at Westminster, 1953.

with her dog to purchase the bitch. The owner of the kennel, upon seeing the dog, informed Mrs. Doherty that he had serious problems, and should not be used for breeding. The bitch eventually was sold to Mrs. Doherty on the condition that she breed the bitch to Ch. Abbeyville Personality. That first bitch went on to become Ch. Melcroft Marigold, granddam of the great dog, Ch. Pugville's Mighty Jim.

Mrs. Doherty is remembered as well for her dedication to the Pug Dog Club of America, having served on the board for 20 consecutive years, from 1954 to 1974. Her positions ranged from a committee member, to board member, to president — an office she held for 16 years! She presided over such topics of debate and discussion as the separation of blacks and fawns (defeated - 1960), the first independent speciality (1957), the first Pug futurity (1968), the first regional Specialty shows (1969), and the incorporation of the Pug Dog Club of America (1973). During those years she also managed to serve numerous times as Trophy Chairman for the National Specialty, as well as Bench Show Chairman, Show Chairman, and even Futurity judge.

Despite all of these outstanding achievements, Mrs. Doherty considers growth in the membership to be her most important contribution to the Pug Dog Club of America. When she first joined the club, total membership consisted of only a handful of people, all simply friends who wanted to help improve the breed. Now the club boasts over 375 members. Mrs. Doherty is a fine example of how just one dedicated person can make a difference.

RICHARD PAISLEY

If Filomena Doherty is the "grande dame" of Pugs, then "Mr. Pug" himself would be Dick Paisley. A champion importer, Dick's Pugs left their mark upon the American scene with such notables as: Eng. & Am. Ch. Phidgity Phircone, Ch. Satan of Rydens, Piccolo Pete of Rydens, Ch. Neubraa Papageno, Ch. Tick Tock of Le Tasyll, and Ch. Hazelbridge Trump High of Le Tasyll. Many of these dogs are still found in the pedigrees of today's Pugs.

Dick was respected by everyone in Pugs, and is a major reason why they are so popular along the East Coast of the United States. He always went out of his way to answer questions and to help anyone, whether a novice owner or a fellow exhibitor. Dick was known all over the United States, and encouraged others with his ever optimistic, charismatic personality.

Not only a friend to all, Dick Paisley also contributed many hours to the early Pug Dog Club of America. Beginning in 1963, he served as Chairman of the Advertising Committee. In 1965, he began his three terms as the Corresponding Secretary. Some of his most influential work for the PDCA was his work on the 1967 National Handbook. Dick also wrote articles for *Pug Talk* magazine on a variety of topics, including colors in the Pug, movement, and whelping. Dick moved up to Recording Secretary of the Pug Dog Club of America in 1970, a post he held until his untimely death in 1973.

What many people remember Dick Paisley for is the rapport he had with his dogs. He was a terrific handler and had that "sixth sense" that it takes to stay one step ahead of the dogs in the show ring. Dick loved the dogs for themselves, not just for their winning abilities. In addition, Dick was one of the first Pug breeders in America to insist that all his dogs be x-rayed and certified free of hip dysplasia. He was a remarkable dog person: judge, exhibitor, importer and friend to all.

(L-R) CH. WISSELWOOD TENDER AMBER, CH. SHEFFIELD'S MIDAS TOUCH, CH. NEUBRAA PAPAGENO, CH. SHEFFIELD'S PALE PUTTY, 1975

GUS & ESTHER WOLF

The dog which may have most influenced the breed in the late 1960s was American and Canadian Ch. Wolf's Li'l Joe, who won 6 Best in Shows, 122 Best of Breeds, and 41 Group firsts. All of this while owner-handled, and never traveling by airplane! Joe was the culmination of 20 years of hard work and dedicated breeding by Gus and Esther Wolf. When speaking of Li'l Joe, Esther describes him as a great dog, a great showman, a fantastic sire, and the sweetest, most lovable, and funniest member of the household.

The influence that Li'l Joe left on the breed is still being felt today.

Many of the top Pugs trace their heritage back to Li'l Joe, sometimes on both sides of the pedigree. Ch. Dhandy's Favorite Woodchuck, for example, was a great-grandson of Li'l Joe's on both his sire's and dam's lines.

CH. GORE'S GABRIELLE, 1967

GORE'S PUGS

Of all the names that appear in modern Pug pedigrees, perhaps none appears more often than the Gore name. Combined with the "Robertson" and "Nunnally" lines (which are simply synonyms for the Gore name, as Louise was Mrs. Robertson for a short time!), a majority of today's quality Pugs trace their ancestry back to the Gore line.

Herman and Louise Gore began their long love affair with the breed after Louise saw a statue of a Pug in the play, "Life With Father" in 1945. Mrs. Gore was so overcome with emotion that she could not concentrate on the plot or the actors. She kept staring at the statue and wondering if there really WAS a dog that looked like that! It wasn't until eight years later, in 1953, that she acquired her first pet Pug.

In almost thirty-five years of breeding and showing, Louise finished over forty champions, owner-handled, including winning the Toy Group on two separate occasions with a class bitch. The first was in 1959 followed by one twelve years later with future champion Reinitz Babe Doll of Gore, who also went on to earn the designation of Register of Merit Dam from the Pug Dog Club of America. Another representative of Gore breeding was Ch. Bassett's Dapper Dan of Gore, winner in 1966 of the Pug Dog Club of America Specialty, the breed at Westminster, and the Chicago Pug Specialty.

Not limiting themselves to the fawn color, the Gores bred some lovely blacks, most notable of which was Ch. Gore's Jack Tarr, who was owned by Russel Hicks. Jack Tarr took back-to-back wins at the first and second Bluebonnet Pug Dog Club Specialties under judges Richard Paisley and Dr. Harry Smith. In 1969, there were three Gore Pugs in the top Pug ratings of the Phillips system: Ch. Heritage Tom Cat of Gore (#1), Ch. Crowell's Little Joe of Gore (#3), and Ch. Gore's Jack Tarr (#10).

The Gore's breeding program was determined by Herman's interest in genetics and pedigrees. To examine the parents and grandparents of Pugs they were considering using in their breeding program, the Gores would often travel across the country to personally look at the dogs behind the pedigrees. Louise and Herman, in planning their breeding programs, decided they would rather fight the faults they could see in the previous known generations and therefore would not breed to unknown dogs.

Early on they decided to use line-breeding as their primary method, but not to be fanatics about it. Later, they did some outcrossing, but only in special situations.

It was Louise's Ch. Gores Up N'Adam, who was Best of Winners at the 1977 Pug Dog Club of America National Specialty who did what Herman had always wanted one of their Pugs to do. In 1975, "Yankee" fulfilled a twenty-year-old dream of Herman and Louise's. In Columbus, Ohio, with an entry of 2000 dogs, Yankee went Best in Show. However, Herman never lived to see it as he had died in 1967. Other well-known recent champions of the Gore line include Ch. Robertson's Bourbon Prince, Ch. Robertson's Fanci Babe (sired by the famous Wolf's Li'l Joe), and Ch. Gore's Fanci Gin Phizz, all Register of Merit award winners.

ALAN & NORMA HARPER

The beginnings of the Harper line started with a family pet. Young Alan, then only 6 years old, had decided that he wanted a pure-bred dog. The family had looked for a Boston Terrier but they found this amazing little dog called a Pug. Winston, Alan's father, loved the puppy on sight and the puppy was waiting for Alan when he got home from school that day. Later, the family decided to get a second Pug for breeding. Alas, they soon discovered that their puppy was not really show quality so they found a better male and with that acquistion, founded the Harper line!

The dogs were Alan's responsibility and he took care of them. When he was 9, the family went to their first show where Dick Paisley was judging. They remember him as being very kind and polite. That experience convinced them to pursue their new found hobby with vigor.

The problem they had to deal with immediately was size, beginning with their bitch, Madam Blossom. She was a 16-pound bitch. However,

CH. PUG HAVEN CACTUS JIM

CH. FIDDLER FAHEY with Judge Percy Roberts, owner Mrs. Jane Fahey and Lena Horne, who donated and presented the trophy, 1965

when bred to a larger dog, she produced three 16-pound girls — the foundation of Harpers Pugs. The girls were Ch. Harper's Fawn C Pants, dam of 2 champions; Ch. Harper's Fawn Nie Girl, who never produced; and Ch. Harper's Fawn Nest Flower, dam of Ch. Harper's Star Sapphire, ROM*, and Best of Opposite at the 1977 PDCA National Specialty. These girls, in turn, passed on the qualities of good movement, nice heads and jawlines, but also big ears!

The Harpers have never bred for a show record, but rather bred their dogs for the qualities they needed. When necessary, they outcrossed to get certain characteristics missing in their dogs. In the past five years they have focused on closer breeding in order to set the type they desired. Their record in the eighties shows them winning consistently with both fawns and blacks.

Alan is now an approved judge of a number of breeds, and Norma continues the breeding plan. They've come a long way from that first pet!

E. N. K. & CHARLOTTE PATTERSON — Ivanwold Kennel

Originally established in Virginia in 1960, the Ivanwold Kennel of Edward and Charlotte Patterson has become an impressive force on the Pug scene. The "ideal Pug" the kennel bred for was modeled on the English Philwil line, as well as the Martlesham line. Early breeding included the names Ch. Walhaven Acrobat (a strong Philwil influence), and Ch. Martlesham Galahad of Bournle (an English import of the late Richard Paisley). Top dogs of the kennel in the '60s included Ch. Ivanwold High Tor, a multiple Group and Specialty winner, Ch. Ivanwold Johnny Appleseed, a Group placement winner, and Ch. Ivanwold High Barbary, a cross of Martlesham and Gore bloodlines.

The kennel was relocated in 1974 to Florida and has since bred over sixty champion Ivanwold Pugs. An important early winner was Ch. Ivanwold Senator Sam who amassed 14 all-breed Best in Show wins (a record at that time), and won the Toy Group at Westminster in 1980. He was also a two-time winner of the PDCA's National Specialty show, along with many other specialty shows.

Following Sam came Ch. Ivanwold Pistol Pete of Rontu, with five BIS all-breeds, as well as a three-time winner of the Bluebonnet Pug Dog Club Specialty. The third win allowed his owners to retire the Jack Keller Memorial Trophy. As far as can be determined, Pistol Pete was the first Pug to win a regional Specialty from the Veterans Class, which occurred at the Pug Dog Club of Greater Cincinnati show in 1982. Pistol Pete also left his mark by producing 37 champion get, winning the Mary Shipman Pickhardt award in 1981 and 1983.

The current "top dog" at the Ivanwold Kennel is Ch. Ivanwold Ancient

CAMEO'S HONEY BEAR, 1988

Mariner, bred by Edward and Charlotte, and owned by Mrs. Alan P. Robson. Sailor was the number one Pug for 1987 and 1988 in the PDCA ratings.

Not to be outdone by their dogs, the Patterson's also handle other Pugs professionally. In six years, they have finished over 100 Pugs to their championships, and handled the number one Pug for 1984, 1985, and 1986, Ch. Charlamar's Ancient Dreamer. Edward has been the breed columnist for the *American Kennel Club Gazette* for a number of years, as well as serving as a representative for many of the regional clubs at the PDCA Board meetings. Charlotte is currently vice-president of the PDCA, and has served on a number of national committees, as well.

BARBARA BRALEY & ANITRA HUTCHISON (DHANDY)

In 1960 Barbara Braley of the Dhandy Pugs, purchased her first Pug, Pug-Haven's Tag Along Jim from the Harley Hornbecks of Pug-Haven Kennels. Her second purchase, Ch. Pug-Haven's Cactus Pandy, a half brother to Tag Along Jim, became the foundation sire of her line. Her future partner, Anitra Hutchison, also purchased her first show Pug in 1958 from the Pug-Haven kennels. This dog was Pug-Haven's Sho Hotei, CDX. She later obtained the beautiful small bitch, Ch. Velvet Tracey, CD, from Dr. Gregory's well-known Velvet line.

In 1963, Velvet Tracey was bred to Barbara's Cactus Pandy, her grandson. Two boys were in the litter: Ch. Dandy's Marco Velvet, whom Barbara finished, was a group winner and a top ten Pug with limited showing.

Ch. Ah-Ya Gung Ho Murphy, the other brother, was shown by Anitra and finished during the heavy January competition on the Florida circuit.

In 1965, Barbara bought Crowell's Pandora, whose breeding emphasized the Fahey line. After completing her championship Pandora was bred to Marco Velvet, that litter producing a number of champions. Later, she was bred to Gung Ho Murphy. That breeding produced Ch. Dandy's Doryson Buccaneer, a group winner, ROM, and Mary Pickhardt award winner for champions produced from 1973-1977. Bucky, in turn, produced Ch. Bleuridge's Link who won the PDCA National in 1974.

This close intertwining of Pugdom's basic bloodlines has led to a winning heritage for Dhandy Pugs who have become known for their distinctive heads and magnificent movement. The culmination of this planned breeding came in the form of a pup named Woodchuck. Ch. Dhandy's Favorite Woodchuck would go on to become the only Pug ever to have won the coveted Best In Show at Westminster. He achieved this prestigious win in 1981.

Since then the Dhandy lines have not been idle. Offspring from Woodchuck have proven to be prepotent, with the bitches especially so. Many young dogs, including Ch. Dhandy's Coopertown Classic and Dhandy's Bitta Butterball, are waiting in the wings for their chance to become the next great Dhandy dog.

MARGERY SHRIVER — Sheffield Pugs

The fascination Margery Shriver has with dogs began in the late thirties when she competed in what was called Childrens Handling Class with borrowed dogs (which was allowed then). After her marriage, Margery continued her interest by securing a bitch from Mary Warner.

Several years were spent learning and observing while raising a few litters. It was not until 1964 that she kept her first homebred bitch, Sheffield's Sunny Peach. The following year she purchased a lovely bitch puppy of mostly English bloodlines from Louise Baker. She became Ch. Serenade of Sheffield. Her three champion offspring, Ch. Sheffield's Rock N'Roll, Ch. Sheffield's Sunday Punch, and Ch. Sheffield's Sally Sunshine, became the foundation of the Sheffield line.

Two champion offspring of Peach and Serenade, Sheffield's Sunday Punch and Ch. Sheffield's Lucy Locket Shogo, produced Ch. Sheffield's Sure-Fire currently the all-time top-producing dam. Sure-Fire was also a show winner, with four Best of Opposite Sex at specialty shows, as well as some Best of Breeds and a Group 4 placement.

Sheffield stud dogs have combined for a total of over 150 champion get. Current Sheffield show winners include Ch. Sheffield's Jersey Bounce with two Best In Shows and five Best in Specialty Shows, and Ch. Sheffield's Spitfire who won the PDCA National Specialty at 17 months of age.

Miss Susan Grahm-Weall and her Phidgity Pugs

CH. HAZELBRIDGE BLACK EROS wins stud dog class at the 1979 PDCA Specialty

In her mind's eye, Margery envisions the ideal Pug patterned after the English type: cobby and square. She has bred or co-bred 68 champions and finished 9 champions bred by others. Her Pugs are almost always owner-handled, and campaigned mostly in the Mid-Atlantic area. She is always willing to give of her time and has been a great help to many novices.

M. MOXLEY & C. CORSON — CHARLAMAR

Two ladies who have influenced the Pug breed in the last ten years are Mary Moxley and Charlotte Corson of Missouri. Their Charlamar name has become one of the most recognized in the country. From early beginnings with black Pugs, they now can list numerous Best In Shows, as well as Group and Specialty winners. Their quality black Pugs are shown throughout the country, and their fawn dogs are much in demand.

From a breeding of their Ch. Charlamar's Billy Joe Black (black) and Ch. Nunnally's Witch Hazel ROM (black), they produced Ch. Charlamar's J. Randall Brown, a fawn dog who would go on to produce two ROM sires. In addition, J. Randall Brown did his share of winning, including taking the Breed from the Bred By Exhibitor class at the Great Lakes Pug Club Specialty. At only 17 pounds, he proved that he could win and also produce, with such offspring as Ch. Charlamar's Louis St. Louis (black), who was Winners Dog from the 6 - 9 month class at the PDCA National, and Ch. Charlamar's Ancient Dreamer, the leading Pug for 1985, 1986 and 1987. The ladies of Charlamar have many up and coming dogs, both fawn and black, that will continue the winning tradition of Charlamar.

PEOPLE TO WATCH

There are many other people who have been active many years in the Pug breed that bear watching. These breeders are the next generation who will influence the breed. In the West, there is Blanche Roberts and "Blaque" Pugs, who consistently has produced quality for many years, as well as Pamela Weaver in Oregon, who has served on the PDCA Board of Directors recently. The "War.joy" name of Warren Hudson in Washington state is one that has quietly meant quality for over twelve years, while Dave and Patty Ricketts of Arizona may, in time, become names to deal with in the Southwest.

In the Midwest, Dori Carnell of Colorado continues to produce good dogs, and Sonja Neu (Iowa) has already made a strong impact with her BIS winning black bitch, Ch. Neu's Enchanting Sorceress. Mrs. Patricia Hallagan has brought the Hallagan kennel name to prominence in Indiana. Geraldine Canary is a steady breeder of quality in that state, as well. Missouri, though, seems to be a hotbed of quality, with Mrs. Jane Fahey and her Fahey Farm Pugs, Mrs. Loretta Wiseman and the Wise-Lore

Pugs, and Mrs. Mary Ann Hall with her beautiful Maridon's Pugs. In Nebraska are Robert and Ann White, breeders as well as judges, while Ohio boasts of Martha Pratt of Paulmar Pugs, Norval and Bonna Webb of the famous Bonjor Pugs, and Mr. and Mrs. Joe Ravotti's Cameo Pugs. Texas, too has numerous breeders, including Herb and Wilma Hyatt, Mrs. Nell Gramigna, Judge Marilynn Ellis, and Jacqueline Siegel and her Stage Door Pugs.

In the Southeast are many good breeders, including the Florida folks: long-time Pug breeder and judge Mrs. Florence Gamburg, Shirley Goodwin, Mr. and Mrs. John Rowell, Dr. and Mrs. Curtis Weston and the Pugs of Weston's Nest, and the Adairs. In Georgia you find Jan and Ronnie Plott, as well as Pat and Larry Shepherd. Mrs. Ann Crowel has bred many fine dogs for many years in Tennessee, while Curtis Rowe has been a strong competitor in Kentucky for a long time. George and Margaret Darden have quietly bred beautiful Pugs in Mississippi for many years, and Brenda Harrower's Pugs of Pern continue their southern tradition of excellence.

The East Coast has long been a stronghold of the Pug breed, with many, many faces, both old and new. It boasts the names of Sue Christensen, Lucille Perzan, Peter and Janet McLaughlin, and the long-established Silvertown Kennels of Polly Lamarine in Connecticut. Maryland is the home of the Van Buskirk family, as well as Carol Gossweiler (Chapel Ridge Pugs) and Marjorie May. Meg Bloxham and Maryellen Castimore of Tori Lane Pugs are located in New Jersey, as well as Carroll and Toni Harrold, and Mrs. Bert Porter. Patricia Scully leads a list of New Yorkers that includes Wanda Hunter (Wanjo), Mrs. Shirley Thomas and long-time breeder Reba Weitz. Life member of the Pug Dog Club of America, Dr. Nancy Riser, DVM, is from Pennsylvania, as well as Andrea J. Belmore, Harry DeGraw and Mrs. Ferman Ritter. Robert and Linda LaBossiere from Rhode Island round out the list of Pug people to watch for tomorrow, as they are making a name for themselves today.

16

Dogs Who Influenced The Breed

CH. PUGVILLE'S MIGHTY JIM

AM. CAN. CUBAN BDA CH. PUGVILLE'S MIGHTY JIM

Whelped: April 5, 1950
Sire: Ch. Melcroft Music Maker
Dam: Am, Can, Cuba Ch. Phyl's Donna Annabelle
Breeder/Owner: Mrs. Philomena Doherty

Considered by Mrs. Doherty the "Boss" of Pugville Kennels and the love of her life, "Jim" was the dog with the greatest all-around show record for his day. Considered to be very elegant, Jim was an aloof dog who demanded every judge to give him the wins he deserved. Described once as "the proud

---

little dog with the doughnut tail," he amassed 172 Best of Breeds (out of 182 times shown), with 65 Group I and 90 additional Group placings. This includes eight Best-In-Show wins, two American-Bred Best-In-Show wins, and four consecutive Best-of-Breed wins at Westminster Kennel Club, including a Group I. Always handled by Walter Foster, Jim's wins were amassed in competition at the larger East Coast show during the first four years of the 50s. By being campaigned week in and week out, Jim brought the Pug breed to prominence in the show ring.

Early on, it was questioned whether Jim could live up to the show record of his dam, Ch. Phyl's Donna Annabelle, which included Group I — an unheard of feat for a bitch in the 1940s! Mrs. Doherty could never show Jim herself, as he always attempted to play with her rather than show. She even remembers him trying to run between her legs and tug on her slip!

Jim was retired at age four (while still on top) to allow his up-and-coming sons their places in the ring. One of them, Int. Ch. Pugville's Maybe Stupendous, had 38 BOB, nine Groups, and many placings prior to being sold from Pugville Kennels. Following him came Ch. Pugville's Mighty Wrinkles who was retired with 35 BOB, eight Groups and numerous Group placings. Both of these sons completed their Championships in just four shows each — shows that included Morris & Essex, Westminster, Boston and Chicago. It is conceivable that Jim could easily have added to his record had he not "abdicated" prematurely in favor of his promising sons. He was, however, returned to the ring at age seven and one-half to add another country's title to his record. In Bermuda, he earned not only his Championship, but also three BOB, two Group Is, one Group placement, and one Best in Show — in three shows.

Jim sired 38 champions, among which were Ch. Pugville's Imperial Imp II owned by the late Duke and Duchess of Windsor, and Ch. Pugville's Might Hope owned by Prince Rainier and the late Princess Grace of Monaco. His legacy continues through numerous bloodlines of today's champions.

CH. BLAYLOCK'S MAR-MA-DUKE

Whelped: March 17, 1956
Sire: Ch. Velvet Tubby   Dam: Blaylock's Cheata
Owner: Mr. Gordon Winders
Breeder: Rolla Blaylock

"Mar-Ma-Duke" was the Pug who next came along to challenge Pugville's Mighty Jim. With 175 total show wins, Mar-Ma-Duke had three consecutive Best-of-Breed wins at the Pug Dog Club of America's National Specialties in 1958, 1959, and 1960, the only dog ever to do so. Mar-Ma-Duke was the product of Mr. and Mrs. Rolla Blaylock's breeding program that was based on the Winna and Melcroft bloodlines. The Blaylocks were well known for

CH. BLAYLOCK'S MAR-MA-DUKE

the champions they sold, as well, including Ch. Gore's Swap, a brother of Mar-Ma-Duke, and Mar-Ma-Duke himself. Mar-Ma-Duke was handled nationally by Jack Funk, and the two were quite a team. Together they racked up 12 Best in Shows (all breed), the three National Specialty wins, another specialty win at the Great Lakes Pug Club Specialty in 1960, 71 toy Group Is, 83 other Group placings, and the 175 Best-of-Breed wins. There is a well known picture of Mar-Ma-Duke's owner, Gordon Winders, standing with his collection of more than 300 trophies and awards won by Mar-Ma-Duke.

Mar-Ma-Duke sired 30 champions, and these dogs in turn continued to improve the breed. Their show records reaffirmed the greatness of their sire. For the years 1961 and 1962, Duke was a Top Sire, with the Phillips System placing him in the Top 10 Dogs of the Toy Group for the years 1957, 1958, 1960, and 1961.

Duke was not only king of the show ring, but was ruler of the Pugs at home. He was a wonderful pet and loved not only by his family and friends, but by the members of royalty and many celebrities.

THE PAISLEY DOGS

An unusual designation, but the late Dick Paisley's kennel included so many sensational dogs that it is difficult to single out one to represent the

---

rest. All of these dogs were whelped in the 1950s and early 1960s. The following dogs were the pride and joy of Dick's kennel:

CH. SATAN OF RYDENS (IMP)

Whelped: Feb. 11, 1962
Sire: Sam of Rydens   Dam: Vanity of Rydens
Breeder: Mrs. Cynthia Young

"Satan" was Dick Paisley's pride and joy among his studs. He was unmatched as a black sire. Some of his winning get include Ch. Satina, a winner at the National Specialty, Ch. Gore's Jack Tarr, Ch. Ewo's Satanson and Ch. Baronrath Travillah. All of these dogs were Toy Group winners, with Jack Tarr and Baronrath Travillah Best-In-Show winners. Ch. Baronrath Travilah was also the first black bitch to go BIS in the United States.

ENG. & AM. CH. PHIDGITY PHIRCONE (IMP)

Whelped: Apr. 4, 1963
Sire: Phidgity Phurze   Dam: L'Esperance Henrietta
Breeder: Lee Walker

English and American Ch. Phidgity Phircone, or "Chunky," was a prolific sire who introduced a new, longer head shape to the Pug breed in America. The 1968 sire of the year, Chunky was for a time the only living English and American champion Pug. With a total of 13 champion offspring, much of Chunky's legacy lives on today through his descendants in the Wisselwood line: Ch. Heathers Honey of Wisselwood ROM, Ch. Wisselwood Legacy of Phircone, Ch. Wisselwood Masked Marvel, and Ch. Wisselwood Mighty Mover. Other well known get include Ch. Auburndale Aquarius, Ch. Freckleton's Aero Queen, Ch. Odalisque's Blossom Time and Ch. Paisley Pickpocket.

CH. TICK TOCK OF LE TASYLL (IMP)

Whelped: Apr. 3, 1967
Sire: Ch. Buster of Rydens   Dam: Hazelbridge Little Toy of LeTasyll
Breeder: D. J. Nash

Ch. Tick Tock of Le Tasyll, or "Fred," as he was called, was also imported by Dick Paisley. He was the first dominant black Pug in America to consistently throw his heavy bone and gorgeous type to nearly every one of his offspring. Dick was especially proud of the fact that Fred's offspring in turn were producing quality get of their own. In many ways, Fred was responsible for upgrading the quality of black Pugs to the level were they could consistently compete with the fawns of the day.

Fred's descendants seen today include: Ch. Porters Pure Gusto, Ch.

CH. MARTLESHAM GALAHAD OF BOURNLE

Wisselwood Wizard of Pug-Pak, Ch. Wisselwood Velvet Tubby, and Ch. Wisselwood Horton Hearsa Who.

CH. MARTLESHAM GALAHAD OF BOURNLE (IMP)

Whelped: April 1967
Sire: Ch. Stormie of Martlesham   Dam: Olive Beaute of Bournle
Breeder: Mrs. D. E. Elbourn

Laddie was a Group and Best-In-Show winner who influenced the breed through a single letter. Bred to Ivanwold Portia's Pride, Laddie produced Ch. Ivanwold Johnny Appleseed, Ch. Ivanwold Orange William, Ch. Ivanwold Alice in Wonderland, and the outstanding Ch. Ivanwold High Tor. Johnny Appleseed was a multiple Group placer, while High Tor was a Group and Specialty winner, as well as a ROM sire in his own right. Orange William and Alice had winning show careers, as well as winning offspring, but it was Ch. Ivanwold High Tor who had the most profound impact on the breed.

CH. NEUBRAA PAPAGENO (Photo by William P. Gilbert)

CH. NEUBRAA PAPAGENO (IMP)

Whelped:
Sire: Ch. Prendergast of Pyebeta   Dam: Edenderry Colanee
Breeder: Sybil Nehring
Owner: Richard Paisley

"Geno" was the last most prolific of Dick's imported studs, coming from the kennel of Sybil Nehring in England. Geno lived with Cmdr. Willis Shaw after Dick's death. His influence was again in the strength of his offspring, with many still well known: Ch. Sheffield's Midas Touch and Ch. Sheffield's Pale Putty coming from a breeding with Ch. Sheffield's Constant Comment ROM*. Ch. Hanover's Cassandra D'Geno and Ch. Hanover's Cassius D'Geno were from a cross with Ivanwold Chelsea of Hy Windy, CD. But, bred to Heathers Honey of Wisselwood, a Register of Merit designated Phidgity Phircone daughter, Geno was spectacular. The resulting get were: Ch. Stonecrusher of Wisselwood ROM, Ch. Wendy the Poo of Wisselwood, Ch. Wisselwood Budweiser, Ch. Wisselwood Tender Amber, and Ch. Wisselwood's Cliff Hanger, all who went on to influence many strains of Pugs.

AM. CAN. CH. WOLF'S LI'L JOE

AM. CAN. CH. WOLF'S LI'L JOE

Whelped: July 1965
Sire: Ch. Cheerio of Even So Dam: Ch. Wolf's Kauffee Royal Rose CD
Breeders/Owners: Gus & Esther Wolf

Perhaps the most famous of all modern Pugs, Am. Can. Ch. Wolf's Li'l Joe was also closest to the hearts of Gus and Esther Wolf. After 18 years of breeding Pugs, the Wolfs considered themselves lucky to have bred him. Esther once said, "Most breeders never breed a BIS dog in their lifetimes. To add to the accomplishment, we showed Joe ourselves — win, lose, or draw — and we did a lot of losing." Also, the fact that Joe was never, ever placed on an airplane to be flown anywhere severely limited the number of shows he was entered in. In spite of all this, Joe eventually won six BIS, 41 Toy Groups, and 144 BOB.

The offspring that descended from Li'l Joe have shown that his influence was not a fluke. Ch. Sheffield's Constant Comment, a daughter owned by Margery Shriver, was BOS at the PDCA National Specialty in both 1975 and 1976. Additionally, nine of his get are Register of Merit Pugs, including: Ch. Li'l Davey of Sheffield, Ch. Shirrayne's Brash Buffi, Ch. Robertson's Fanci Babe, and Ch. Li'l Sugar of MSJ. Li'l Joe tied for top Pug sire in 1969 and was the top sire for 1970. He also tied for top Toy Sire, all toy breeds, in 1970.

SHEFFIELD

Another group designation must go to the dogs of Margery Shriver and her Sheffield line. Since the 1970s, her dogs have been well known throughout the country for their quality and prepotent genes. Many times, a quick look at a dog is enough to determine that it is a Sheffield dog. A few stand out as those who have (and still are) influenced the breed:

CH. SHEFFIELD'S LITTLE RED WAGON

Whelped: Nov. 12, 1981
Sire: Ch. Sheffield's Rose Tattoo   Dam: Ch. Sheffield's Country Cousin
Breeder/Owner: Margery Shriver

"Reddy" is one of the top sires today, with more than 37 champion get. Sired by Ch. Sheffield's Rose Tattoo (Ch. Sheffield's Sneaky Pete, ROM X Ch. Sheffield's Second Hand Rose, ROM), Reddy is a third-generation ROM-designated sire. His winning get include: Ch. Gerrie's Rory of Charlamar, Ch. Katsu Honeybun of Maridon (a Best in Specialty Show winner), Ch. Maridon's Texas Tiger, Ch. Porter's Spirit of Eighty-Six, and Ch. Sheffield's Spitfire, winner of the PDCA National Specialty at the age of 17 months. Reddy is still siring quality puppies.

CH. SHEFFIELD'S LITTLE RED WAGON

CH. SHEFFIELD'S STUFF'N NONSENSE

Whelped: Nov. 19, 1978
Sire: Ch. Samet Paul of Paramin (Eng. Imp.)
Dam: Ch. Sheffield's Sweeter Than Wine
Breeder/Owner: Margery Shriver

"Stuffy" is the number-two dog in terms of champions produced, with 65, and he is still actively producing. The long-standing record of Wolf's Li'l Joe may soon fall.

Stuffy has sired two BIS winners to date, and numerous Group and Breed winners. Many of the top sires and winners of today are sons or grandsons of Stuffy. He is the sire of three Register of Merit sires, Ch. Bonjor Peter Parker, Ch. Bornfree Phire Fox (both sires of ROM dogs, and Ch. Sheffield's Life of the Party. He also has five ROM daughters: Cameo's Very Vanilla, Ch. Chapel Ridge Queen Anne Lace, Donaldson's Apricot Brandi, Ch. Ivanwold Honeysuckle Rose, and Manalapan's September Song, dam of the current winning dogs, Ch. Sheffield's Jersey Bounce, Ch. Porter's Spirit of Eighty-Six, Ch. Sheffield's Jersey Joe porter, and Ch. Sheffield's Spitfire. Three of these dogs are in the Top Ten Pugs for 1988.

CH. DANDY'S FAVORITE WOODCHUCK

CH. DHANDY'S FAVORITE WOODCHUCK

Whelped: Feb. 21, 1977
Sire: Ch. Chen's A Favorite of the Gods
Dam: Ch. Heritage Wicked Witch
Breeder: Barbara Braley & Anitra Hutchison
Owner: R. Hauslohner

"Woodchuck" was literally born on the road in the back of Barbara's station wagon during a mad dash to the veterinarian because his entry into this world was not going smoothly. After he finally arrived, the trip to the vet continued and Chipmunk (Ch. Dhandy's Favorite Chipmunk) arrived. Woodchuck and Chipmunk finished quickly with Barbara and Anitra, and Woodchuck had eight Group wins in casual jaunts close to home — four handled by Barbara and four by Anitra. In 1979, Woodchuck went to Robert A. Hauslohner to be campaigned. Mr. Hauslohner has had many outstanding winners through the years, but Woodchuck was his first Pug.

The favorite memory of Woodchuck's winning career was in February 1981, when a group of about 30 Florida dog exhibitors gathered in a small motel to watch cable television — and Westminster. As the people there had assorted breeds, comments were heard on the various dogs they saw and those they had heard of, but never seen before. When the Toy Group was going into the ring, Bobby Barlow's (Woodchuck's handler) red coat was seen as the camera panned down the line of dogs. When "Chucky" gaited, the whole room applauded and when he won the Group — shouts and more applause. Hometown boy makes good! When the final six were in the ring, the TV announcer gave a vast amount of background on most of the final winners: who was favored, who had won before, who was going to retire, etc. When Woodchuck was finally gaited the background of swelling applause at Westminster could be heard as the commentator said, "This little dog seems to have won the hearts of the spectators." When Judge Langdon Skarda pointed to Chucky for Best in Show, the motel as well as the Garden went wild. Barbara and Anitra stayed at the motel until 3 a.m. to watch the replay all over again! Woodchuck, or Chucky, was the first Pug to win a BIS at Westminster.

The legacy that Chucky left Pugs is through his offspring, as he died in an accident the summer after his win at Westminster. Notably, the bitches sired by Woodchuck have been outstanding: nine designated as Register of Merit by the Pug Dog Club of America, and their get are turning out to be top producers themselves.

SECTION VII

Representative Winning Dogs and Bitches

- *Great Winning Dogs of the Recent Past*
- *Great Winning Bitches of the Recent Past*

CHAPTER 17

Great Winning Dogs
of the Recent Past

The 33 Pugs pictured in this chapter are some of America's top winning male champions in the recent past. Though unable to depict every top winning, male Pug, this representative sampling of winning Pugs, both fawn and black, portrays some of the best that America has offered during the last decade or so.

CH. LKK'S FLY'N TIGER OF ROSEVILLE

CH. BLAQUE'S STREAKIN DEACON

CH. SHEFFIELD'S STUFF'N NONSENSE, ROM
CH. SHEFFIELD'S STAGE DOOR JOHNNY
CH. SHEFFIELD'S WILDFLOWER
CH. BLAQUE'S STREAKIN DEACON
Ken M's Starskipper
CH. BLAQUE'S KITTY MAE
Jo Nol's Blaque Amber

Breeder/Owner: Blanche Roberts
Handler: Ann Storniolo

"Deacon," winner of the PDCA Specialty Show at the AKC Centennial, has gone on to many other Specialty and All Breed show wins.

He is an excellent dog with a good head. He also has a short body and fine movement His offspring have inherited his fine qualities.

CH. BONJOR THE SPORTIN' MAN

CH. HARPER'S TOMMY TUNE
CH. HARPER'S HUIE LEWIS
Harper's Jewell of Denham, ROM
CH. BONJOR THE SPORTIN' MAN
CH. BONJOR CLARK KENT
Bonjor Pirouette
Bonjor Ballerina

Breeder: Bonna Webb
Owner: John & Linda Rowell & Bonna Webb

A proven Breed winner, "Sport" has excellent bone and type, as well as being short and cobby. He also passes on to his get his large head.

CH. CAMEO'S ORANGE JULIUS

CH. SAMET PAUL OF PARAMIN (ENG. IMP)
CH. SHEFFIELD'S STUFF'N NONSENSE, ROM
CH. SHEFFIELD'S SWEETER THAN WINE
CH. CAMEO'S ORANGE JULIUS
CAN. CH. ROSENED'S TOMAC
Rosend's Lotus Blossom
Rosend's Precious Penelope

Breeder/Owner: Jan Ravotti
Handler Judy Hemmerling

"Julius" is a proven, consistent producer of puppies. His hips X-ray excellent and he has a straight front. Possibly his best feature, though, is his marvelous broad head. These are qualities that are passed on to his offspring. Julius was designated a Register of Merit Sire by the Pug Dog Club of America in 1989.

CH. CAMEO'S SUPER STUFF

```
                    CH. SHEFFIELD'S STUFF'N NONSENSE
         CH. BONJOR CLARK KENT
                    CH. BONJOR ANGEL OF CHARITY
CH. CAMEO'S SUPER STUFF, ROM
                    CH. TERYTAM TASKMASTER, ROM
         CH. ROWELL'S TOUCH OF TIFFANY, ROM
                    CH. ROWELL'S DHANDY GYPSY ROSE, ROM
```

Breeder: Joe & Jan Ravotti
Owner: Linda G. & John Rowell Jr.
and Joe & Jan Ravotti

"Super" amassed quite a show record after moving to Florida. A top-ten Pug for 1986 and 1987, he qualified for the Purina Invitational Show, was in the top twenty Pugs PDCA Showcase in 1987, and won a Best in Specialty show at the hotly contested Tampa Bay Pug Club show in 1987. His show career includes 48 Best of Breeds including five Group Is at all-Breed shows, and 23 other Group placings.

CH. CHAPEL RIDGE'S THEODORE

CH. SAMET PAUL OF PARAMIN (ENG. IMP)
CH. SHEFFIELD'S SNEAKY PETE
CH. SHEFFIELD'S CONSTANT COMMENT
CH. CHAPEL RIDGE'S THEODORE
CH. FRECKLETON'S AREO KING
Chapel Ridge's Angelus Belle
Shirrayne's Doodlebug

Breeder/Owner: Dr. & Mrs. Robert L. Gossweiler

"Teddy" finished in style with an all-Breed Best in Show at Pennsylvania Treaty K.C. That day he beat 2389 dogs at only 11 months of age. He has begun producing very nice puppies who should do well in the show ring.

CH. CHAUNCELEAR'S DHANDY ANDY

CH. DHANDY'S SKY RIDER
CH. DHANDY'S TOBY JOE YOUNG
CH. DHANDY'S WOODEN SHOE
CH. CHAUNCELEAR'S DHANDY ANDY
CH. DHANDY'S FAVORITE WOODCHUCK
CH. CHAUNCELEAR'S BITTA DHANDY
CH. CHAUNCLEAR'S GOLDEN GIRL, ROM

Breeder: Patricia A. Park
Owners: Patricia A. Park & Barbara A. Braley

"Andy" went Best of Winners from the Puppy Class on his very first weekend of shows. Before finishing he had two Best of Breeds and a Group III under his belt! His dam is a specialty winning Woodchuck daughter, while his sire is a specialty winning grandson of Ch. Dhandy's Favorite Woodchuck. Andy continued the family tradition when he won Best of Breed at the 12th Tampa Bay Pug Club Specialty.

CH. CHELSEA'S CHECKMATE

CH. BROUGHCASTL BALLADEER
CH. CHAUNCELEAR'S GOODTIME CHARLEY
CH. CHAUNCELEAR'S GOLDEN GIRL
CH. CHELSEA'S CHECKMATE
CH DONALDSON'S TIPPI CANOE
CH. CHELSEA'S HIDE AND SEEK, ROM
CH. RITTER'S GOLDEN DAWN

Breeder: Cindy Stover
Owner: Patti Lin & Cindy Stover

Ch. Chelsea's Checkmate is pictured winning Best of Breed at the Minnesota River Valley Kennel Club on April 15, 1988.

BEST OF BREED
MN. RIVER VALLEY K.C.
APRIL 15, 1988
OLSON PHOTO - TERI

CH. CROWELL'S REBEL ROUSER OF GORE

CH. GORE'S UP N' ADAM
CH. GORE'S FANCI ADAM
CH. ROBERTSON'S FANCI BABE
CH. CROWELL'S REBEL ROUSER OF GORE
CH. NALLEY'S ELEGANT ED
Nalley's Li'l Skimper
Dant's Katie Did

Breeder: Carolyn June Ricke
Owner: Ann D. Crowell

The picture shows "rebel" going Best of Breed from the classes over Specials for his first major at the Mid-Kentucky Kennel Club show in August of 1986. After finishing his championship he was retired, a multiple Breed winner and Group placer. A beautiful apricot with outstanding showmanship, his first litter was all show quality.

CH. DARDEN'S B.A. WINNER

CH. DARDEN'S MUS' BE MATTHEW
CH. DARDEN'S SOLDIER OF FORTUNE
Darden's Miss Behavin
CH. DARDEN'S B.A. WINNER
CH. DARDEN'S LITTLE JOHN OF GORE
CH. DARDEN'S MEE TU
Darden's Gee Whiz of Southland, ROM

Breeder/Owner: George Darden
Handler: Brenda Harrower

Darden's B.A. Winner, "Man," went Best of Winners at the Greater Atlanta Pug Specialty for a four-point major in the Spring of 1988. He completed his championship handled by a novice. He is now siring the traditionally excellent Darden type puppies.

CH. DARDEN'S DUIT DONOVAN

CH. BROUGHCASTL BOMBADIER
CH. DARDEN'S MUS' BE MATTHEW
Darden's Gee Whiz of Southland, ROM
CH. DARDEN'S DUIT DONOVAN
Paulmars Super Trooper
CH. DARDEN'S LILY OF BRITTANY
Cameo's Very Vanilla

Breeder: Margaret J. Darden
Owner: Brenda Harrower

"Donovan" is a campaigning little dog achieving his championship in only six shows! A true line-bred Pug, Donovan went on to back-to-back Best of Breeds the following weekend, with a group I on the second day. We expect many things from this little man.

CH. DARDEN'S LITTLE JOHN OF GORE

CH. ROBERTSON'S PINTO
CH. ROBERTSON'S TALK TO ME JOHN
Robertson's Milo
CH. DARDEN'S LITTLE JOHN OF GORE
CH. GORE'S UP'N ADAM, ROM
CH. GORE'S UP'N FANCY BEBE
CH. ROBERTSON'S FANCI BABE, ROM

Breeder: Louis Gore
Owners: George & Margaret Darden

"Little John" is the sire of champions at Darden Pugs and the top stud as well. He went Best of Winners at the 1981 Great Lakes Specialty from an outstanding class. Shown as a Special on a limited basis; always capable of wins over top ten pugs. He was retired with multiple Best of Breed and Group placements. His offspring are now out and winning, often following their father's footsteps by going Best of Winners at Specialties.

CH. DARDEN'S MUS' BE MATTHEW

Gais Rufty Tufty (Eng Imp), ROM
CH. BROUGHCASTL BOMBADIER
CH. BONJOR'S SUSAN B. ANTHONY
CH. DARDEN'S MUS' BE MATTHEW
CH. GORE'S UP'N ADAM, ROM
Darden's Gee Whiz of Southland, ROM
CH. SOUTHLAND'S DIXIE OF CROWELL

Breeder/Owner: Margaret J. Darden

"Matthew" congratulates his kids and grandkids on their wins: Ch. Darden's Soldier of Fortune going Best of Winners at the PDCA regional and finishing with four majors; Ch. Darden's Moonflower, who went Best of Opposite Sex over Specials for a four-point major, and others. He consistently passes winning attributes on to his get.

CH. GOODWIN'S GANDY DANCER

CH. PRELLY'S ROLLY ROISTER
CH. CHENS A FAVORITE OF THE GODS
CH. ALEXANDER'S VILLAGE IDIOT
CH. GOODWIN'S GANDY DANCER
Goodwin's Anxious Andy
Goodwin's Dixie Darling, ROM
CH. GOODWIN'S GEORGY GIRL

Breeder/Owner/Handler: Shirley J. Goodwin

This dog lived up to his name and danced to his championship (enjoying every moment) in rugged competition. His wins to his title included Best of Winners at Greater Daytona under renowned breeder/judge, Mrs. Esther Wolf.

CH. IVANWOLD HIGH JINKS

Gais Rufty Tufty (Eng. Imp), ROM

CH. BROUGHCASTL BALLADEER

CH. BONJOR'S SUSAN B. ANTHONY

CH. IVANWOLD HIGH JINKS

CH. IVANWOLD HIGH TOR

CH. IVANWOLD HIGH BARBARY

Electra of Gayberry

Breeders: E.N.K Patterson & John D. Cobb

Owner/Handlers: E.N.K. & Charlotte Patterson

This very correct dog compared well with his better-known sire. He was the second champion bred and shown by Ivanwold Kennel in one year, finishing at the Montgomery Kennel Club show in tough competition.

CH. IVANWOLD SENATOR SAM

Gais Rufty Tufty (Eng. Imp), ROM
CH. BROUGHCASTL BALLADEER
CH. BONJOR'S SUSAN B. ANTHONY
CH. IVANWOLD SENATOR SAM
CH. IVANWOLD HIGH TOR
CH. IVANWOLD GAYBERRY CAROLINA, CD, ROM
CH. GAYBERRY VICTORIA OF GORE

Breeder: Edward & Charlotte Patterson
Owner: Mrs. R.V. Clark, Jr.
Handler: Roy Holloway

The number one Pug for 1978 and 1979, Sam set a then-record with 14 all-Breed Best In Shows. His record also included Best of Breeds and Group placings. Sam did a lot to make judges conscious of the breed in the Toy Group, and the Best in Show ring. He was one of five brothers to finish from this litter. the others being: Ch. Ivanwold Pistol Pete of Rontu, Ch. Ivanwold Broadway Joe Willie, Ch. Glen Glow Rock of Ivanwold and Ch. Ivanwold Gorgeous George.

CH. JAC'S DIAMOND JIM

CH. CHARLAMAR'S J RANDALL BROWN
CH. CHARLAMAR'S ANCIENT DREAMER
Charlamar's Alpha Omega

CH. JAC'S DIAMOND JIM

CH. GAMBURG'S OLLETIME SHOW OFF
Gamburg's Pitter Patter
Sheffield's Wild Irish Rose

Breeder: Florence Gamburg
Owner: Judi Crowe

"Jimmy" is tops with us! Finishing in 1986 with a four-point major at only fifteen months of age. He is already the sire of ten extremely nice puppies. He was shown as a Special on a limited basis.

CH. KATSU HONEYBUN OF MARIDON'S

CH. SHEFFIELD'S ROSE TATTOO
CH. SHEFFIELD'S LITTLE RED WAGON
CH. SHEFFIELD'S COUNTRY COUSIN
CH. KATSU HONEYBUN OF MARIDON'S
CH. DHANDY'S FAVORITE WOODCHUCK
CH. MARIDON'S WOODCHOPPER OF GORE
CH. GORE'S FANCI GIN PHIZZ

Breeder/Handler: Mary Ann Hall
Owner: Sue & Kate Jennings

"Zu" finished at the Houston Kennel Club shows going Best of Winners on Friday, repeating the win on Saturday and then finishing the three-day weekend with a Best of Breed on Sunday! He went on to other Best of Breed wins including a back-to-back Group I weekend. He also won a Best In Specialty Show award at the Bluebonnet Pug Dog Club. He has sired lovely puppies who carry on his nice head and movement.

AM. BDA. CH. KENDORIC'S HOT CONNECTION

INT. CH. SHEFFIELD'S KENDORIC HOT STUFF
INT. CH. KENDORIC'S PIPIN HOT
Bretchase Daisychain (Eng. Imp.)
AM. BDA CH. KENDORIC'S HOT CONNECTION
CH. SAMET PAUL OF PARAMIN (Eng. Imp.)
AM. CAN. CH. KENDORIC'S FRENCH CONNECTION
Kendoric Double Play

Breeder/Owner: Doris Aldrich

"Corey Jr." follows in his dad's footsteps and produces outstanding puppies. He is strong in both front and rear with a good topline and a beautiful head. His pigmentation is excellent.

INT. CH. KENDORIC'S PIPIN HOT

CH. SHEFFIELD'S TUFF STUFF
AM. CAN. CH. SHEFFIELD'S KENDORIC HOT STUFF
CH. SHEFFIELD'S SHASTA
INT. CH. KENDORIC'S PIPIN HOT
Cobby's Jeremy Fisher of Martlesham
Brentchase Daisychain (Eng. Imp.)
CH. ROBERTSON'S GODELLE

Breeder/Owner/Handler: Doris Aldrich

"Corey" went Best of Winners for a five point major to finish his championship. He later went all the way to Group I from the classes at the International Dog Shows in Bermuda. He has sired lovely puppies in both sexes.

CH. LKK'S FLY'N TIGER OF ROSEVILLE

CH. SAMET PAUL OF PARAMIN (ENG IMP)
CH. PARAGON'S AMERICAN CLASSIC
Paragon's California Dreamer
CH. LKK'S FLY'N TIGER OF ROSEVILLE
CH. BRUNO LE NOYRE OF TOR
LKK'S Maraglenn Genuine Risk
LKK'S Sassy Imp

Breeder: Linda K. Reisdorff
Owner/Handler: Linda La Bossiere

"Tiger" was a remarkable puppy finishing his championship at 11 months of age with four majors. This included two Best of Breeds over Specials and a Group III achieved at eight months. He was owner handled all the way.

His record to date is 51 Best of Breeds and 11 Group placements and still going. He is siring winning puppies.

CH. PAULMAR'S TRACE OF EXCELLENCE

CH. ROBERTSON'S BOURBON PRINCE, ROM
CH. GORE'S UP'N ADAM, ROM
CH. ROBERTSON'S GODELLE
CH. PAULMAR'S TRACE OF EXCELLENCE
Rosend's Oriental Tobi Tong
CH. ROSEND'S LOVIN ABBY
Rosend's Jumping Judy

Breeder/Owner: Martha Pratt

"Corky" excels in type and movement. He finished with five majors at just 15 months of age.

CH. RITTER'S WOODEN NICKEL

CH. PAULMAR'S TRACE OF ANTIQUITY
CH. PAULMAR'S LITTLE LUKE
Paulmar's Favorite Dolly
CH. RITTER'S WOODEN NICKEL
CH. SHEFFIELD'S CHARLATAN
CH. RITTER'S HAPPY DAYS
CH. RITTER'S KERRI-ON

Breeder/Owner/Handler: Virginia Ritter

'Woody" is Ritter's 29th Champion Pug. He won in the classes under judges Mrs. William Lahnig and Dr. Bernard Esporite and finished under Mrs. Sadie Thorn. He is a proven sire of show-quality puppies, carrying on the Ritter line.

AM. CAN. CH. RITTER'S RUSTY NAIL

CH. IVANWOLD HIGH TOR
AM. CAN. CH. RITTER'S SUPER STAR
CH. RITTER'S SESAME STREET
AM. CAN. CH. RITTER'S RUSTY NAIL
CH. RITTER'S MONACO OF WESTDALE
CH. RITTER'S MINI MUFFIN
CH. WESTON'S ISADOLL

Breeder/Owner/Handler: Virginia Ritter

"Rusty's" first time out as a Special saw him go Best of Breed and on to Group IV at the Fort Stueben Kennel Club show. He went on to more Group placements including Group I. He completed his Canadian championship in four shows which included Group placings from the classes.

CH. ROWELL'S TONKA TOY MASTER

CH. BROUGHCASTL BALLADEER
CH. TERYTAM TASKMASTER, ROM
CH. TERYTAM'S TALLYHO OF PARAGON
CH. ROWELL'S TONKA TOY MASTER
CH. CHEN'S A FAVORITE OF THE GODS
CH. ROWELL'S DHANDY GYPSY ROSE, ROM
CH. DHANDY'S SKYLARK

Breeder/Owner/Handler: John & Linda Rowell

"Tonka" began his Specials career with a bang, taking five Best of Breeds (placing twice in the Group.) He defeated 75 Pugs in winning those five breed wins. He has gone on to become a fine example of Rowell Pugs: Quality that "shows and wins."

CH. SHEFFIELD'S JERSEY BOUNCE

CH. SHEFFIELD'S ROSE TATTOO
CH. SHEFFIELD'S LITTLE RED WAGON
CH. SHEFFIELD'S COUNTRY COUSIN
CH. SHEFFIELD'S JERSEY BOUNCE
CH. SHEFFIELD'S STUFF'N NONSENSE
Manalapan's September Song
Sheffield's Gingersnap

Breeder: Bert Porter
Owner: Mrs. Alan Robson
Handler: Margery Shriver

"Bounce" began his career with a bang: An all-Breed Best in Match at five months of age! He finished in style as well, with his first major coming at the Philadelphia Kennel Club show while still just eight months of age. Through June of 1988, Bounce had won two all-Breed Best in Shows, three Specialty Best in Shows, and Best of Breed twice at Westminster. He also accumulated 18 Group Is. He is a cobby dog with a large head and plenty of bone. He has sired beautiful puppies.

CH. SHEP'S LI'L GOLDEN ROOSTER, ROM

CH. DANDY'S DORYSON BUCCANEER

CH. MERRIMAKER'S TAWNY TOKAY

Reiman's Saucy Soya

CH. SHEP'S LI'L GOLDEN ROOSTER, ROM

CH. SHEP'S LI'L GOLDEN TOM BOY

CH. LI'L GOLDEN TI LEI OF SHANGRA-LA

Shep's Glowing Yoyo

Breeders/Owners: Larry & Pat Shepherd

"Rooster", with only limited showing, won many Best of Breeds and numerous group placings. The number-four dog for 1984 (Canine Chronicle System), he has sired champion offspring. He passes on to his puppies his good front, excellent rear and topline, and his very showy personality.

CH. SHEP'S RISING SON

CH. SHEFFIELD'S SUNDAY PUNCH

CH. SHEP'S SASSAFRAS COCA

Shep's Li'l Tamu of Dunroamin, ROM

CH. SHEP'S RISING SON

CH. SHEP'S LI'L GOLDEN ROOSTER, ROM

CH. SHEP'S HIGHFALUTIN FLOOZY

CH. SHEP'S AFTERNOON DELITE

Breeders/Owners/ Handlers: Larry & Pat Shepherd

"Sonny" salutes his multiple Best in Show daughter, Ch. Rowell's Solo Moon Rising on her win of the prestigious Toy Group at the 1989 Westminster Kennel Club show! He is the sire of other lovely puppies who are doing well in the show ring.

CH. SOUTHLAND'S TOP BONANA OF GORE

                    CH. ROBERTSON'S BOURBON PRINCE
        CH. GORE'S UP'N ADAM, ROM
                    CH. ROBERTSON'S GODELLE
CH. SOUTHLAND'S TOP BONANA OF GORE
                    CH. GORE'S UP'N ADAM, ROM
        CH. ROBERTSON'S FANCI BEBE
                    CH. ROBERTSON'S FANCI BABE

Breeder: Louise Gore
Owner/Handler: Billie Sue Baker

"Bo" finished at the Bayou Kennel club by going Best of Breed of Specials. His other notable wins were three- and four-point majors. Bo was always owner handled.

AM. CAN. CH. THAT OLD BLAQUE MAGIC

CH. SHEFFIELD'S STUFF'N NONSENSE, ROM
CH. BORNFREE PHIRE FOX, ROM
CH. BORNFREE LIZZIE TISH
AM. CAN. CH. THAT OLD BLAQUE MAGIC
Ken M's Starskipper
Blaque's Butterscotch, ROM
CH. BERNALEE VENUS

Breeder: Blanche Roberts
Owners/Handlers: Bob & Ann White

Butler is a consistent Breed winner and Group placing dog with multiple Groups and Best in Show wins. His American Championship was completed at eleven months of age and his Canadian title was achieved at 13 months.

He was awarded his first Best in Show win at the young age of 15 months. Among Butler's most notable wins are his Best of Breed and Group III at the 1988 Purina Invitational show and receiving the Award of Merit at the Pug Dog Club of America's Top Twenty Showcase in 1988. At the first Manitoba Canine Classic Invitational, a show for winners of Group firsts and Best in Show winners, he was awarded a Toy Group 1st and went on to Best in Show.

CH. WISSELWOOD FOR SEVEN ISLANDS

ENG. CH. PRENDERGAST OF PYEBETA
CH. NEUBRAA PAPAGENO (Eng. Imp.)
Edenderry Coolanee
CH. WISSELWOOD FOR SEVEN ISLANDS
CH. PHIDGITY PHIRCONE (Eng. Imp)
CH. HEATHERS HONEY OF WISSELWOOD
Morfa Madcap (Can. Imp.)

Breeder: Lorene M. Vickers
Owners: Lorene M. Vickers & Terry J. Smith
Handler: Terry J. Smith

A full brother to Ch. Stonecrusher of Wisselwood, this boy's accomplishments include Best of Winners at the Great Lakes Pug Club Specialty. After he matured he won other Best of Breeds including the Toledo Kennel Club show.

CH. WISSELWOOD RAVEN SOUL

CH. BUSTER OF RYDENS
CH. TICK TOCK OF LE TASYLL (ENG. IMP.)
Hazelbridge Little Toy of LeTasy II
CH. WISSELWOOD RAVEN SOUL
Pug-Pak Beamish Boy
Wisselwood Touch of Class
Wisselwood Witch Hazel

Breeder/Owner. Handler: Lorene Vickers

"Henry" finished from the Puppy class with two five-point Specialty majors as well as a Grand Sweepstakes win at the Pug Dog Club of Greater New York Specialty. He is a solid black with no white hairs.

CH. WISSELWOOD NIGHT MUSIC

AM. CAN. CH. EBONY'S MARMADUKE OF HAVEN
CH. WISSELWOOD VELVET TUBBY, ROM
Wisselwood Cotton Tasyll
CH. WISSELWOOD NIGHT MUSIC
CH. JAY BEE'S MR. STUBBS
CH. WISSELWOOD JAY BEE SHORTCAKE, ROM
Jay Bee's Little Complainer

Breeder: Lorene Vickers-Smith
Owners/Handlers: Lonny & Tedda Burton

"Peter" was owner-handled and shown sparingly. He is standard size and weight with good bone, good head wrinkle and a cobby body. He is quite the showman displaying excellent animation coupled with proper movement. His wins include Best in Specialty show at the Central Indiana Pug Club show in 1986.

18

Great Winning Bitches
of the Recent Past

The 32 Pug ladies pictured in this chapter are some of America's top winners of the recent past. And, while unable to depict every winning bitch, this is a representative sampling of winners, both fawn and black. These are the bitches to look for as Register of Merit winners in the near future, and the up and coming breeders associated with them.

CH. ROWELL'S SOLO MOON RISING

CH. CAMEO'S COVER GIRL

CH. SHEFFIELD'S STUFF'N NONSENSE, ROM
CH. CAMEO'S ORANGE JULIUS, ROM
Rosened's Lotus Blossom
CH. CAMEO'S COVER GIRL
Paulmar's Super Trouper
CH. PAULMAR'S STELLA BY STARLIGHT
CH. CAMEO'S VERY VANILLA

Breeder: Jan Ravotti
Owner: Joe & Jan Ravotti

"Bunny" is shown placing second in the Group just six weeks after whelping nine puppies, By six months of age she had two majors. She is an extremely sound bitch with hips that X-rayed excellent. She is the winner of a number of specialties, groups and group placings as well as three all-breed Best in Shows.

CH. CHARLAMAR'S LADY BEAR

CH. CHARLAMAR'S BILLY JOE BLACK
CH. CHARLAMAR'S J RANDALL BROWN
CH. NUNNALLY'S WITCH HAZEL, ROM
CH. CHARLAMAR'S LADY BEAR
CH. BONJOR CLARK KENT
Broughcastl Amy of Charlamar
CH. HESTER'S AMBER LADY

Breeders/Owners: Mary Moxley & Charlotte Corson

Our breeders dream come true was Ch. Charlamar's Lady Bear. She
was whelped December 13, 1984 and finished handily. She is "decidedly
square and cobby."

CH. KAOTIC KT OF DARDEN

CH. ROBERTSON'S TALK TO ME JOHN
CH. DARDEN'S LITTLE JOHN OF GORE
CH. GORE'S UP 'N' FANCI BEBE
CH. KAOTIC KT OF DARDEN
CH. GORE'S FANCI ADAM
Darden's Hei Yu of Gore, ROM
CH. GORE'S PINK LADY

Breeder: Margaret Darden
Owners: Ralph & Betty Cook

"Katie" is shown going Best of Winners at the Missouri Valley Pug Fanciers Regional Specialty for her finishing major under breeder/judge Ann White. She was owner handled to this important win, after taking time off to whelp her first litter of pups.

CH. DARDEN'S LILY OF BRITTANY

CH. DHANDY'S FAVORITE WOODCHUCK
Paulmar's Super Trouper
CH. PAULMAR'S LUK-E-LOLLIPOP
CH. DARDEN'S LILY OF BRITTANY
CH. SHEFFIELD'S STUFF'N NONSENSE
CH. CAMEO'S VERY VANILLA, ROM
Rosend's Lotus Blossom

Breeder: Jan Ravotti
Owners: George & Margaret Darden

"Lily" with four 4 -point majors, including Best of Winners at the Carolina Kennel Club. She is a proven brood bitch, with a number of finished champions, including a Group winner. She is the love of Margaret's life.

CH. DARDEN'S MOONFLOWER

                    CH. BROUGHCASTL BOMBADIER
        CH. DARDEN'S MUS' BE MATTHEW
                    Darden's Gee Whiz of Southland, ROM
CH. DARDEN'S MOONFLOWER
                    CH. PAULMAR'S SUPER TROOPER
        CH. DARDEN'S LILY OF BRITTANY
                    CH. CAMEO'S VERY VANILLA, ROM

Breeder: Margaret Darden
Owner: Brenda Harrower

"Moonie's" biggest win was going Best of Opposite Sex over a number of Specials for four points at the Griffin Kennel Club Show under judge Emil Klinckhardt. She is a litter mate to a Group winning dog.

CH. DHANDY'S POLISHED PEBBLE

CH. JIAN'S 00 BUCKSHOT
CH. PUG-PAK CROWN ME HENRY
CH. PUG-PAK DHANDY'S SHORTCAKE
CH. DHANDY'S POLISHED PEBBLE
CH. DHANDY'S FAVORITE WOODCHUCK
CH. DHANDY'S WOODEN SHOE
CH. GOODWIN'S MISTY DAWN

Breeder/Owner/Handlers: Barbara Braley and Anitra Hutchison

This 1986 Champion is one half of a Best in Show Brace! The other member is her mother, Ch. Dhandy's Wooden Shoe. Pebble was also first in Junior bitches and Best in Sweepstakes at the Tampa Bay Pug Club Specialty in 1986, while her brother, Ch. Dhandy's Favorite McMurphy was reserve winners Dog at the same show.

CH. DONALDSON'S MEGAN

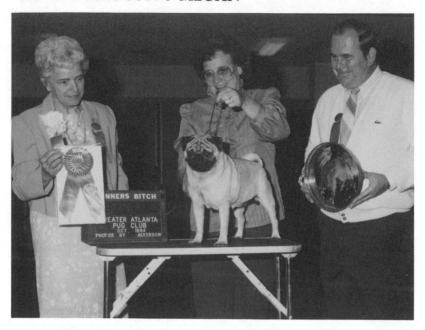

<table>
<tr><td></td><td></td><td>Heritage Great Gusto</td></tr>
<tr><td></td><td>Donaldson's Rocki</td><td></td></tr>
<tr><td></td><td></td><td>Donaldson's Fanci</td></tr>
</table>

                Heritage Great Gusto
       Donaldson's Rocki
                Donaldson's Fanci
CH. DONALDSON'S MEGAN
                CH. GAIS TIPKINS
       Donaldson's Raquel
                Heritage Wildwood Flower

Breeder/Owner/Handler: Marie Donaldson

"Megan" finished with three five-point majors, two of them being at the Specialties of the Bluebonnet Pug Dog Club and the Atlanta Pug Club. She is always owner handled.

CH. EDEN'S BLAQUE MADRIGAL

		CH. SAMET PAUL OF PARAMIN (ENG. IMP.)
	CH. SHEFFIELD'S STUFF'N NONSENSE, ROM	
		CH. SHEFFIELD'S SWEETER THAN WINE
CH. EDEN'S BLAQUE MADRIGAL		
		CH. SHEFFIELD'S STAGE DOOR JOHNNY
	CH. BLAQUE EDEN'S STORMI WEATHER, ROM	
		CH. BLAQUE KITTY MAE, ROM

Breeder: Blanche C Roberts & Eileen Rutmayer
Owners: Ray & Pat Kolesar

"Maddy" finished quickly with a Best of Breed win from the classes. She is a dear little dog.

CH. EDEN'S MAGICAL MAIDEN

CH. SHEFFIELD'S STUFF'N NONSENSE, ROM

CH. BORNFREE PHIREFOX, ROM

CH. BORNFREE LIZZIE TISH

CH. EDEN'S MAGICAL MAIDEN

CH. SHEFFIELD'S STAGE DOOR JOHNNY

CH. BLAQUE EDEN'S STORMI WEATHER, ROM

CH. BLAQUE'S KITTY MAE, ROM

Breeders: Blanche C. Roberts & Eileen C. Rutmayer

Owner: Blanche C. Roberts

This little girl is a multiple Best of Breed winner and Group placer. She was also the 1989 Miss February in the Mighty Dog Calender. She is from a litter of three champions.

CH. GOODWIN'S THUMBELINA ROWELL

CH. SAMET PAUL OF PARAMIN, ROM
CH. SHEFFIELD'S STUFF'N NONSENSE, ROM
CH. SHEFFIELD'S SWEETER THAN WINE
CH. GOODWIN'S THUMBELINA ROWELL
CH. TERYTAM TASKMASTER
CH. ROWELL'S SASSY SCRUPLES
CH. ROWELL'S DHANDY GYPSY ROSE, ROM

Breeders: Linda & John Rowell
Owner: Shirley J. Goodwin

"Good things come in small packages," and that describes Thumbelina!
At sixteen months of age Thumbelina went Winners Bitch and Best of
Opposite Sex at the Sara-Bay Kennel Club show under Forrest McCoy.
She completed her championship with three majors at 21 months of age.
She is a cobby 15 1/2 pound bitch, with dark eyes, and personality plus!

CH. GORE'S PINK LADY

                    CH. CHEN'S A FAVORITE OF THE GODS
          CH. DHANDY'S FAVORITE WOODCHUCK
                    CH. HERITAGE WICKED WITCH
CH. GORE'S PINK LADY
                    CH. ROBERTSON'S BOURBON PRINCE
          CH. GORE'S FANCI GIN PHIZZ
                    CH. ROBERTSON'S FANCI BABE

Breeder/Owner: Louise V. Gore

This lady is the product of over nine generations of Gore breeding, tracing back to one of the original Gore Pugs of the sixties: Gore's Atlas. Along the way, her heritage includes Ch. Gore's Sir Flip, Ch. Gore's Linebacker, Nunnally's Derby Doll, and Ch. Robertson's Bourbon Prince. She is a true "Gore Pug."

CH. HARPER'S IN A NUT SHELL

```
                    CH. KESANDER'S SPEAK OF D'DEBBEL
          CH. BARBLAND'S HOT PEPPER
                    Barbland's Cinder Bits
CH. HARPER'S IN A NUT SHELL
                    CH. BONJOR I'M THE GREATEST O'ANDOR
          Harper's Xanadu
                    CH. HARPER'S AMADEUS
```

Breeder/Owner/Handler: Norma S. & Alan Harper

"Shelly" is the fourth generation of black Pugs for the Harpers. Her first time shown she was Grand Sweepstakes Winner, as well as Winners Bitch for 5 points at the Pug Dog Club of Maryland Specialty. She has gone on to win Best of Breed at the Yankee Pug Dog Club fall specialty show. Shelly is an elegant, feminine, showy single-coated, coal-black bitch.

AM. CAN. CH. KENDORIC'S FRENCH CONNECTION

Phirefly of Paramin
CH. SAMET PAUL OF PARAMIN (ENG. IMP.)
Paramin Paulette
AM. CAN. CH. KENDORIC'S FRENCH CONNECTION
CH. RAVENCROFTS KENDORIC GAMBLER
Kendoric Double Play
CAN. CH. AL TORA PEANUT GIRL

Breeder/Owner/Handler: Doris Aldrich

Her biggest win was going Winners Bitch, Best of Winners, and Best of Breed over four Specials for a three point major. She went on from there to be the Grand Sweepstakes winner at Westchester, and one week later went Winners Bitch and Best of Winners at the Pug Dog Club of America show for a five-point major to finish. She is now an American and Canadian Champion.

CH. KENDORIC'S KISS ME KATE

AM. CAN. CH. TED'S KAUFFEE ROYAL RUPERT
CH. KENDORIC RUPERT ON THE ROCKS
Kendoric's Li'l Bibup
CH. KENDORIC'S KISS ME KATE
AM. CAN. CH. KENDORIC'S SILVERTOWN NUGGET
CH. KENDORIC'S KATY-DID OF KAE-JAC
Kae-Jac's Royal Princess

Breeder/Owner/Handler: Doris Aldrich

"Kate" is just one of 25 American champions bred at Kendoric, and she continues the tradition of quality and excellence there. All dogs are owner-handled at Kendoric, which has also produced 15 Canadian champions, 9 Bermuda champions, and four Register of Merit Pugs.

CH. LIMON LADY CHELSEA

Donaldson's Apache Chief
CH. DONALDSON'S PEPPERRIDGE MACK
Donaldson's Honeysuckle Rose
CH. LIMON LADY CHELSEA
CH. SILVERTOWN GRAND SLAM
Gale's Pumpkin Patch, CD
CH. NAZREP PLAY ME A MELODY

Breeder/Owner: Helen Gale

"Chelsea" finished royally, with five majors and always owner-handled. She was Best of Opposite Sex at the Yankee Pug Dog Club's first specialty show in 1986. She is short, cobby, 16 lb. bitch with a straight front, strong rear, and excellent movement.

CH. NEU'S ENCHANTING SORCERESS

CH. CHARLAMAR'S J. RANDALL BROWN, ROM
CH. CHARLAMAR'S ANCIENT DREAMER, ROM
Charlamar's Alpha Omega
CH. NEU'S ENCHANTING SORCERESS
CH. CHARLAMAR'S LOUIS ST. LOUIS
CH. NEU DOLLY OF PRIS
CH. PRIS' BLACK LUV PACKAGE

Breeder/Owner/Handler: Sonja Neu

"Molly" has been called the fawn Pug in a black mink coat. She started her career by going Best of Winners and Best of Opposite Sex over 22 bitch specials at the 1986 National under Michelle Billings. The same weekend, she received her first Group I! Molly has four Best in Specialty Show wins covering all parts of the country. She retired the Fahey's Fancy Pants Memorial Trophy by winning Best of Opposite Sex three consecutive times at National and Regional specialties. She received the honor of winning back-to-back, the 1987 and 1988 Pug Dog Club of America Top Twenty Showcase, as well as the 1989 Pug Dog Club of America National Specialty Show itself.

CH. RITTER'S CHINESE FORTUNE

CH. SAMET PAUL OF PARAMIN (ENG. IMP.)
CH. SHEFFIELD'S CHARLATAN, ROM
CH. SHEFFIELD'S SURE FIRE
CH. RITTER'S CHINESE FORTUNE
CH. RITTER'S SUPERSTAR
AM. CAN. CH. RITTER'S NO NONSENSE, ROM
CH. WESTON'S ISADOLL

Breeder/Owner/Handler: Virginia Ritter

This gal's wins include the one shown in the photograph, Winners Bitch at the Ravenna Kennel Club. "Tea" finished in style, going to Best of Opposite Sex for a major under James Nickerson. Her lasting value, though, has been in the offspring she has produced for the Ritter line, including Ch. Ritter's Country Lace and Ch. Ritter's Just Right.

CH. RITTER'S COUNTRY LACE

CH. PAULMAR'S LITTLE LUKE
CH. RITTER'S WOODEN NICKEL
CH. RITTER'S HAPPY DAYS
CH. RITTER'S COUNTRY LACE
CH. SHEFFIELD'S CHARLATAN, ROM
CH. RITTER'S CHINESE FORTUNE
CH. RITTER'S NO NONSENSE

Breeder/Owner/Handler: Virginia Ritter

"Lace," her first time in the show ring, went Winners Bitch and Best of Winners for a three point major. She finished her championship with a nice win going Winners Bitch, Best of Winners and Best of Opposite Sex (over two bitch specials) at the Baltimore County Kennel Club.

CH. RITTER KENDORIC SWEET DREAMS

CH. SHEFFIELD KENDORIC HOT STUFF
INT. CH. KENDORIC PIPIN HOT
Brentchase Daisychain, ROM
CH. RITTER KENDORIC SWEET DREAMS
CH. SAMET PAUL OF PARAMIN (EMG. IMP.)
AM. CAN. CH. KENDORIC'S FRENCH CONNECTION
Kendoric Double Play

Breeder: Doris Aldrich
Owner/Handler: Virginia Ritter

Shown going Best of Winners and Best of Opposite Sex at the Crawford County Kennel Club in 1986, this gal is a sister to the well known-winner, Ch. Kendoric's Hot Connection.

CH. ROWELL'S SOLO MOON RISING

CH. SHEP'S SASSAFRAS COCA

CH. SHEP'S RISING SON

CH. SHEP'S HIGHFALUTIN FLOOZY

CH. ROWELL'S SOLO MOON RISING

CH. TERYTAM TASKMASTER, ROM

CH. ROWELL'S SASSY SCRUPLES, ROM

CH. ROWELL'S DHANDY GYPSY ROSE, ROM

Breder/Owner: Linda & John Rowell, Jr.
Handler: Linda Rowell

"Solo" is no ordinary bitch, she is SPECIAL! Now the top-winning bitch in Pug history (Kennel Review through 3/89), Solo has nine all-breed Best in Show wins. She also took a Toy Group I at the prestigious Westminster Kennel Club show in 1989, and has numerous Best in Specialty Show wins, as well.

CH. SHEFFIELD'S KITTEN ON THE KEYS

CH. SAMET PAUL OF PARAMIN (ENG. IMP.)
CH. STUFF'N NONSENSE, ROM
CH. SHEFFIELD'S WILD CLOVER
CH. SHEFFIELD'S KITTEN ON THE KEYS
CH. SHEFFIELD'S SNEAKY PETE
CH. SHEFFIELD'S WILD CLOVER
CH. SHEFFIELD'S SECOND HAND ROSE

Breeder/Owner/Handler: Margery A. Shriver

"Kitten" finished at eleven months of age, winning three five point majors, three days in a row. What makes this achievement special, is that the first day was the National Specialty! She was shown a total of five times to achieve her championship. In 1982, she returned to Redding, Pennsylvania where she was Best in Specialty Show at the Pug Dog Club of America National, as well as Best in Specialty Show at the Pug Dog Club of Maryland Specialty the same year. She is the sixth generation of homebred champion bitches for Sheffield. She had only five puppies; both of her daughters are champions.

CH. SHEFFIELD'S SPITFIRE

CH. SHEFFIELD'S ROSE TATTOO
CH. SHEFFIELD'S LITTLE RED WAGON, ROM
CH. SHEFFIELD'S COUNTRY COUSIN

CH. SHEFFIELD'S SPITFIRE

CH. SHEFFIELD'S STUFF'N NONSENSE, ROM
Manaplan's September Song
Sheffield's Gingersnap

Breeder: Bert Porter
Owner/Handler: Margery A. Shriver

"Bun" finished at 12 months of age, winning six out of ten shows she was entered in. She was Best of Breed over male specials her first time out as a special herself, and went on to a Group III. At the age of 17 months she won the National Specialty with over 180 entries; about 60 of those were specials. She has over 40 Best of Breeds, three Group Is and many placements. Her breed wins were always over male specials.

CH. SHEP'S CASSIA OF HOLLY SPRINGS

CH. HERITAGE TOM CAT OF GORE
CH. SHEP'S MAJOR TOP CAT
Shep's L'il Tamu of Dunroamin, ROM
CH. SHEP'S CASSIA OF HOLLY SPRINGS
CH. SHEP'S SUNDANCE KID
CH. MENEHUNE FANDANCER OF SHEP'S
Paragon's X-Citation

Breeders: Pat & Larry Shepherd
Owner: Anne Wood

This girl has been quite a producer for the Holly Springs line, with Ch. Holly Springs Jacaranda and Ch. Holly Springs Honeycomb being just two of her offspring.

CH. SHEP'S HIGHFALUTIN FLOOZY

CH. MERRIMAKER'S TAWNY TOKAY
CH. SHEP'S LI'L GOLDEN ROOSTER
CH. LI'L GOLDEN TILEI OF SHANGRA-LA
CH. SHEP'S HIGHFALUTIN FLOOZY
CH. SHEP'S MAJOR TOP CAT
CH. SHEP'S AFTERNOON DELITE
CH. SHEP'S PEACH PUDDIN

Breeder/Owner/Handlers: Pat & Larry Shepherd

"Floozy" is a producing brood bitch now whose son, Ch. Shep's Rising Son, is the sire of Ch. Rowell's Solo Moon Rising, Group winner at the 1988 Westminster Kennel Club.

CH. SHIRRAYNE'S VIVID VANESSA

CH. ANCHORAGE MATTHEW
Shirrayne's Notable Nimrod
CH. SHIRRAYNE'S BRASH BUFFI
CH. SHIRRAYNE'S VIVID VANESSA
Shirrayne's Golden Gaymark
CH. SHIRRAYNE'S LOTS OF LOVING
CH. GREENTUB'S BUSY BEE

Breeder: Shirley Thomas
Owners/Handler: Dan & Ann Fischetti

"Vanessa" went Best of Opposite Sex at the Rockland County Kennel Club (pictured). She has produced three champion bitch offspring, as well: Ch. Vandonna's Cheerio, Ch. Vandonna's Diggy of Shirrayne, and Ch. Vandonna's Golly Gee.

CH. SILVERTOWN NO FOOLIN'

BEST OF
BREED OR VARIETY

TRAP FALLS
KENNEL CLUB
MAR
1987
TATHAM PHOTO

```
                              CH. DONALDSON'S TIPPI CANOE
            CH. BORNFREE TOM FOOLERY
                              CH. IVANWOLD PANHANDLE PIXIE
CH. SILVERTOWN NO FOOLIN'
                              CH. RIVERRIDGE POTENT PASHA
            CH. SILVERTOWN KATRINA
                              CH. SILVERTOWN SURPRISE PACKAGE
```

Breeder: Polly J. Lamarine
Owner: Doris Aldrich

One of Silvertown Kennel's most memorable moments was when this girl went Best of Winners at the Yankee Pug Dog Club Specialty. The same year she was Grand Sweepstakes winner at the Pug Dog Club of Maryland Specialty show. She finished as a puppy with a total of four majors, making her the fourth generation of Champion bitches bred from our foundation, Am. Can. Ch. Sabbaday Favor, ROM.

CH. SOUTHLAND'S DIXIE OF CROWELL

CH. ROBERTSON'S BUC O' NUNNALLY
CH. ROBERTSON'S BOURBON PRINCE
Nunnally's Derby Doll
CH. SOUTHLAND'S DIXIE OF CROWELL
CH. WOLF'S LI'L JOE, ROM
Carol's Sassy Caper of Crowell
Haigwood's FiFi De Romega

Breeder/Owner/Handler: Billie Sue Baker

"Dixie" went Winners Bitch and Best of Opposite Sex at the Gulfport show of the Mississippi State Kennel Club. She is the dam of numerous champions and ROM offspring.

CH. TORI LANES OH ELIZABETH

CH. BORNFREE PHIREFOX
CH. BORNFREE JAC DANIEL OF TORI
CH. IVANWOLD PANHANDLE PIXIE
CH. TORI LANES OH ELIZABETH
CH. GORE'S FANCY ADAM
Tori Lanes You Are My Sunshine, ROM
CH. TORI LANE'S DADDY'S GIRL

Breeders/Owners: Maryellen Castimore & Meb Bloxham

"Elizabeth" finished at eight months of age, and is currently being specialed. Her presence is being felt in the Group ring!

CH. TORI LANE PISTOL PACKIN MAMA

CH. BORNFREE PHIRE FOX
CH. BORNFREE JAC DANIEL OF TORI
CH. IVANWOLD PANHANDLE PIXIE
CH. TORI LANE PISTOL PACKIN MAMA
CH. DHANDY'S FAVORITE WOODCHUCK
CH. TORI LANE'S DADDY'S GIRL
Windage Farm's Tolly Golly

Breeders/Owners: Maryellen Castimore & Meb Bloxham

"Babe" was a champion at 14 months of age. One of three daughters of our foundation bitch, she brought us our first Best in Show win. The #1 Pug in Canada for 1988, Babe is the mother of two beautiful girls being shown in the U.S. and Canada.

CH. WINDY ACRE'S HOLLY OF WODEMORE

CH. SHEFFIELD'S MIDAS TOUCH
CH. LKK'S SIR GENO OF SHEFFIELD
Lkk's Baby Doll of Robertson
CH. WINDY ACRE'S HOLLY OF WODEMORE
CH. WESTON'S BO-EDWARD
Weston's Bo-Poppin, ROM
Weston's Sarah Koch

Owners: Amara & Gretta Grittinger
Co-Owner/Breeder/Handler: Linda Buss

"Holly" was one of the prettiest puppies! From her dam, she inherited the ability to produce quality pups, as well as pretty ones.

CH. WISSELWOOD SEMI-SWEET KISSES

AM. CAN. CH. EBONY'S MARMADUKE OF HAVEN

CH. WISSELWOOD VELVET TUBBY

Wisselwood Cotton Tasyll

CH. WISSELWOOD SEMI-SWEET KISSES

Wisselwood Gee Whillickers

Wisselwood Moon Unit

Paragon's Curiosity Shop

Breeder: Terry Smith & Lorene Vickers-Smith
Owner: Nancy A. McCorkle
Handler: Jeannie Deimler

Shown finishing at Pug Dog Club of Maryland Specialty under breeder-judge Alan Harper, she was also a winner of the open class at the Pug Dog Club of New York Specialty in 1988. This is one of a line of quality black Pugs.

CH. WISSELWOOD SUZY SHARPTEETH

CH. PARAGON'S PAGE OF WISSELWOOD
CH. PARAGON'S AMERICAN HERITAGE
CH. PARAGON'S DELTA DAWN
CH. WISSELWOOD SUZY SHARPTEETH
Wisselwood Gee Whillickers
Wisselwood Whippdip
Paragon's Curiosity Shop

Breeder/Owner/Handler: Lorene Vickers-Smith

"Suzy" went Best of Winners at the Pug Dog Club of America National Specialty under breeder-judge Joan Alexander in September of 1985. Suzy is one of a long line of Paragon and Wisselwood breeding for excellence.

SECTION VIII
Top Producing
Dogs and Bitches

- *The Register of Merit Sires*
- *The Register of Merit Dams*

CHAPTER 19

Register of Merit Sires

(Statistics complete through PDCA's 1988 year)

The awarding of the designation Register Of Merit, or ROM, was begun by the Pug Dog Club of America in 1979. The current requirements to be awarded the Register of Merit are: A Pug sire, owned by a Pug Dog Club of America member (or members, if co-owners) that has produced six Champion get whose Championships are published in the AKC Gazette within a particular five-year period will be eligible.

Further recognition is afforded to a sire by the addition of stars to the ROM Certificate. A star is awarded to a Pug for each additional group of six Champions he sires. For this purpose, the requirement that this occur during a five-year period is replaced by an eight-year time span. A Pug cannot receive stars until the requirements for the ROM award itself are first met. Also, it is not required that the two time spans, for the ROM and the star(s), overlap, making it possible for a Pug to have all of its Champion offspring qualify for this award, regardless of the length of time involved.

The ROM appellation may be used in pedigrees, as in: Ch. Bozo The Clown ROM**. This would indicate that Bozo sired 18 Champions in eight years, at least six of which were published during a given five-year period.

Perhaps the most interesting feature is that the ROM award is not automatically granted by the club; the owner(s) of the dog must apply for it. No statistics are compiled by the PDCA. The club then verifies the application prior to awarding the ROM Certificate. When the ROM designation was begun in 1979, there was a time limit that required owners to file for the award within two years of the date the dog was eligible. That requirement no longer exists, but many dogs from previous years, deserving of the designation, do not have their ROMs.

An analysis of the dogs on this list confirms the concept that quality produces quality. Many of the more recent ROM dogs are sons of ROM sires. Incredibly, at one point there is a direct line of five generations of ROM breeding. Not unexpectedly, this line is strongly influenced by Sheffield blood. Ch. Wolf's Li'l Joe, the all-time top producer of Pug Champions, is the ROM sire of Ch. Sheffield's Sweeter Than Wine. She was bred to Ch. Samet Paul of Paramin, a ROM sire to produce Ch. Sheffield's Stuff'N Nonsense. Stuffy is second in the total number of Pug Champions produced, and the third generation to be designated ROM. Both Ch. Bonjor Peter Parker (out of Ch. Bonjor Angel of Charity) and Ch. Bornfree Phire Fox (out of Ch. Bornfree Lizzie Tish) are ROM sons of Stuffy, and each has a ROM son of his own: Ch. Harper's Tommy Tune and Ch. Bornfree Jac Daniel of Tori, respectively. It is important to point out that Tommy Tune was sired by Ch. Harper's Star Sapphire, a ROM dam, and the daughter of Ch. Harper's Fawn Nest Flower, daughter of another ROM sire, Ch. Dandy's Doryson Buccaneer.

Only one other line comes close to repeating this phenomenal breeding heritage, that of the Charlamar line. Ch. Nunnally's Witch Hazel, a black ROM bitch, produced Ch. Charlamar's J Randall Brown. He, in turn, is the sire of Ch. Charlamar's Ancient Dreamer and Ch. Charlamar's Louis St. Louis, both ROM sires. It is Dreamer who has continued the line so far, producing Ch. Ivanwold Ancient Mariner, the latest in the line to receive the ROM designation.

CH. ANIDEE'S REPETE* (Gordon & Mary Phillips) Merriveen With Cream X CH. MC GEE'S DARKLU OF SAPPHIRE (1980) (1981*)
    CH. ANIDEE'S BLACK I. S. BEAUTIFUL
    CH. ANIDEE'S C TOO FULLMER
    CH. ANIDEE'S CHIEF OF STAFF
    CH. ANIDEE'S CHRISTMAS JOY
    CH. ANIDEE'S IMPERIAL DYNASTY
    CH. ANIDEE'S TONI CERA T
    CH. ANIDEE'S LOLA-FA-LANA
    CH. ANIDEE'S WEE WONDER
    CH. ANIDEE'S ANGELLE PHACE OF JUAL
    CH. BLAQUE SHAHANSHAH OF PAULAINE
    CH. PAULAINE'S WEE PING A DANDY
    CH. PAULAINE'S WEE PING A DINGER
    CH. WISSELWOOD APRIL SHOWERS
    CH. WISSELWOOD DREAM WEAVER

CH. BLAQUE SHAHANSHAH OF PAULAINE

CH. BLAQUE SHAHANSHAH OF PAULAINE* (Blanche C. Roberts)
CH. ANIDEE'S REPETE X CH. REKO'S WEE PING-A-PUG (1982)
(1985*)
    CH. BLAQUE'S BIMINI CRICKET
    CH. BLAQUE'S RAGING SEA OF EDEN'S
    CH. CON BRIO BLOSSOM OF BLAQUE
    CH. EDEN'S GUENIVERE OF BLAQUE
    CH. EDEN'S HARRIGAN OF BLAQUE
    CH. EDEN'S SWEET PEA OF BLAQUE
    CH. HILTON'S CROWN PRINCE
    CH. JO NOL'S BLAQUE AMBER
    CH. JO NOL'S BLAQUE RAFFITY
    CH. JO NOL'S CARRIE BLAQUE
    CH. OLIVER TWIST BLAQUE
    CH. PAJI'S TAFI A DISASTER O BLAQUE

CH. BOGEY WEST OF WISSELWOOD (Mrs. Ralph C. West) CH.
WISSELWOOD RAVEN SOUL X Domo Blak Smak of Nunnally
(1987)

  CH. MENSING'S ARNIE PALMER OF WEST
  CH. NEU DUFFER OF WEST
  CH. POLLARD'S DIVOT OF WEST
  CH. PUG-PAK WILD WILD WEST
  CH. SAL E WAG'S BUNKER TEE OF WEST
  CH. WISSELWOOD JAY BEE SHORTCAKE

CH. BOLDERBUSTER OF FEATHERWOOD

CH. BOLDERBUSTER OF FEATHERWOOD (Charmaine Widmor)
CH. STONECRUSHER OF WISSELWOOD X Wisselwood Silver
Slipper (1986)

  CH. FEATHERWOOD BOLD ELWOOD
  CH. FEATHERWOOD BOLD PRODUCTION
  CH. FEATHERWOOD GINGER SNAP
  CH. SEVEN ISLAND TOOT-DOLES
  CH. SEVEN ISLAND TULIP ROSE
  CH. WEDJWOOD CAMEO OF FEATHERWOOD

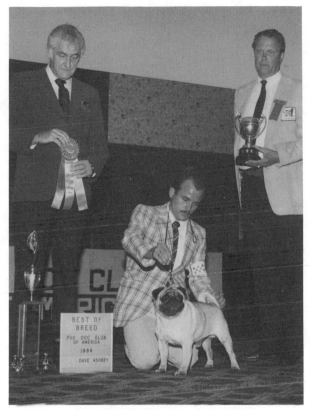

CH. BONJOR PETER PARKER

CH. BONJOR PETER PARKER (Bonna Webb & Alan Harper)
  CH. SHEFFIELD'S STUFF'N NONSENSE X CH. BONJOR
  ANGEL OF CHARITY (1986)
      CH. BONJOR BENITO JUAREZ
      CH. CHAPEL RIDGE'S BEAU BRUMMELL
      CH. CHAPEL RIDGE'S CASANOVA
      CH. HARPER'S DRESS CIRCLE T.S. ELLIOT
      CH. HARPER'S TOMMY TUNE
      CH. HARPER'S WHITT VAN WRINKLE
      CH. YOUNGFORD'S THE TEMPEST

CH. BORNFREE JAC DANIEL OF TORI (on right)

CH. BORNFREE JAC DANIEL OF TORI (Maryellen Castimore & Meg Bloxham) CH. BORNFREE PHIRE FOX X CH. IVANWOLD PANHANDLE PIXIE (1988)

    CH. ALABEE BILLIE JEAN
    CH. DOVAN FRANKLIN MINT
    CH. PRIS PEACH BRANDY
    CH. TORI LANE APOLLO
    CH. TORI LANE PISTOL PACKIN MAMA
    CH. TORI LANES I LOVE LUCY

CH. BORNFREE PHIRE FOX

CH. BORNFREE PHIRE FOX* (Blanche C. Roberts) CH. SHEFFIELD'S
STUFF'N NONSENSE X CH. BORNFREE LIZZIE TISH (1987)
(1988*)
    CH. BLAQUE MERRI'D XERES
    CH. BLAQUE MINOR DETAIL OF HILTON
    CH. BLAQUE'S MARATAYA PHIRE
    CH. BLAQUE'S LOOKING FOR TROUBLE
    CH. BORNFREE JACK DANIEL OF TORI
    CH. BORNFREE PRINCESS MEE TOO
    CH. CON BRIO LOVELY TO LOOK AT
    CH. CON BRIO SIMPLY SMASH'N
    CH. NEU'S MYSTICAL WARLOCK
    CH. PRIS' NEU BLACK KEWPIE DOLL
    CH. STABRADAV'S DREAM MACHINE
    CH. YAWN'S SADIE

CH. CHARLAMAR'S ANCIENT DREAMER

CH. CHARLAMAR'S ANCIENT DREAMER**** (Mrs. Alan R. Robson)
CH. CHARLAMAR'S J. RANDALL BROWN X Charlamar's Alpha
Omega
> CH. IVANWOLD CHINABERRY
> CH. IVANWOLD PRINCESS JASMINE
> CH. IVANWOLD ANCIENT MARINER
> CH. STABRADAV'S DREAM MACHINE
> CH. NEU'S MYSTICAL WARLOCK
> CH. NEU'S MIDNIGHT REGENCY
> CH. ALBELARM MASTER CHARGE
> CH. JAC'S DIAMOND JIM
> CH. GAMBURG'S WOOFMAN JAC
> CH. GAMBURG'S CENTERFOLD
> CH. ALBELARM AMERICAN EXPRESS
> CH. NEU'S ENCHANTING SORCERESS
> CH. ALBELARM CREDIT CARD
> CH. KEURIG'S SHERMAN TANK
> CH. PRIS' NEW BLACK KEWPIE DOLL

CH. EU BET'S NEU DREAM COME TRUE
CH. NEU GRACIOUS GARBO
CH. IVANWOLD MARGARET ROSE
CH. LARIZADEY'S LEADING LADY
CH. HUGAPUG'S TIGER LILY
CH. HUGAPUG'S SUNDANCE KID
CH. FAIRCLOTH'S POLLY POPPINS
CH. GERI'S MANDARIN POPPY
CH. YAWN'S SADIE
CH. HARRISON'S DUTCH TREAT
CH. STABRADAV'S PRUNELLA
CH. ALBELARM CHARGE IT
CH. KESANDER'S TOWN CRIER
CH. KEURIG'S IN A NEW YORK MINUTE
CH. ALBELARM VISA

CH. CHARLAMAR'S LOUIS ST. LOUIS

CH. CHARLAMAR'S LOUIS ST. LOUIS (Blk) (Mary Moxley & Charlotte Corson) CH. CHARLAMAR'S J RANDALL BROWN, ROM X Charlamar's Alpha Omega (1986)
    CH. BARBLAND'S DAPPER DAN
    CH. BARBLAND'S KENTUCKY BELLE
    CH. BE BO'S HANNIBAL
    CH. ECHOING OAKS ET OF KESANDER
    CH. NEU DOLLY OF PRIS
    CH. PRIS' BLACK JACK

CH. CHARLAMAR'S J RANDALL BROWN

CH. CHARLAMAR'S J RANDALL BROWN* (Dog) (Mary Moxley & Charlotte Corson) CH. CHARLAMAR'S BILLY JOE BLACK X CH. NUNNALLY'S WITCH HAZEL, ROM (1986) (1988*)
 CH. BONJOR JESSIE OWNES
 CH. CHARLAMAR'S ANCIENT DREAMER
 CH. CHARLAMAR'S BLACK SILHOUETTE
 CH. CHARLAMAR'S BUNNY BOO BLACK
 CH. CHARLAMAR'S FESTIVE ELEGANCE
 CH. CHARLAMAR'S LACE AT PUGNOOK
 CH. CHARLAMAR'S LADY BEAR
 CH. CHARLAMAR'S LOUIS ST. LOUIS
 CH. CHARLAMAR'S MISS TOOIE
 CH. GRAMIGNA'S BEAR
 CH. GRAMIGNA'S TEXAS CHARLAMAR
 CH. GRAMIGNA'S BLACK LACE

CH. DANDY'S DORYSON BUCCANEER

CH. DHANDY'S DORYSON BUCCANEER (Mrs. W.J. Braley & Mrs.
R.J. Hutchinson) CH. AY YA GUNG HO MURPHY X CH.
CROWELL'S PANDORA (1979)

    CH. BLEURIDGE'S LINK
    CH. DHANDY'S BLEURIDGE BERRY
    CH. CH. DHANDY'S BUCKINGHAM HIGGS
    CH. DHANDY'S GOODWIN DAFFODIL
    CH. GOODWIN'S PATTY CAKE
    CH. HARPER'S FAWN C. PANTS
    CH. HARPER'S FAWN NEST FLOWER
    CH. HARPER'S FAWN NIE GIRL
    CH. MERRIMAKER'S BUSTER BROWN
    CH. MERRIMAKER'S LITTLE LULU
    CH. MERRIMAKER'S TAWNY TOKAY
    CH. OUR TIGER HIGGS

CH. DHANDY'S SKY HIGH

CH. DHANDY'S SKY HIGH (Nell Gramigna) CH. CHEN'S A FAVORITE
OF THE GODS X CH. DHANDY'S SKYLARK (1986)
    CH. BILBEV'S DUDLEY OF GRAMIGNA
    CH. CEDARS GRAMIGNA GO-GETTER
    CH. DUNNINGS JOY OF GRAMIGNA
    CH. GRAMIGNA'S JEZEBEL
    CH. GRAMIGNA'S MAX A MILLION
    CH. GRAMIGNA'S PATRICK
    CH. GRAMIGNA'S SAMSON

CH. DONALDSON'S RINESTONE COWBOY

CH. DONALDSON'S RINESTONE COWBOY (Marie Donaldson)
Donaldson's Gold Nugget X CH. DONALDSON'S RAGGIDY
ANN (1983)
CH. DONALDSON'S NICK-A-DEMUS
CH. DONALDSON'S THE FONZ
CH. DORISTAN'S SIGMOND FROWN
CH. FABERGE CZARINA OF WISE LORE
CH. FELICITY'S TILL DO IT MY WAY
CH. STEPHENS TOBETTA OF WISE-LORE

CH. DONALDSON'S TIPPI CANOE

CH. DONALDSON'S TIPPI CANOE* (Anita & Ivan Crowell)
AM. CAN. CH. GAIS TIPKINS (Eng. Imp) X CH.
DONALDSON'S LITTLE BO-PEEP (1984) (1985*)

> CH. BORNFREE LET'S DANCE
> CH. BORNFREE LIZZIE TISH
> CH. BORNFREE MISTER BO GART
> CH. BORNFREE TOM FOOLERY
> CH. CHELSEA DAWN'S FIRST EDITION
> CH. GOODTIME'S CENTERFOLD
> CH. HALLAGAN'S HOOSIER TARA
> CH. LIL KATE SMITH OF MSJ
> CH. LOURA LOVE OF MSJ
> CH. SHEPHEN'S GARNER BEAU BLEU
> CH. SUNNY TU CHANCE OF MSJ
> CH. TONQUIN ACRES CHELSEA TIA

Gais Rufty Tufty (Eng. Imp) (Mrs. Curtis R. Weston) Gais Peter Rabbit
 X Gais Pigwig (1979)
> CH. BONJORS DIFFERENT DRUMMER
> CH. BONJORS CALAMITY JANE
> CH. BONJORS WILD BILL HICKOK
> CH. BROUGHCASTL BALLADEER
> CH. C J'S IMACHIGAL
> CH. C J'S IMACHIGUY
> CH. C J'S MISTER BUMBLE
> CH. CAMBRROKES KOJAK

AM. CAN. CH. GAIS TIPKINS** (Mrs. C.R. Weston) Paramin Peter Pan
 of Slepe X Gais Penny (1981) (1987*)
> CH. DONALDSON'S LADY SNOOKUMS
> CH. CONALDSON'S LADY VICTORIA
> CH. DONALDSON'S NOTHERN EXPLORER
> CH. DONALDSON'S TIPPI CANOE
> CH. DORRELL'S BEAU VISAGE
> CH. FELICITY'S DIE FLEDERMOUS
> CH. HARPER'S SANGUINE LADY
> CH. HARPER'S SUMPIN' SPECIAL
> CH. HESTERS AMBER LADY
> CH. HESTERS ATTA BOY AMOS
> CH. HESTERS ATTA BOY ANDY
> CH. IVANWOLD TIP TOP
> CH. KOCH'S MISS DOLLY OF MAR DU
> CH. KOCH'S MISS JENNIFER OF MAR DU
> CH. KOCH'S SIR WINSTON OF RAYBROOK
> CH. WESTON'S HEARTS'N FLOWERS
> CH. WESTON'S PRIDE'N JOY
> CH. WESTON'S TEDDY BEAR

CH. GORE'S UP N'ADAM

CH. GORE'S UP 'N ADAM (Louise Gore) CH. ROBERTSON'S
BOURBON PRINCE X CH. ROBERTSON'S GODELLE (1983)
        CH. CROWELLS BLACK JACK OF GORE
        CH. ESSONS SHOW-NUFF GORE
        CH. GORE'S FANCI ADAM
        CH. GORE'S UP N'FANCI BEBE
        CH. GORE'S UP N'HI WENDY TRINKET
        CH. PAULMARS TRACE OF ANTIQUITY
        CH. PAULMARS TRACE OF EXCELLENCE
        CH. PAULMARS TRACE OF VIRTUE
        CH. PAULMARS WAGGA DE ANN
        CH. SOUTHLANDS TOP BONANA O'GORE

CH. HARPER'S FLY'IN HIGH

CH. HARPER'S FLY'IN HIGH (Norma S. Harper) CH. IVANWOLD
HIGH TOR X CH. HARPER'S STAR SAPPHIRE (1987)
CH. HARPER'S AMADEUS
CH. HARPER'S AS I BEE
CH. HARPER'S KISS ME KATE
CH. HARPER'S PANDA SAN OF TATHAM
CH. HARPER'S SEATTLE SUE
CH. HARPER'S SIZZLE

CH. HARPER'S TOMMY TUNE

CH. HARPER'S TOMMY TUNE (Alan L. Harper) CH. BONJOR PETER PARKER X CH. HARPER'S STAR SAPPHIRE, ROM (1987)
CH. HARPER'S BENNY HILL
CH. HARPER'S CINDY LAUPER
CH. HARPER'S HUIE LEWIS
CH. SCHONEWALD'S RAISIN CANE
CH. VANDONNA'S K O KATIE
CH. YOUNGFORD'S BLUE CHIP

CH. HAZELBRIDGE BLACK EROS

CH. HAZELBRIDGE BLACK EROS (Blk. Imp.) (Joe Martha) ENG. CH.
WHAT OH OF RYDENS X Hazelbridge Black Ann (1980)
    CH. KENDORICS SILVERTOWN NUGGET
    CH. MARNINA'S DIABLO
    CH. PUG PAK STEEL CURTAIN
    CH. SILVERTOWN JASPER
    CH. WALLS INKY OF KINGS RIDGE
    CH. WALLS JOEY OF KINGS RIDGE
    CH. WALLS PHIL OF KINGS RIDGE

CH. IVANWOLD'S ANCIENT MARINER

CH. IVANWOLD ANCIENT MARINER (Mrs. Alan R. Robson)
CH. CHARLAMAR'S ANCIENT DREAMER, ROM X CH.
IVANWOLD HONEYSUCKLE ROSE, ROM (1988)
    CH. IVANWOLD ALADEAN'S CHINA LORD
    CH. IVANWOLD CHINA CLIPPER
    CH. IVANWOLD CHINATOWN EXPRESS
    CH. ROYAL A'S MAGICAL MARINER
    CH. ROYAL A'S MERRY MARINER
    CH. ROYAL A'S MYSTICAL MARINER

CH. IVANWOLD HIGH TOR (Janet Patterson) CH. MARTLESHAM
GALAHAD OF BOURNLE X Ivanwold Portia's Pride (1979)
    CH. BRUNO LE NOYRE OF TOR
    CH. CROWELL'S HIGH KING
    CH. EMBEE ROBIN OF TOR
    CH. FOWLER'S MERWYN OF GAYBERRY
    CH. HARPER'S FLY'IN HIGH
    CH. IVANWOLD ACE HIGH OF CROWELL
    CH. IVANWOLD FIGARO FIGARO
    CH. IVANWOLD GAYBERRY CAROLINA
    CH. IVANWOLD HIGH BARBARY
    CH. IVANWOLD PINAFORE OF HYWINDY
    CH. MAR LOS WILD HONEY EX TOR
    CH. RITTER'S SUPER STAR
    CH. ROBERTSON'S GOLDELLE
    CH. RONTU NAPOLEON
    CH. THE TOOTH FAIRY OF TOR

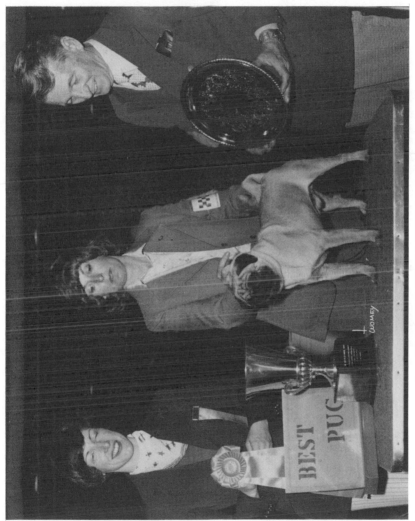

CH. IVANWOLD PISTOL PETE OF RONTU

CH. IVANWOLD PISTOL PETE OF RONTU***** (E.N.K. &
C. Patterson & J. & P. Cobb) CH. BROUGHCASTL BALLADEER
X CH. IVANWOLD GAYBERRY CAROLINA (1981) (1983*)
(1984***) (1987*)

    CH. ALADEAN'S TWEET-SEY OF ROBEL
    CH. HARCOR'S OLIVIA
    CH. HARPER'S BIZZI BODI
    CH. HATIKVAH ISHMAEL
    CH. HEAVY ARTILLERY OF ERROW
    CH. HOWLAND CASHMERE CLOWN
    CH. HOWLAND DELICATE DANDELION
    CH. HOWLAND MUPPET MUNCHKIN
    CH. IVANWOLD ARKANSAS TRAVELLER
    CH. IVANWOLD BEAU OF HALLAGAN
    CH. IVANWOLD DESIREE OF NICE
    CH. IVANWOLD ELIZABETH REGINA
    CH. IVANWOLD GIGI OF ALADEAN
    CH. IVANWOLD LI'L OSCAR
    CH. IVANWOLD LORD CECIL
    CH. IVANWOLD MATILDA OF CAMARADE
    CH. IVANWOLD MEMPHIS BELLE
    CH. IVANWOLD PANHANDLE PIXIE
    CH. IVANWOLD PETERBILT
    CH. IVANWOLD PISTOL PACKIN' MAMA
    CH. IVANWOLD VICTORIA REGINA
    CH. LAIRD MALCOLM OF YORKHILL
    CH. LI'L MEMORY OF MSJ
    CH. PUGTOWNE'S CHINA HOLLYBERRY
    CH. ROWELL'S BAD BAD LEROY BROWN
    CH. RUSSO'S TUFFY THE SECOND
    CH. SOUTHERN DEBUTANTE OF ERROW
    CH. STABRDAV'S SHAYNA OF HATIKVAH
    CH. TIKAS BOHEMIAN RHAPSODY
    CH. TIKAS INCREDIBLE HULK
    CH. TIKAS LITTLE PISTOL OF PETE
    CH. TIKAS TIFFIE TOO
    CH. TOM'S BRAW LADDIE OF YORKHILL
    CH. WIND OF DESTIN

CH. KESANDER'S SIWASHER

CH. KESANDER'S SIWASHER (Bob & Jean Anderson) CH. BONJOR
WILD BILL HICKOK X Kesander's Dandy Darlin' (1985)
    CH. KESANDER'S GISMO GAL OF MARMAG
    CH. KESANDER'S P-R MAN
    CH. MARMAGS LUKKI OF WINDY ACRES
    CH. MARMAGS SILVER SNEAKER
    CH. MARMAGS WHIZZER OF KOTH
    CH. STEPHEN'S GREAT SEBASTIAN

CH.KESANDER'S SPEAK OF D'DEBBEL, C.D.

CH. KESANDER'S SPEAK OF D'DEBBEL, C.D. (Blk.) (Bob & Jean
Anderson) CH. KESANDER'S DOUBLE DEBBEL X CH.
KESANDER'S SASSY LASSY (1985)
> CH. BECCA'S D'DEBBEL'S ADVOCATE
> CH. J-K'S MIA MOOSETTE OF KESANDER
> CH. PIXIE FARM GIVEMHELL HARRY
> CH. PRIS' BUNKSHUS
> CH. THISTLEDOWN SANDMAN
> CH. THISTLEDOWN VICTORY BLACK

CH. LI'L DAVY OF SHEFFIELD

CH. LI'L DAVEY OF SHEFFIELD (Marie Donaldson) CH. WOLF'S
LI'L JOE X CH. SHEFFIELD'S SURE FIRE (1983)
    CH. DONALDSON'S GOLDEN GIRL
    CH. DONALDSON'S LEVI'S TRADEMARK
    CH. FAHEY'S FANCY PANTS
    CH. FAHEY'S GREAT BALL OF FIRE
    CH. SHEFFIELD'S BOBBY SHAFTOE
    CH. SHEFFIELD'S FORTUNE TELLER
    CH. STEPHEN'S TRUE GRIT CARNEYBEAU

CH. NEUBRAA PAPAGENO

CH. NEUBRAA PAPAGENO (Eng. Imp) (Willis Shaw) ENG. CH.
PRENDERGAST OF PYEBETA X Edenderry Coolanee (1979)
    CH. AYME TU WYN KWI
    CH. HANOVER'S CASSANDRA D'GENO
    CH. HANOVER'S CASSIUS D'GENO
    CH. J AND J'S ROLLING STONE
    CH. LITTLE TOMMY TUCKER
    CH. PRINCESS CHERYL OF MELCAR
    CH. SHEFFIELD'S MIDAS TOUCH
    CH. SHEFFIELD'S PALE PUTTY
    CH. STONECRUSHER OF WISSELWOOD
    CH. TOBOLL'S GENO DARLING
    CH. WENDY THE POO OF WISSELWOOD
    CH. WHISPERING LANE'S LE KERAI
    CH. WISSELWOOD BUDWEISER
    CH. WISSELWOOD TENDER AMBER
    CH. WISSELWOOD'S CLIFF HANGER

CH. PAMAJO'S LITTLE TOMMY TUCKER (Pam & Margaret Weaver)
    CH. PAMAJO'S SHERMAN TANK X Pamajo's Dear Abby (1986)
    CH. DEYOUNG'S MR. IMPORTANT
    CH. MISSY'S SCOOKUMS
    CH. SANCHI'S CHINA DOLL OF PAMAJO
    CH. SANCHI'S GRIZZLY BEAR
    CH. SANCHI'S JUNE BUG
    CH. SANCHI'S KERMIT

CH. PANDA MISTERY JOEY OF HARDWAY

CH. PANDA MISTERY JOEY OF HARDWAY* (Marvin Werth)
CH. WOLF'S LI'L JOE X CH. BO'S SUNSHINE MISS OF
LARIMAR (1980)

      CH. MARVIE CLARE DE LOONE
      CH. MARVIE KATHLEEN JOY
      CH. MARVIE MISTERY PANDY BOYCE
      CH. MARVIE PANABELL MISTERY
      CH. MARVIE PANAROSE LANE
      CH. MARVIE PANCELIA MISTERY
      CH. MARVIE PANCHOO BOY MISTERY
      CH. MARVIE PANDALENA MISTERY
      CH. MARVIE PANDELLA RAE
      CH. MARVIE PANDJOE OF SUNSHINE
      CH. MARVIE PANWENDOWAY MISTERY
      CH. MARVIE ROSEMARYS LAST ROSE
      CH. SURE SWEET CANDY KISS
      CH. SURE SWEET COOKIE
      CH. SURE SWEET HONEY BUN

CH. PEER'S JOHN - JOHN (Mary Peer) CH. BLAYLOCK'S GOLIATH
X Garden Lane Merry Poppins (1980)
    CH. LEE SU BUM
    CH. MASON'S PUTTER
    CH. PEERS AUDIE
    CH. PEERS KANDY KANE
    CH. PEERS KOONIE
    CH. PEERS RONNIE JOE
    CH. PEERS THUNDER
    CH. PEERS TINY JUDY

AM. CAN. CH. PELSHIRE'S EXCALIBUR (Susan B. Christensen)
AM. CAN. CH. KENDORIC SILVERTOWN NUGGET X AM.
CAN. CH. PELSHIRE'S WISSELWOOD MAGIC, C.D. (1986)
    CH. BEECHWOOD MAGNUM FORCE
    CH. PELSHIRE'S MAGIC MARK
    CH. PELSHIRE'S MAGIC QUILL
    CH. WATERSIDE BELL RINGER
    CH. WATERSIDE ROYAL MAGIC
    CH. WATERSIDE SORCERER
    CH. WATERSIDE THE IRISH REBEL

AM. CAN. CH. RITTER'S SUPER STAR

CH. RITTER'S SUPER STAR (Virginia Ritter) CH. IVANWOLD
HIGH TOR X CH. RITTER'S SESAME STREET (1981)
    CH. CANDICE SEAMAN
    CH. DOBER PUG'S APRIL HEIRESS
    CH. DOBER PUG'S JIM E CRICKET
    CH. DOBER PUG'S STAR TREK

CH. DOBER PUG'S TOM E GEE
CH. IVANWOLD MEMPHIS BELLE
CH. RITTER'S NO NONSENSE
CH. RITTER'S ROAD RUNNER
CH. RITTER'S RUSTY NAIL

CH. ROBERTSON'S BOURBON PRINCE (Louise Gore) CH.
ROBERTSON'S BUC-O-NUNNALLY X Nunnally's Derby Doll (1982)
    CH. CROWELL'S WICKED WANDA O'GORE
    CH. GORE'S FANCI GIN PHIZZ
    CH. GORE'S UP'N ADAM
    CH. ROBERTSON'S OH SUSIE, CD
    CH. ROBERTSON'S PRINCESS ROSE
    CH. SOUTHLAND'S DIXIE OF CROWELL

CH. SAMET PAUL OF PARAMIN

CH. SAMET PAUL OF PARAMIN*** (Eng. Imp.) (Margery Shriver)
Phirefly of Paramin X Paramin Paulette (1980*) (1983**)
    CH. BERNALEE MARS
    CH. BERNALEE SATURN
    CH. BERNALEE VENUS
    CH. GAS HOLLOW'S WHIFF N POOF
    CH. HUGAPUG MR. SQUIGGENBOTHAM
    CH. KENDORIC'S FRENCH CONNECTION
    CH. LOWES PURPLE OF BERNALEE
    CH. MIKEMAR'S GEM OF ALBELARM
    CH. PARAGON'S AMERICAN CLASSIC

CH. PARAGON'S MISS AMERICA
CH. PUGTOWNES JENNY VALENTINE
CH. SHEFFIELD OLD FASHIONED GIRL
CH. SHEFFIELD'S CELTIC SOLDIER
CH. SHEFFIELD'S CHARLATAN
CH. SHEFFIELD'S COUNTRY COUSIN
CH. SHEFFIELD'S GREEN APPLE
CH. SHEFFIELD'S ORANGE PEKOE
CH. SHEFFIELD'S PIPE DREAMS
CH. SHEFFIELD'S SNEAKY PETE
CH. SHEFFIELD'S STARGAZER
CH. SHEFFIELD'S STUFF'N NONSENSE
CH. SHEFFIELD'S SUNKIST
CH. SHEFFIELD'S TAM PIERCE
CH. SHEFFIELD'S DARLING EVE
CH. SIR OSCAR OF HEINEFURST II

CH. SHEFFIELD'S CHARLATAN

CH. SHEFFIELD'S CHARLATAN (Virginia Ritter) CH. SAMET PAUL
OF PARAMIN X CH. SHEFFIELD'S SURE FIRE (1983)
CH. PITTINGER'S SPECTACULAR BID
CH. RITTER'S CALL ME MAXI
CH. RITTER'S LUCKY LYNX
CH. RITTER'S RAINDANCE
CH. RITTER'S SOMEBODY LOVES ME
CH. THEO-DEANS SPARKLING JEWELL

CH. SHEFFIELD'S DANCING TIGER

CH. SHEFFIELD'S DANCING TIGER* (M. Shriver & Michael Wolf)
    CH. WOLF'S LI'L JOE X CH. SHEFFIELD'S SURE FIRE (1979*)
        CH. DHANDY'S SKYLARK
        CH. DHANDY'S WHIPPOORWILL
        CH. DOR ANN'S KELLY GIRL
        CH. GAMBURG'S OLLETIME SHOW OFF
        CH. GAMBURG'S OLLETIME TIGER BOI
        CH. HEATHERLANE BLUERIDGE BENNY
        CH. HERITAGE FRIVOLOUS PHANNY
        CH. HERITAGE JUBILANT JELLYBEAN
        CH. HERITAGE LUSCIOUS LOLLIPOP
        CH. HERITAGE WICKED WITCH
        CH. JAN'S CRACKER JACK
        CH. JEFFORDS' PARTNERS' CHOICE
        CH. SHEFFIELD'S MISTER MUSTARD
        CH. SHEFFIELD'S TASTYKAKE
        CH. SHEP'S LI'L GOLDEN TOM BOY
        CH. SHEP'S SUNDANCE KID

CH. SHEFFIELD'S LIFE OF THE PARTY

CH. SHEFFIELD'S LIFE OF THE PARTY* (Loretta B. Wiseman)
CH. SHEFFIELD'S STUFF'N NONSENSE X CH. SHEFFIELD'S
CHARMING EYES (1986) (1988*)
CH. FAHEY'S COUNTRY GENTLEMAN
CH. FAHEY'S FOR GOODNESS SAKE
CH. FAHEY'S GOODIE GO GETT'EM
CH. FAHEY'S HOT PANTS
CH. FAHEY'S I'M FANCY
CH. FAHEY'S MISSOURI FARMER
CH. FAHEY'S PARADING PRINCESS
CH. SHEAD'S CHARLEMAGNE
CH. TERI-LAR'S LI'L MIKE HAMMER
CH. WISE-LORE'S CHAMPAGNE LADY
CH. WISE-LORE'S WING COMMANDER
CH. WISE-LORE'S WRAPPED 'N RAINBOWS

CH. SHEFFIELD'S LITTLE RED WAGON

CH. SHEFFIELD'S LITTLE RED WAGON**** (Margery Shriver)
CH. SHEFFIELD'S ROSE TATTO X CH. SHEFFIELD'S COUNTY
COUSIN (1986*) (1987**) (1988*)
 CH. ALBELARM SOUND THE ALARM
 CH. ALCAR'S GRATOM GABRIELLE
 CH. BOXWYN'S PUGNACIOUS
 CH. BOXWYN THE PUGALIST
 CH. CHAPEL RIDGE'S LADY SLIPPER
 CH. CHAPEL RIDGE'S WONDERBOY
 CH. GAS HOLLOW'S K-K-K KATIE
 CH. GAS HOLLOW'S LOG CABIN
 CH. GERRIE'S DAN O'MINE
 CH. GERRIE'S RORY OF CHARLAMAR
 CH. IMPERIAL COOKIE CRUSHER
 CH. IMPERIAL PING T'U FEI LEGAYLE
 CH. IVANWOLD HOOSIER OF GERRIE
 CH. KATSU HONYEYBUN OF MARIDON
 CH. MANALAPAN'S GOLDEN BUDDHA
 CH. MARIDON'S ALTHEA
 CH. MARIDON'S FLAME OF LIBERTY

CH. MARIDON'S PRINCE COMUS
CH. MARIDON'S TEXAS TIGER
CH. NEU'S KONIGSSEE OF MARIDON
CH. PORTER'S COOL CALVIN
CH. PORTER'S SPIRIT OF EIGHTY-SIX
CH. SHEFFIELD'S ONE TRICK PONY
CH. SHEFFIELD'S SPITFIRE

CH. SHEFFIELD'S SNEAKY PETE

CH. SHEFFIELD'S SNEAKY PETE**** (Margery Shriver) CH. SAMET
PAUL OF PARAMIN (Eng. Imp.) X CH. SHEFFIELD'S
CONSTANT COMMENT (1984*) (1986***)
CH. BIG E'NUF'S SPARKLIN SHERRI
CH. CHAPEL RIDGE'S MISS CHIEF
CH. CHAPEL RIDGE'S MY ANGEL
CH. CHAPEL RIDGE'S SHOW GIRL
CH. CHAPEL RIDGE'S THEODORE
CH. HALLAGAN'S BLARNEY MIST O'ERIN
CH. IVANWOLD TESS OF MENUHUNE
CH. KOKOMO'S MOON SHADOW
CH. PUGLO'S COUNTRY ROADS
CH. RICKSHAW'S CLYDE BARROW
CH. SHEFFIELD'S CHARMING EYES
CH. SHEFFIELD'S ROSE TATTOO
CH. SHEFFIELD'S LITTLE NIGHT MUSIC
CH. SHEFFIELD'S SNOW FIRE
CH. SHEFFIELD'S SPRING FLOWER
CH. SHEFFIELD'S WILD CLOVER
CH. SHEFFIELD'S WYNDSHYRE LASS
CH. WANJO'S SUE Z QUE

VARIETY GROUP
THIRD
UPPER POTOMAC
VALLEY
JUNE 1980

PHOTO BY *Graham*

CH. SHEFFIELD'S STUFF'N NONSENSE*********** (Margery Shriver) CH. SAMET PAUL OF PARAMIN, ROM (Eng. Imp.) X CH. SHEFFIELD'S SWEETER THAN WINE (1984**) (1985*) (1986***) (1987*) (1988*)

 CH. ALCAR'S FRISCO BAY BOY
 CH. BELORIK KENDORIC BLACK WINDY
 CH. BORNFREE MY DIANE
 CH. BORNFREE PHIRE FOX
 CH. BORNFREE THAT'S INCREDIBLE
 CH. CAMEO'S ORANGE JULIUS
 CH. CAMEO'S SWEET MAGNOLIA
 CH. CAMEO'S VERY VANILLA
 CH. CHAHARY ANDREW OF SHEFFIELD
 CH. CHAHARY ATIEN OF SHEFFIELD
 CH. CHAPEL RIDGE'S BUBBLING OVER
 CH. CHAPEL RIDGE'S CATS PAJAMAS
 CH. CHAPEL RIDGE'S CHERUB
 CH. CHAPEL RIDGE'S DOLL FACE
 CH. CHAPEL RIDGE'S EXCALIBUR
 CH. CHAPEL RIDGE'S ROBIN HOOD
 CH. CHAPEL RIDGE QUEEN ANN LACE
 CH. CHOPSTIX OF THE PINES
 CH. DONALDSON'S KNIGHTRIDER
 CH. DONALDSON'S PLAY BOY
 CH. EDEN'S BLAQUE MADRIGAL
 CH. FASHION DOLL VON SAN REMO
 CH. FLIRTATION VON SAN REMO
 CH. GOODWIN'S THUMBELINA ROWELL
 CH. HALLIGANS KATIE OF ERIN
 CH. IVANWOLD CAPITOL GAIN
 CH. IVANWOLD HONYSUCKLE ROSE
 CH. IVANWOLD ROSE VELVET
 CH. JULIE'S POPPY SWEET SANDY
 CH. KESANDER'S JINGLIN' JAIMIE
 CH. KESANDER'S JINGLIN' JORDIE
 CH. KESANDER'S JINGLING JOSIE
 CH. LAUGHING WATERS JAMI
 CH. MENEHUNE HOLIDAY CHEER
 CH. MIKE-MAR'S TEMPLE BELLS
 CH. MY-TEE STUFF OF THE PINES
 CH. PELSHIRE'S MAGIC PHIDDLER
 CH. RAINELL'S EDWARD DEE
 CH. SHEFFIELD'S COTTON EYED JOE
 CH. SHEFFIELD'S CRYSTAL BALL

CH. SHEFFIELD'S LIFE OF THE PARTY
CH. SHEFFIELD'S RAGTIME
CH. SHEFFIELD'S SECOND SEQUENCE
CH. SHEFFIELD'S STAGE DOOR JOHNNY
CH. SOUTHLAND'S DUTCHESS
CH. SPIKE BEEBE GIBBS
CH. STUFFED SHIRT OF THE PINES

AM. & CAN. CH. SHEFFIELD'S SUNDAY PUNCH* (Margery Shriver)
CH. WALL'S WARRIOR OF PARAMIN X CH. SERENADE OF
SHEFFIELD (1979*)
CH. MAR LOS HOLLY OF SHEFFIELD
CH. MAR LOS KNICK KNACK
CH. MAR LOS PADDY WHACK
CH. MAR LOS POPPY OF SHEFFIELD
CH. NAZREP LADY KISMET
CH. SHEFFIELD'S BACHELOR BUTTON
CH. SHEFFIELD'S QUEEN OF HEARTS
CH. SHEFFIELD'S SONTATA OF MARLOS
CH. SHEFFIELD'S SURE FIRE
CH. SHEFFIELD'S YUM YUM SHOGO
CH. SHEP'S LI'L GOLDEN SUNDAY NIP
CH. SHEPS SASSAFRAS COCA

CH. SHEP'S MAJOR TOP CAT

CH. SHEP'S MAJOR TOP CAT (James L. Shepherd) CH. HERITAGE
TOM CAT OF GORE X Shep's Li'l Tamu of Dunroamin' (1980)
CH. COUNTESS BOUSHA AGGIE
CH. SHEP'S AFTERNOON DELITE

CH. SHEP'S BUTCH CASSIDY
CH. SHEP'S LLAMA OF SHANGRA LA
CH. SHEP'S MAGIC MOMENT
CH. SHEP'S MR MIKE OF NARDILA
CH. SHEP'S PEACH PUDDIN
CH. SHEP'S PENNY FROM HEAVEN

AM. CAN. CH. SILVERTOWN GRAND SLAM

AM. CAN. CH. SILVERTOWN GRAND SLAM (Polly Lamarine)
CH. SILVERTOWN CAPRICORN'S CAPER X CH. SILVERTOWN
SURPRISE PACKAGE, ROM (1987)
CH. GALE BE MY VALENTINE OF NAZREP
CH. GALE KRINGLE IN TIME
CH. GALE'S POSEY OF WARWICK
CH. RICKY TICK PENNYROYAL
CH. SILVERTOWN SEQUEL
CH. SUNSET PRINCE WILLIAM

CH. STONECRUSHER OF WISSELWOOD

CH. STONECRUSHER OF WISSELWOOD (Lorene Vickers) CH.
NEUBRAA PAPAGENO X CH HEATHER'S HONEY OF
WISSELWOOD (1979)
    CH. BOLDERBUSTER OF FEATHERWOOD
    CH. FEATHERWOODS STONEY SILENCE
    CH. FEATHERWOOD STONE OF DESTINY
    CH. HARPER'S MISS IN A MINUTE
    CH. HARPER'S ROCK AND ROLL
    CH. MIKSAN'S WAR BONNET
    CH. PITTINGER'S CHICO OF RITTER
    CH. RITTER'S LUCEA OF WA KAY
    CH. STONEWOOD'S DELTA MISS
    CH. WISSELWOOD L S KENNEDY
    CH. WISSELWOOD WAR LORD
    CH. WOHLFORD'S SNICKERDOODLE
    CH. WOHLFORD'S WILLIE WONKA

CH. TERYTAM TASKMASTER

CH. TERYTAM TASKMASTER (Linda & John Rowell, Jr.) CH.
BROUGHCASTL BALLADEER X CH. TERYTAM'S TALLYHO OF
PARAGON (1985)
   CH. D AND D'S BLACK JACK DAVY
   CH. HATIKVAH RUFNTUFNFULOSTUF
   CH. ROWELL'S DIAMONDS ARE FOREVER
   CH. ROWELL'S SASSY SCRUPLES
   CH. ROWELL'S TONKA TOY MASTER
   CH. ROWELL'S TOUCH OF TIFFANY

CH. WALL'S INKY OF KING'S RIDGE (Blk) (Sue Wall) AM. CH. HAZELBRIDGE EROS, ROM (Blk. Eng. Imp.) X Wall's Doris of King's Ridge (1987)

    CH. GERRIE'S CUPCAKE OF CHARLAMAR
    CH. GERRIE'S I LOVE LUCY
    CH. GERRIE'S JORDAN OF CHARLAMAR
    CH. MARNINAS AFRO DOLLI
    CH. MARNINAS FAWN TEU
    CH. WALLS SUSIE OF KINGS RIDGE

CH. WALL'S INKY OF KINGS RIDGE, C.D.

CH. WARJOY'S COAL CRUSHER

CH. WARJOY'S COAL CRUSHER (Blk.) (Warren D. Hudson) CH. MAY'S
BLARNEY STONE (Blk.) X Embee Sugarplum of Trinket (1988)
    CH. LUVPUG'S GOODTIME CHARLIE
    CH. LUVPUG'S LITTLE RICHARD
    CH. WARJOY'S AXLE GREASE
    CH. WARJOY'S BLACK DRAGON
    CH. WARJOY'S JACQUELINE
    CH. WARJOY'S LITTLE HUNK
    CH. WARJOY'S PAYNE'S LITTLE WARYOR

CH. WISSELWOOD VELVET TUBBY

CH. WISSELWOOD VELVET TUBBY (Blk) (Lorene Vickers-Smith)
AM. CAN. CH. EBONY'S MARMADUKE OF HAVEN X
Wisselwood Cotton Tasyll (1987)
      CH. MIKSAN'S VILLAGE SQUIRE
      CH. WISSELWOOD ADAIR'S TISHA
      CH. WISSELWOOD MARVELOUS MARVIN
      CH. WISSELWOOD NIGHT MUSIC
      CH. WISSELWOOD WIZARD OF PUG-PAK
      CH. YOUNGFORD'S BLACK BART

AM. CAN. CH. WOLF'S LI'L JOE* (Gus & Esther Wolf) CH. CHEERIO
OF EVEN SO X CH. WOLF'S KAUFFEE ROYAL ROSE (1979***)
      CH. ALEXANDER'S DOCTOR GOOFEE
      CH. ALEXANDER'S HO HO HO
      CH. ALEXANDER'S MERI XMAS
      CH. ALEXANDER'S VILLAGE IDIOT
      CH. B AND B'S EXPLORER OF PARAGON
      CH. BLEURIDGE'S SANDI OF HERITAGE
      CH. CEALYANNE'S AIRY GINGERSNAP
      CH. CHAR MILY'S LI'L JOE'S BAMBI
      CH. CHAR MILY'S LI'L JOE'S DYN A MITE
      CH. CHAR MILY'S JOE'S LI'L TEDDI
      CH. DOR ANN'S DELIGHT OF PARAGON
      CH. FAHEY'S FOLLOW ME
      CH. FAHEY'S FOR GOODNESS SAKE
      CH. FAHEY'S IN FASHION
      CH. FARMER JOE FAHEY
      CH. FERGIS LTTLE KAUFFEE ROYAL
      CH. FICHTER FAYE'S DIC TRACEE

AM. CAN. CH. WOLF'S L'IL JOE

      CH. FOWLER'S JODOLL OF ROBERTSON
      CH. GRAMIGNA'S LI'L JOE GIRL
      CH. HALVOR'S JUSO EVR OF THE PINES
      CH. HAPPY MELODIE OF DUXBURY
      CH. JAN'S HARMONICA MAN

CH. JULIE'S JOE OF MAR LOS
CH. KAUFFEE ROYAL BRANDY WINE
CH. KAUFFEE ROYAL LI'L MR SATCHMO
CH. KAUFFEE ROYAL LI'L JOE
CH. KELLY'S BRANDY JOE
CH. KELLY'S CHERUB STAR OF DREAMER
CH. KELLY'S OZARK PHILWIL
CH. KELLY'S QUACHITA JOEY
CH. KELLY'S ROYAL GRETTA GO GIRL
CH. KELLY'S WALTER CHARLIE
CH. KOCH'S I'M CHIPPER OF PARAGON
CH. LI'L DAVEY OF SHEFFIELD
CH. LI'L JOE'S LI'L JOE
CH. LI'L SUGAR OF MSJ
CH. LKK'S SUSIE'S LI'L JOSEPHINE
CH. LKK'S SUSIE'S LI'L BACHELOR JOE
CH. MARVIE CRISTY RAE OF SUNSHINE
CH. MORAN'S BITTERSWEET MOLLY
CH. NOBLES DERBY JOE OF PARAGON
CH. PANDA MISTERY JOEY OF HARDWAY
CH. PARAGON'S DELTA DAWN
CH. PARAGON'S LITTLE CENTURION
CH. PREIFER'S LI'L ODD JOB
CH. PREIFER'S PENELOPE
CH. PUG HILL'S LI'L JOE
CH. PUGSLY OF FROSTACRES
CH. RITTER'S TRAVELIN APACHE
CH. ROBERTSON'S FANCI BABE
CH. SHEFFIELD'S JOHNNY COME LATELY
CH. SHEFFIELD'S CARELESS LOVE
CH. SHEFFIELD'S CONSTANT COMMENT
CH. SHEFFIELD'S DANCING TIGER
CH. SHEFFIELD'S LAVENDAR BLUE
CH. SHEFFIELD'S PENNY SERENADE
CH. SHEFFIELD'S SECOND HAND ROSE
CH. SHEFFIELD'S SHORTENING BREAD
CH. SHEFFIELD'S STAR TREK
CH. SHEFFIELD'S SWEETER THAN WINE
CH. SHIRRAYNE'S BASHFUL BIFF
CH. SHIRRAYNE'S BRASH BUFFI
CH. SIR BUFFINGTON OF IRON BLUFF
CH. SLAPSY MAXIE, CD
CH. SY LIN'S IT'S HAPPENED
CH. TERYTAM'S ODE TO JOEY

CH. TERYTAM'S TALLYHO OF PARAGON
CH. THE HERITAGE BRAT OF DECRIS
CH. WISE LORE'S JOMAHA
CH. WISE LORE'S SHOWDOWN SHERMAN
CH. WISE LORE'S U OTTA KNO WHO
CH. WOLF'S KAUFFEE OF CROZIER

20

Register of Merit Dams

(Statistics complete through PDCA's 1988 year)

The awarding of the designation Register of Merit, or ROM, was begun by the Pug Dog Club of America in 1979. The current requirements to be awarded the Register of Merit are: a Pug dam, owned by a Pug Dog Club of America member (or members, if co-owners), must have produced three Champion get whose Championships are published in the AKC *Gazette* within a particular five-year period.

Further recognition is afforded to a dam by the addition of stars to the ROM Certificate. A star is awarded for each additional group of three Champions she whelps. For this purpose, the requirement that they finish during a five-year period is replaced by an eight-year time span. A Pug cannot receive stars until the requirements for the ROM award itself are first met. Also, it is not required that the two time spans, for the ROM and the star(s), overlap, making it possible for a Pug to have all of its Champion offspring qualify for this award, regardless of the length of time involved.

The ROM appellation may be used in pedigrees, as in: Ch. Clara The Clown ROM*. This would indicate that Clara whelped six Champions in eight years, at least three of which were published during a given five-year period.

An analysis of the dams on this list confirms the concept that quality produces quality. Many of these dams have one or more ROM-designated parents. Only three, though, come from a ROM X ROM breeding. They are: Ch. Bornfree Lizzie Tish ROM, Ch. Rowell's Sassy Scruples ROM, and Ch. Rowell's Touch of Tiffany.

After the listing of the ROM sires, it is not unexpected to learn that Ch. Sheffield's Stuff'N Nonsense ROM and Ch. Wolf's Li'l Joe ROM are tied with six ROM-designated female offspring. It is interesting to note that Ch. Dhandy's Favorite Woodchuck, while not a ROM dog himself, has two ROM daughters.

By kennel name, again, Sheffield leads the list, with six ROM dams. That is followed by the Ivanwold dogs with five, the Chapel Ridge Pugs of Carol V.S. Gossweiler, Virginia Ritter, and Betty Weston, each tied at four ROM dams. The top-producing Pug dam is Ch. Sheffield's Sure Fire, who had eleven Champions. Others who are close include Shep's Li'l Tamu of Dunroamin, Ch. Laughing Waters Upsie, Ch. Sheffeild's

Sally Sunshine, and Ch. Heather's Honey of Wisslewood ROM, all with nine Champion get.

While there are many ROM dams with ROM daughters, there are only a few with more than one. They are: Ch. Sabbaday Favor ROM, dam of Ch. Silvertown Surprise Package ROM, Silvertwon Onyx ROM, and Sabbaday Fantasy ROM. Generationally speaking, the Sheffield dams again lead the way, with four generations descending from Ch. Sheffield's Sunday Punch ROM: his daughter, Ch. Sheffield's Sure Fire ROM, her daughter, Ch. Sheffield's Second Hand Rose ROM, and *her* daughter, Ch. Sheffield's Wilds Clover ROM, out of Ch. Sheffield's Sneaky Pete ROM.

Again, only one other line comes close to to repeating this achievement: Carol Gossweiler and the Chapel Ridge Pugs. Her Chapel Ridge Angelus Bell ROM is the dam of two ROM bitches, one being Chapel Ridge Belszon ROM, who is the dam of Ch. Chapel Ridge Queen Anne Lace ROM.

CH. ALABEE'S ASTA RISK (Abby & Allen Fox) CH. SHIRRAYNE'S VICTORIOUS VANCE X CH. VANDONNA'S FLICKA OF ALABEE (1988)

> CH. ALABEE'S BARZEN MARGE
> CH. ALABEE'S BILLIE JEAN
> CH. ALABEE'S BROADWAY DANNY ROSE

Aladean's Suzie Que (Doreen F. Martin) Aladean's Lucky Lad (Eng. Imp.) X Martins Southern Crescent (1986)

> CH. ALADEAN'S BILLY BOY
> CH. ALADEAN'S EMMA SUE
> CH. ALADEAN'S TWEET-SEY OF ROBIE

CH. ANIDEE'S WEE WONDER (Blk.) (Gordon & Mary Phillips) CH. ANIDEE'S REPETE X Anidee's Black Magic (1981)

> CH. ANIDEE'S BLACK I. S. BEAUTIFUL
> CH. ANIDEE'S CHIEF OF STAFF
> CH. ANIDEE'S LO-LA-FALANA
> CH. ANIDEE'S TONI CERA T

CH. AVONA'S SAN JAUN KUTIE (Patricia A. Mitchell) CH. DE YOUNG'S FANCY FREE, ROM X Koch's Suzy Que of Avona (1986)

> CH. TI KAS INCREADIBLE HULK
> CH. TI KAS LIL PISTOL OF PETE
> CH. TI KAS TIFFIE TOO

BLACK PUFF OF HAPPINESS

Black Puff of Happiness (Blk.) (M. Moxley & C. Corson) CH. MAY'S PEPPER
(Blk.) X Gore's Debutante (Blk.) (1979)
      CH. BROUGHCASTL LICORICE STICK
      CH. CHARLAMAR'S PREACHER BLACK
      CH. LI'L BUDDY HOTEI

Blaque's Butterscotch (Blanche C. Roberts) Ken M's Starskipper
   X CH. BERNALEE VENUS (1988)
      CH. BLAQUE JAN'S TWO STAR GENERAL
      CH. BLAQUE'S LOOKING FOR TROUBLE
      CH. THAT OLD BLAQUE MAGIC

BLAQUE EDEN'S STORMI WEATHER (Blanche C. Roberts)
   CH. SHEFFIELD'S STAGE DOOR JOHNNY X CH. BLAQUE'S
   KITTY MAE (1988)
      CH. BLAQUE'S MERRI-D XERES
      CH. EDEN'S BLAQUE MADRIGAL
      CH. ELEN'S MAGICAL MAIDEN

Bleuridge's Natasha (Marie Donaldson) CH. BLEURIDGES'S TUFFY'S BOY
X Bleuridge's Image (1980)
    CH. HERITAGE JUBILANT JELLYBEAN
    CH. HERITAGE LUSCIOUS LOLLIPOP
    CH. HERITAGE WICKED WITCH
    CH. THE HERITAGE BRAT OF DECRIS

CH. BORNFREE LIZZIE TISH (Andrew & Diane Gregory)
CH. DONALDSON'S TIPPI CANOE, ROM X CH. IVANWOLD
PANHANDLE PIXIE, ROM (1986)
    CH. BORNFREE MY DIANE
    CH. BORNFREE PHIRE FOX
    CH. BORNFREE THAT'S INCREDIBLE

BRANDENDORF'S TAMY

Brandendorf's Tamy (Carol & Fred Schmidt) CH. BITTERWELL BROTH
OF A BOY X CH. POMARA'S GOLDEN LADY (1980)
    CH. PINEWOODS BETTY BOOP
    CH. PINEWOOD'S BONNIE BLUE BUTLER
    CH. SHIRRAYNE'S OH OH OLIVIA
    CH. SHIRRAYNE'S OKAY OZZIE

BRENTCHASE DAISYCHAIN

Brentchase Daisychain (Eng. Imp.) (Doris Aldrich) Cobby's Jeremy Fisher of Maitlesham X Brentchase Dolly Bird (1986)
    CH. KENDORIC BY RESERVATION ONLY
    CH. KENDORIC'S MARC ANTONY
    CH. KENDORIC'S PIPIN HOT

(Photo by Martin Booth)

BROUGHCASTL AMY OF CHARLAMAR

Broughcastl Amy of Charlamar (Mary Moxley and Charlotte Corson)
    CH. BONJOR CLARK KENT X CH. HESTER'S AMBER LADY
(1988)
        CH. CHARLAMAR'S LACE AT PUGNOOK
        CH. CHARLAMAR'S LADY BEAR
        CH. CHARLAMAR'S FESTIVE ELEGANCE

Cameo's Very Vanilla (R. A. Bacon) CH. SHEFFIELD'S STUFF'N
NONSENSE X Rosened's Lotus Blossom (1986)
  CH. BRITTANY ROSIE ROSEANNA ROSE
  CH. MAJOR BONAPARTE
  CH. PAULMAR'S DAPHNE DELIGHT
  CH. PAULMAR'S STELLA BY STARLIGHT

CH. CANDICE SEAMAN (Stanley & Paulaine Hughes) CH. RITTER'S
SUPER STAR X Samantha XXVI (1983)
  CH. RITTER'S CALL ME MAXI
  CH. VIP HARTBRIDGE BRADY BRAT
  CH. VIP HARTBRIDGE MASTER FINLEY

CHAPEL RIDGE'S ANGELUS BELLE

Chapel Ridge Angelus Belle (Carol V.S. Gossweiler) CH. FRECKELTON'S
AERO KING X Shirrayne's Doodlebug (1984)
  CH. CHAPEL RIDGE'S MISS CHIEF
  CH. CHAPEL RIDGE'S MY ANGEL
  CH. CHAPEL RIDGE'S SHOW GIRL
  CH. CHAPEL RIDGE'S THEODORE

Chapel Ridge's Belszon (Carol V.S. Gossweiler) CH. SHEFFIELD'S
SNEAKY PETE X Chapel Ridge Angelus Belle (1986)
  CH. CHAPEL RIDGE QUEEN ANNE LACE
  CH. CHAPEL RIDGE'S ROBIN HOOD
  CH. MIKE-MAR'S TEMPLE BELLS

CH. CHAPEL RIDGE'S MISS-CHIEF

CH. CHAPEL RIDGE'S MISS-CHIEF (Carol V.S. Gossweiler)
CH. SHEFFIELD'S SNEAKY PETE X Chapel Ridge Angelus Belle
(1986)
    CH. CHAPEL RIDGE'S BUBBLING OVER
    CH. CHAPEL RIDGE'S CAT'S PAJAMAS
    CH. CHAPEL RIDGE'S CHERUB
    CH. CHAPEL RIDGE'S DOLL FACE
    CH. CHAPEL RIDGE'S EXCALIBUR

CH. CHAPEL RIDGE QUEEN ANNE LACE

CHARLAMAR'S ALPHA OMEGA

CH. CHAPEL RIDGE QUEEN ANNE LACE (Carol V.S. Gossweiler)
CH. SHEFFIELD'S STUFF'N NONSENSE X Chapel Ridge's Belszon
(1987)
>CH. CHAPEL RIDGE'S BEAU BRUMMEL
>CH. CHAPEL RIDGE'S CASANOVA
>CH. CHAPEL RIDGE'S LACY VALENTINE
>CH. CHAPEL RIDGE'S LADY SLIPPER
>CH. CHAPEL RIDGE'S WONDER BOY

Charlamar's Alpha Omega (Blk.) (Mary Moxley & Charlotte Corson)
CH. HAZELBRIDGE BLACK EROS, ROM (Eng. Imp.) X Black Puff
of Happiness (1984)
>CH. CHARLAMAR'S ANCIENT DREAMER
>CH. CHARLAMAR'S BUNNY BOO BLACK
>CH. CHARLAMAR'S LOUIS ST. LOUIS

CH. CHAUNCELEAR'S GOLDEN GIRL

CH. CHAUNCELEAR'S GOLDEN GIRL (Patricia L. Park)
CH. CHAUNCELEAR'S HIYELLA X Chauncelear's April Angel
(1982)
>CH. BROUGHCASTL BOOTLEGGER
>CH. CHAUNCELEAR'S BALLADEER BOY
>CH. CHAUNCELEAR'S BITTA DHANDY

CH. CHELSEA'S HIDE AND SEEK

CHELSEA'S HIDE AND SEEK (Cindy Stover) CH. DONALDSON'S TIPPI CANOE X. CH. RITTER'S GOLDEN DAWN (1987)
    CH. CHELSEA'S CHECK MATE
    CH. CHELSEA'S NAUGHTY BITS
    CH. CHELSEA'S QUICK MISS
    CH. RITTER'S BENSON OF CHELSEA

Chris-Mar's Little Muppet (Judy Ybarra) Mighty Angus X Chris-Mar's Polk Salad Annie (1986)
    CH. PEPPERIDGE KRIS-TO-FUR
    CH. PEPPERIDGE MR. BO-JANGLES
    CH. PEPPERIDGE TUFF-E-NUFF

Darden's Gee Whiz of Southland (Margaret J. Darden) CH. GORE'S UP'N ADAM X CH. SOUTHLAND'S DIXIE OF CROWELL (1985)
    CH. DARDEN'S MEET MR. WALLACE
    CH. DARDEN'S MEE TU
    CH. DARDEN'S MUS' BE MATTHEW

Darden's Hei Yu of Gore (Marvin Nellie) CH. GORE'S FANCI ADAM X CH. GORE'S PINK LADY (1987)
    CH. CK'S KAOTIC KT OF DARDEN
    CH. DARDEN'S JOHNNY ON THE SPOT
    CH. NELLI'S NAUGHTY ELIJAH

DENHAM'S JEWEL OF HARPER

Denham's Jewel of Harper (Norma S. Harper) CH. GOODWIN'S
GANDY DANCER X Harper's Tiffany Topaz (1986) (1988*)
    CH. HARPER'S BENNY HILL
    CH. HARPER'S BILLY ODD BALL
    CH. HARPER'S CINDY LAUPER
    CH. HARPER'S HARD HEARTED HANNAH
    CH. HARPER'S HUIE LEWIS
    CH. HARPER'S PHANDA SAN OF TATHAM

CH. DHANDY'S SKYLARK

CH. DHANDY'S WOODEN SHOE

CH. DHANDY'S SKYLARK* (Mrs. W. J. Braley & Mrs. Kaspar)
CH. SHEFFIELD'S DANCING TIGER X Dhandy's Bleuridge Robin
(1979) (1986*)
>CH. DHANDY'S SKY HIGH
>CH. DHANDY'S SKY RIDER
>CH. DHANDY'S SKY ROCKET
>CH. PUG-PAK DHANDY STORMY SKY
>CH. ROWELL'S DHANDY GYPSY ROSE

CH. DHANDY'S WOODEN SHOE (Mrs. W. J. Braley & Mrs. R. D.
Hutchinson) CH. DHANDY'S FAVORITE WOODCHUCK X CH.
GOODWIN'S MISTY DAWN (1986)
>CH. DHANDY'S FAVORITE MCMURPHY
>CH. DHANDY'S TOBY JOE YOUNG
>CH. DHANDY'S WIZARD
>CH. DHANDY'S WOODEN BRIDGE

Dober-Pug's Little Gigi (Mary E. & Phillip L. Hein) AM. CAN. CH.
RITTER'S MONACO OF WESTDALE X AM. CAN. CH. DOBER-
PUG'S LITTLE CINDERELLA (1982)
>CH. DOBER PUG'S APRIL HEIRESS
>CH. DOBER PUG'S JIM E CRICKET
>CH. DOBER PUG'S STAR TREK
>CH. DOBER PUG'S TOM E. GEE

DONALDSON'S APRICOT BRANDI

Donaldson's Apricot Brandi (Marie Donaldson) CH. SHEFFIELD'S
STUFF'N NONSENSE X Donaldson's Raquel (1987)
>CH. DONALDSON'S I'M NOT HERB
>CH. DONALDSON'S SOLID GOLD
>CH. DONALDSON'S SYLVESTER
>CH. DONALDSON'S TONI

Donaldson's Heritage Kitty (Marie Donaldson) CH. HERITAGE TOM
CAT OF GORE X Gore's Why Not Kookie (1983)
      CH. DONALDSON'S GOODTIME CHARLIE
      CH. DONALDSON'S LEVI'S TRADEMARK
      CH. DONALDSON'S LITTLE BO PEEP
      CH. DONALDSON'S NICK-A-DEMUS

CH. DONALDSON'S RAGGIDY ANN

CH. DONALDSON'S RAGGIDY ANN (Marie Donaldson)
CH. DONALDSON'S LI'L ABNER X Gore's Why Not Kookie
(1983)
      CH. DONALDSON RINESTONE COWGIRL
      CH. DONALDSON'S GOLDEN GIRL
      CH. DONALDSON'S RINESTONE COWBOY

CH. FAHEY'S FALLING IN LOVE (Jane Fahey) CH. LI'L DAVEY OF
SHEFFIELD, ROM X CH. FAHEY'S GOODIE GRAMIGNA, ROM
(1986)
> CH. FAHEY'S COUNTRY GENTLEMAN
> CH. FAHEY'S MISSOURI FARMER
> CH. FAHEY'S PARADING PRINCESS

FAHEY'S GOODIE GRAMIGNA (Jane Fahey) AM. CAN. CH. FAHEY'S
FRIENDLY X Gramigna's Ginny Sue (1986)
> CH. FAHEY'S FANCY PANTS
> CH. FAHEY'S FUN TO WATCH
> CH. FAHEY'S GREAT BALLS OF FIRE

Felicity's Sweetasnuff for Me (Kelvin J. & Barbara A. Hill) CH.
DOUGAN'S SILVER JO JO C.D.X. X Little Miss Muffet V (1983)
> CH. FELICITY'S BELIEVE IN YOU
> CH. FELICITY'S SASSY MISS
> CH. FELICITY'S TAKE IT TO THE LIMIT

First Lady of Yoda (Andrea Belmore) Sir Winston of Wise-Lore X
Wise-Lore's Golden Faberge (1985)
> CH. GAS HOLLOW'S MICKEY SAN
> CH. GAS HOLLOW'S QUIZZY URCHIN
> CH. GAS HOLLOW'S RUFFLES N LACE

CH. GALE BE BY VALENTINE OF NAZREP (Lucille Perzan and
Diana Gardner) CH. SILVERTOWN GRAND SLAM X CH.
NAZREP PLAY ME A MELODY (1988)
> CH. CADO TSAI TASI
> CH. NAZREP'S INCREDIBLE FACE
> CH. NAZREP'S INVINCIBLE PHOENIX

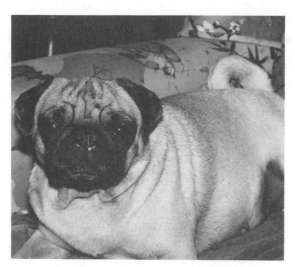

GAMBURG'S PITTER PATTER

GOODWIN'S DIXIE DARLING

Gamburg's Pitter Patter (Judi Crowe) CH. GAMBURG'S OLLETIME
SHOW OFF X Sheffield's Wild Irish Rose (1988)
    CH. GAMBURGS CENTERFOLD
    CH. GAMBURGS WOOFMAN JAC
    CH. JAC'S DIAMOND JIM

Gerrie's Gypsy of Charlamar (Geraldine Canary) CH. CHARLAMAR'S
ANCIENT DREAMER, ROM X CH. GERRIE'S GINGER NO
NAME (1988)
    CH. GERRIE'S DAN 'O MINE
    CH. GERRIE'S RORY OF CHARLAMAR
    CH. IVANWOLD HOOSIER OF GERRIE

Gerrie's Midget of Charlamar (Blk) (Rosemary King, M. Moxley, &
C. Corson) CH. CHARLAMAR'S J RANDALL BROWN, ROM X
Gerrie's Missliza of Trinket (1987)
    CH. GERRIE'S CUPCAKE OF CHARLAMAR
    CH. GERRIE'S I LOVE LUCY
    CH. GERRIE'S JORDAN OF CHARLAMAR

Goodwin's Dixie Darling (Mrs. Goodwin) Goodwin's Anxious Andy
X CH. GOODWIN'S GEORGY GIRL (1979)
    CH. GOODWIN'S FASCINATION
    CH. GOODWIN'S GANDY DANCER
    CH. GOODWIN'S MISTI DAWN
    CH. GOODWIN'S PUTT PUTT

CH. GORE'S FANCI GIN PHIZZ (Louise V. Gore) CH. ROBERTSON'S
BOURBON PRINCE X CH. ROBERTSON'S FANCI BABE (1983)
    CH. CHE J'S GORE GEOUS WOODCHICK
    CH. GORE'S PINK LADY
    CH. MARIDON'S WOODCHOPPER OF GORE

(Photo by Martin Booth)

CH. GORE'S FANCI GIN PHIZZ

Gramigna's Ginny Sue (Nell Gramigna) CH. LITTLE TORMENTOR
X Hazel Black Sherry (Eng. Imp.) (9184)
      CH. FAHEY'S GOODIE GRAMIGNA
      CH. GRAMIGNA'S CORKY
      CH. GRAMIGNA'S MOLLY

CH. GRAMIGNA'S MOLLI

CH. GRAMIGNA'S MOLLI (Blk) (Nell Gramigna) Gramigna's Black
George X Gramigna's Ginny Sue (1986)
      CH. GRAMIGNA'S BEAU
      CH. GRAMIGNA'S BLACK JEWEL
      CH. GRAMIGNA'S TEXAS CHARLAMAR

CH. GRAMIGNA'S NANCI

Gramigna's Nanci* (Nell Gramigna) Gramigna's Black George X Gramigna's
Ginny Sue (1985) (1986*)

    CH. BILBEV'S DUDLEY OF GRAMIGNA
    CH. CEDARS GRAMIGNA GO-GETTER
    CH. DUNNING'S JOY OF GRAMIGNA
    CH. GRAMIGNA'S JEZEBEL
    CH. GRAMIGNA'S PATRICK
    CH. GRAMIGNA'S SAMSON

CH. HARPER'S AMADEUS

CH. HARPER'S AMADEUS (Blk) (Norma S. & Alan L. Harper)
    CH. HARPER'S FLY'IN HIGH X Harper's Rumour Has It (1987)
        CH. HARPER'S AS I BEE
        CH. HARPER'S DRESS CIRCLE STANZA
        CH. HARPER'S SEATTLE SUE

CH. HARPER'S STAR SAPPHIRE

CH. HARPER'S STAR SAPPHIRE* (Norma S. & Alan L. Harper)
CH. WISSELWOOD MIGHTY MOVER X CH. HARPER'S
FAWNNEST FLOWER (1982) (1985*)
 CH. DORRELL'S BEAU VISAGE
 CH. HARPER'S BIZZI BODI
 CH. HARPER'S FLY'IN HIGH
 CH. HARPER'S SANGUINE LADY
 CH. HARPER'S SUMP'IN SPECIAL
 CH. HARPER'S TIFFANY TOPAZ
 CH. HARPER'S TOMMY TUNE

CH. HEATHERS HONEY OF WISSELWOOD

(Photo by William P. Gilbert)

CH. HEATHER'S HONEY OF WISSELWOOD* (Lorene Vickers-Smith)
CH. PHIDGITY PHIRCONE (Eng. Imp.) X Morfa Madcap (Can.
Imp.) (1980) (1986*)
> CH. PARAGON'S PAGE OF WISSELWOOD
> CH. WISSELWOOD APRIL SHOWER
> CH. WISSELWOOD BUDWEISER
> CH. WISSELWOOD DREAM WEAVER
> CH. WISSELWOOD FOR SEVEN ISLANDS
> CH. WISSELWOOD TENDER AMBER

Homet's Liddie (Sue Burnham Christensen) CH. STONECRUSHER OF
WISSELWOOD X LKK'S Express to Mammrick (1979)
> CH. MACCAUGHEY'S PRIDE OF JOY
> CH. PELSHIRE'S WISSELWOOD MAGIC
> CH. WATERSIDE BLACKBERRY IMP
> CH. WATERSIDE CARROUSEL

CH. IVANWOLD CHINABERRY

CH. IVANWOLD CHINABERRY (E.N.K. & Charlotte P. Patterson)
CH. CHARLAMAR'S ANCIENT DREAMER X CH.
PUGTOWNE'S CHINA HOLLYBERRY (1988)
    CH. IVANWOLD ALADEAN'S CHINA LORD
    CH. IVANWOLD CHINA CLIPPER
    CH. IVANWOLD CHINATOWN EXPRESS

CH.IVANWOLD GAYBERRY CAROLINA, C.D.* (Romola Hicks &
E. & C. Patterson) CH. IVANWOLD HIGH TOR X CH.
GAYBERRY VICTORIA OF GORE (1979)
    CH. GLEN GLOW ROCK OR IVANWOLD
    CH. IVANWOLD BROADWAY JOE WILLIE
    CH. IVANWOLD GORGEOUS GEORGE
    CH. IVANWOLD MIGHTY LAK A ROSE
    CH. IVANWOLD PISTOL PETE OF RONTU
    CH. IVANWOLD PORTERFIELDS PIXIE
    CH. IVANWOLD SENATOR SAM

CH. IVANWOLD GAYBERRY CAROLINA

CH. IVANWOLD HONEYSUCKLE ROSE

CH. IVANWOLD HONEYSUCKLE ROSE (E.N.K. & Charlotte P. Patterson) CH. SHEFFIELD'S STUFF'N NONSENSE X Ivanwold Autumn Rose (1988)
> CH. IVANWOLD ANCIENT MARINER
> CH. IVANWOLD MARGARET ROSE
> CH. LARIZADY'S LEADING LADY

CH. IVANWOLD PANHANDLE PIXIE* (Andrew & Diane Gregory) CH. IVANWOLD PISTOL PETE OF RONTU X CH. HODOWN'S ECHO AM (1985) (1986*)
> CH. BORNFREE JAC DANIEL OF TORI
> CH. BORNFREE LET'S DANCE
> CH. BORNFREE LIZZIE TISH
> CH. BORNFREE PRINCESS MEE-TOO
> CH. BORNFREE TOM FOOLERY
> CH. BORNFREE WILLIE THE KID

CH. IVANWOLD TIP TOP

CH. IVANWOLD TIP TOP* (Edward & Charlotte Patterson) AM. CAN.
  CH. GAIS TIPKINS, ROM X Rontu Ivanwold Tara (1984)
      CH. IVANWOLD BEAU OF HALLAGAN
      CH. IVANWOLD DESIREE OF NICE
      CH. IVANWOLD FINEST KIND
      CH. IVANWOLD LORD CECIL
      CH. IVANWOLD MATILDA OF CAMARADE
      CH. IVANWOLD MEMPHIS BELLE

CH. JO NOL'S BLAQUE AMBER (Blanche Roberts) CH. BLAQUE'S
  SHAHANSHAH OF PAULAINE X CH. JO NOL'S HOLIDAY
  HARMONY (1987)
      CH. BLAQUE'S DOCTOR'S ORDERS
      CH. BLAQUE'S KITTY MAE
      CH. NIETS TUFF NUFF OF BLAQUE

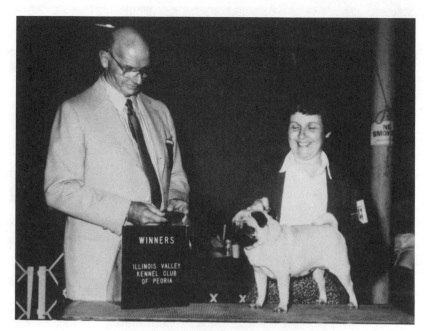

CH. KESANDER'S BUDGIE

CH. KESANDER'S SASSY LASSY

CH. KESANDER'S BUDGIE (Robert & Jean Anderson)
CH. KESANDER'S P.R. MAN X CH. KESANDER'S SASSY LASSY
(1987)
    CH. KESANDER'S JINGLIN' JAIMIE
    CH. KESANDER'S JINGLIN' JORDIE
    CH. KESANDER'S JINGLIN' JOSIE

Kesander's Dandy Darlin' (Robert & Jean Anderson) CH. KESANDER'S
JIMI'S DANDY X Kesander's Darlin Debbel (1982)
    CH. KESANDER'S ANNE WELLINGTON, CD
    CH. KESANDER'S MISS NO BODY
    CH. KESANDER'S SIWASHER

CH. KESANDER'S SASSY LASSY (Bob & Jean Anderson)
CH. KESANDER'S JIMI'S DANDY X Ming Dingeling (1985)
    CH. J-K'S Q.P. DOLL OF KESANDER
    CH. KESANDER'S BUDGIE
    CH. KESANDER'S SPEAK OF D'DEBBEL, C.D.

CH. LAUGHING WATER'S TRINKEL (Toni Harrold) CH. HIGMAN'S
LITTLE HELLER X CH. LAUGHING WATERS DESIREE (1984)
    CH. LAUGHING WATER'S BRONCO
    CH. LAUGHING WATER'S BUS BOY
    CH. LAUGHING WATER'S UPSIE II

CH. LAUGHING WATER'S TRINKEL

CH. LAUGHING WATER'S UPSIE II

CH. LAUGHING WATER'S UPSIE II (Carroll & Toni Harrold) CH. GRAMIGNA'S CORKY X CH. LAUGHING WATER'S TRINKEL (1988)
      CH. LAUGHING WATERS JAMI
      CH. LAUGHING WATERS JASON
      CH. LAUGHING WATERS JINI-SU

Laughing Waters Valerie (Elizabeth Page) CAN. CH. MARQUIS OF HAZELBRIDGE X CH. LAUGHING WATER UPSIE (1979)
      CH. PUG PAK DANDY DON
      CH. PUG PAK JOE WILLIE
      CH. PUG PAK PAUL REVERE

CH. LI'L DARKEYED SUGAR OF MSJ

AM. BDA. CAN. MEX. INT. AMERICAS. WORLD CH. LI'L DARKEYED SUGAR OF MSJ* (Marianne S. Johnson) CH. ANGEL'S ACE HI OF CAROL MAR X CH. LI'L SUGAR OF MSJ (1982) (1985*)

    CH. LI'L CHEW OF MSJ
    CH. LI'L CHOP OF MSJ
    CH. LI'L KATE SMITH OF MSJ
    CH. LI'L LUMP OF MSJ
    CH. LI'L TAURUS OF MSJ
    CH. SUNNY TU CHANCE OF MSJ

LI'L SUGAR OF MSJ

CH. LI'L SUGAR OF MSJ (Marianne Johnson) CH. WOLF'S LI'L JOE
  X Donaldson's Sweety Pie of Gore (1980)
    CH. KINGS LI'L EASTER PUG OF MSJ
    CH. LI'L CHARMIN OF MSJ
    CH. LI'L DARKEYED SUGAR OF MSJ
    CH. LI'L SUGAR ROZ OF MSJ

LKK'S CAMEO JEWELL

LKK's Cameo Jewell (Robert and Linda LaBossiere) CH. LKK'S LI'L
GUNG HO X Donaldson's Beauchamp (1988)
    CH. ROSEVILLE'S JAY JAY WALKER
    CH. ROSEVILLE'S ROAD WARRIOR
    CH. ROSEVILLE'S TANGLEWOOD TOP GUN

CH. LUBA'S DIXIE GIRL, C.D. (Virginia C. Ford) CH. EWO'S
JOHNNY REB X Luba of Mukden (1985)
    CH. SPRINGFIELD'S VA. CUSHAW
    CH. VIRGINIA'S LADY BOMAR
    CH. VIRGINIA'S TAKI DRAGON FLOWER

CH. MANALAPAN'S CARTE BLANCHE (Mrs. Alan R. Robson)
CH. BORN FREE TOM FOOLERY X CH. MANALAPAN'S
OCEAN GEM (1987)
    CH. ALBELARM AMERICAN EXPRESS
    CH. ALBELARM CREDIT CARD
    CH. ALBELARM MASTER CHARGE

CH. MANALAPAN'S CARTE BLANCHE

MANALAPAN'S SEPTEMBER SONG

Manalapan's September Song* (Bert Porter) CH. SHEFFIELD'S STUFF'N
NONSENSE X Sheffield's Gingersnap (1987) (1988*)
    CH. SHEFFIELD'S JERSEY BOUNCE
    CH. PORTERS COOL CALVIN
    CH. PORTER'S FEARLESS FRED
    CH. PORTER'S PAUL REVERE
    CH. PORTER'S SPIRIT OF EIGHTY-SIX
    CH. SHEFFIELD'S JERSEY JOE PORTER
    CH. SHEFFIELD'S SPITFIRE

CH. MARIDON'S WOODCHOPPER OF GORE* (Mary Ann Hall)
CH. DHANDY'S FAVORITE WOODCHUCK X CH. GORE'S
FANCI GIN PHIZZ (1986) (1988*)
    CH. KATSU HONEYBUN OF MARIDON'S
    CH. MARIDON'S ALTHEA
    CH. MARIDON'S FLAME OF LIBERTY
    CH. MARIDON'S PRINCE COMUS
    CH. MARIDON'S TEXAS TIGER
    CH. NEU'S KONIGSSEE OF MARIDONS

CH. MARIDON'S WOODCHOPPER OF GORE

MAR-LOS TROUBLES

MarLos Troubles (Nadine Ludwig) Whitman's Lucky Charm X Terrells
    Toy Ming (1983)
        CH. KNICK KNACK
        CH. PADDY WHACK
        CH. MAR-LOS-BABY-RUTH-OF-SWEETUTH

CH. MARVIE ROSEMARY RAE

CH. MARVIE ROSEMARY RAE (Marvin Werth) CH. FAHEY FOLLOW ME X Lady Josephine (1980)
>
> CH. MARVIE KATHLEEN JOY
> CH. MARIVE PANCHOO BOY MISTERY
> CH. MARVIE PANDALENA MISTERY
> CH. MARVIE PANDELLA RAE
> CH. MARVIE PANDELANA ROSEMARYS LAST ROSE

CH. MAY'S IVANWOLD AFRICAN QUEEN (Blk.) (Margorie May) CH. TICK TOCK OF LE TASYLL X. CH. MAYS DINA MITE (1979)
>
> CH. IVANWOLD AFRICAN EXPLORER
> CH. IVANWOLD AFRICAN VIOLET
> CH. MAY'S MYSTIC MELANIE

CH. MISS BIRDIE WEST OF TRINKET (Blk.) (Mrs. Raplph L. West) CH. CHARLAMAR'S PREACHER BLACK X Missella Black of Trinket (1987)
>
> CH. NEU DUFFER OF WEST
> CH. POLLARD'S DIVOT OF WEST
> CH. WISSELWOOD JAY BEE SHORTCAKE

CH. MORFA MOPSELENA

CH. MORFA MOPSELENA (Lorene Vickers) CH. MORFA MEDICINE
   MAN X Adoram Amaryllis (Eng. Imp) (1988)
      CH. WISSELWOOD LEGACY OF PHIRCONE
      CH. WISSELWOOD L.S. KENNEDY
      CH. WISSELWOOD WAR LORD

CH. NAZREP'S PLAY ME A MELODY

CH. NAZREP'S PLAY ME A MELODY (Robert & Helen Gale)
CH. SHEFFIELD'S BOBBY SHAFTOE X CH. NAZREP
CHINGACHGOOK (1986)
    CH. GALE BE MY VALENTINE OF NAZREP
    CH. GALE KRINGLE IN TIME
    CH. GALE'S POSEY OF WARWICK

(Photo by Martin Booth)

CH. NEU DOLLY OF PRIS

CH. NEU DOLLY OF PRIS* (Blk.) (Sonja E. Neu) CH. CHARLAMAR'S
LOUIS ST. LOUIS X CH. PRIS' BLACK LUV PACKAGE (1987)
(1988*)
    CH. EU-BETTE NEU DREAM COME TRUE
    CH. NEU'S ENCHANTING SORCERESS
    CH. NEU GRACIOUS GARBO
    CH. NEU'S MIDNIGHT REGENCY
    CH. NEU'S MYSTICAL WARLOCK
    CH. PRIS' NEU BLACK KEWPIE DOLL

CH. NUNNALLY'S WITCH HAZEL

CH. NUNNALLY'S WITCH HAZEL (Blk.) (Mary Moxley & Charlotte Corson) Nunnally's Blackmail X Whitman's Miss Sapphire (1982)
    CH. CHARLAMAR'S J RANDALL BROWN
    CH. CHARLAMAR'S MISS PIGGIE
    CH. TABITHA BLACK OF CHARLAMAR

Paragon's X-Citation (Frank & Micki Theisen) CH. PARAGON'S PAGE OF WISSELWOOD X Paragon's Curiosity Shop (1982)
    CH. IVANWOLD TESS OF MENEHUNE
    CH. MENEHUNE FANDANCER OF SHEP'S
    CH. MENEHUNE MIMILO OKOLE
    CH. MENEHUNE NANI WAHINE

Paulaine's Gazetta (Al and Carolyn Bradshaw) CH. SEACREST'S ANDY OF BLAQUE X Paulaine's Korkee (1988)
    CH. ALCAR'S AIN'T MISBEHAVIN
    CH. ALCAR'S LORD NELSON
    CH. ALCAR'S SLUGGO

CH. PAULAINE'S WEE-PING-A-DINGER

CH. PELSHIRES MAGIC PHANTASY

CH. PAULAINE'S WEE PING-A-DINGER (Paul & Elaine Lipka) CH. ANIDEE'S RE-PETE X CH. REKO'S WEE-PING-A-PUG (1979)
    CH. BLAQUE'S MAGGIE OF PAULAINE
    CH. PAULAINE'S JOLLA BY DINGER
    CH. PAULAINE'S LIGHTFOOT
    CH. PAULAINE'S LOUD SPEAKER
    CH. PAULAINE'S TEDDY BEAR
    CH. PAULAINE'S TIC A LONG
    CH. YULO NATASCO OF PAULAINE

CH. PELSHIRE'S MAGIC PHANTASY (Doris Aldrich) CH. SHEFFIELD'S STUFF'N NONSENSE X CH. PELSHIRE'S MAGIC KRISTAL (1988)
    CH. KENDORIC'S ANGEL ON A STRING
    CH. KENDORIC'S MAGIC PHLYER
    CH. KENDORIC'S MAGIC PHORTUNE

CH. PELSHIRE'S WISSELWOOD MAGIC, C.D. (Sue Burnham Christensen) Homet's Fred X Homet's Liddie (1979)
    CH. PELSHIRES EXCALIBUR
    CH. PELSHIRES MAGIC BANNER
    CH. PELSHIRES MAGIC CHANCE
    CH. PELSHIRES MAGIC WIZARD OF OZ

CH. PRIS' BLACK LUV PACKAGE (Blk.) (Priscilla Brown & James Hupp) Pris' Preacher's Kid X CH. PRIS' MISS ANNABELLE (1986)
    CH. NEU DOLLY OF PRIS
    CH. PRIS' BLACK JACK
    CH. PRIS' BLACK JELLYBEAN

CH. RITTER'S GOLDEN DAWN

CH. RITTER'S GOLDEN DAWN (Cindy Stover & Virginia Ritter)
CH. RITTER'S RUSTY NAIL X CH. RITTER'S RAIN DANCE
(1985)
  CH. CHELSEA DAWN'S FIRST EDITION
  CH. CHELSEA'S HIDE AND SEEK
  CH. CHELSEA'S PITTER PATTER
  CH. TONQUIN ACRES CHELSEA TIA

CH. RITTER'S NO NONSENSE

AM. CAN. CH. RITTER'S NO NONSENSE (Virginia Ritter) CH.
RITTER'S SUPERSTAR X CH. WESTON'S ISADOLL (1987)
  CH. RITTER'S CHANGING TIMES
  CH. RITTER'S CHINESE FORTUNE
  CH. RITTER'S SOMEBODY LOVES ME

(Photo by Martin Booth)

CH. RITTER'S RAIN DANCE

CH. RITTER'S RAIN DANCE (Virginia Ritter) CH. SHEFFIELD'S
  CHARLATAN X Ritter's Nick Nack (1984)
     CH. RITTER'S GOLDEN DAWN
     CH. RITTER'S JUSTA CHARM
     CH. RITTER'S PIGGY BANK

Ritter's Trick or Treat (Virginia Ritter) AM. CAN. CH. RITTER'S RUSTY
  NAIL X CH. RITTER'S RAIN DANCE (1987)
     CH. RITTER'S MAD MAX
     CH. RITTER'S SHOW ME
     CH. RITTER'S TUFF E NUFF

CH. ROBERTSON'S FANCI BABE (Louise Gore) CH. WOLF'S LI'L JOE
  X CH. REINITZ BABE DOLL OF GORE (1981)
     CH. GORE'S FANCI ADAM
     CH. GORE'S FANCI GIN PHIZZ
     CH. GORE'S UP N'FANCI BEBE
     CH. ROBERTSON'S PRINCESS ROSE
     CH. SOUTHLAND'S TOP BONANA O'GORE

CH. ROBERTSON'S PRINCESS ROSE

CH. ROSENED'S LOVIN ABBEY

CH. ROBERTSON'S PRINCESS ROSE (Mary Moxley & Patricia Taylor Hokenson) CH. ROBERTSON'S BOURBON PRINCE X CH. ROBERTSON'S FANCI BABE (1983)
 CH. GERRI'S GINGER NO NAME
 CH. FOXFIRE'S GLITTERING TINSEL
 CH. FOXFIRE'S STOCKING STUFFER

CH. ROSENED'S LOVIN' ABBY* (Martha J. Pratt) Rosened's Oriental Tobi Tong x Rosened's Jumping Judy (1983) (1985)
 CH. PAULMAR'S SERENE SERENA
 CH. PAULMAR'S TRACE OF ANTIQUITY
 CH. PAULMAR'S TRACE OF EXCELLENCE
 CH. PAULMAR'S TRACE OF FAC'INATION, C.D.
 CH. PAULMAR'S TRACE OF VIRTUE
 CH. PAULMAR'S WAGGA DE ANN

CH. ROWELL'S DHANDY GYPSY ROSE

ROWELL'S DHANDY GYPSY ROSE (Linda G. & John H. Rowell, Jr.) CH. CHEN'S A FAVORITE OF THE GODS X CH. DHANDY'S SKYLARK (1983)
 CH. ROWELL'S BAD BAD LEROY BROWN
 CH. ROWELL'S SASSY SCRUPLES
 CH. ROWELL'S TOUCH OF TIFFANY

CH. ROWELL'S SASSY SCRUPLES

CH. ROWELL'S SASSY SCRUPLES (John & Linda Rowell) CH.
TERYTAM TASKMASTER, ROM X CH. ROWELL'S DHANDY
GYPSY ROSE, ROM (1987)
     CH. GOODWIN'S THUMBELINA ROWELL
     CH. ROWELL'S SILVER BULLET
     CH. ROWELL'S SOLO MOON RISING

CH. ROWELL'S TOUCH OF TIFFANY

CH. ROWELL'S TOUCH OF TIFFANY* (John & Linda Rowell) CH.
TERYTAM TASKMASTER X CH. ROWELL'S DHANDY GYPSY
ROSE (1985) (1986*)
> CH. CAMEO'S GOLDEN TOUCH
> CH. CAMEO'S GOLDILOCKS
> CH. CAMEO'S IVANWOLD TRIXIE LA RUE
> CH. CAMEO'S MINYA
> CH. CAMEO'S SUPER STUFF
> CH. CAMEO'S VELVET TOUCH

CH. ROYAL A'S TASHA OF BRITTANY (Richard and Judy Alstrom)
Paulmar's Super Trouper X CH. CAMEO'S VERY VANILLA, ROM
(1988)
> CH. ROYAL A'S MAGICAL MARINER
> CH. ROYAL A'S MERRY MARINER
> CH. ROYAL A'S MYSTICAL MARINER

Sabbaday Fantasy (Jane Lamarine) AM. CAN. CH. SABBADAY CAPTAIN'S
KIDD X AM. CAN. CH. SABBADAY FAVOR (1979)
> CH. SABBADAY FRANCES OF FOXDEN
> CH. SABBADAY PROMISE
> CH. SABBADAY SEAN
> CH. SABBADAY TITUS

AM. CAN. CH. SABBADAY FAVOR

AM. CAN. CH. SABBADAY FAVOR (Polly Lamarine) CH. SABBADAY
BONANZA X Sabbaday Amanda (1979)
    CH. SABBADAY FULL OF IT
    CH. SABBADAY KIDD'S CAPRICORN
    CH. SABBADAY SABRINA
    CH. SABBADAY SUPRISE PACKAGE

CH. SHAW'S DOTTIE (Winona Shaw) CH. SHAW'S RAMBLIN' ROGUE
X Shaw's Misty Morn' (1984)
    CH. SHAW'S CHIP
    CH. SHAW'S SMOKEY SMUGGLER
    CH. SHAW'S TOBY

CH. SHAW'S DOTTIE

Sheffield's Angelica (Margery Shriver) CH. SHEFFIELD'S STAR TREK
X Sheffield's Merry Molly (1981)
    CH. SHEFFIELD'S BOBBY SHAFTOE
    CH. SHEFFIELD'S FORTUNE TELLER
    CH. SHEFFIELD'S MISTER MUSTARD
    CH. SHEFFIELD'S TASTYKAKE

CH. SHEFFIELD'S CONSTANT COMMENT

CH. SHEFFIELD'S CONSTANT COMMENT* (Margery Shriver)
CH. WOLF'S LI'L JOE X CH. SHEFFIELD'S SALLY SUNSHINE
(1979)
    CH. SHEFFIELD'S COUNTY COUSIN
    CH. SHEFFIELD'S MIDAS TOUCH
    CH. SHEFFIELD'S ORANGE PEKOE
    CH. SHEFFIELD'S PALE PUTTY
    CH. SHEFFIELD'S PIPE DREAMS
    CH. SHEFFIELD'S SNEAKY PETE
    CH. SHEFFIELD'S TAM PIERCE

Sheffield's Seaside Charmer (Margery Shriver) CH. SAMET PAUL OF
PARAMIN X Sheffield's Starry Eyes (1984)
    CH. SHEFFIELD'S MARCO POLO
    CH. SHEFFIELD'S PLAIN POCKETS
    CH. SHEFFIELD'S TUFF STUFF

CH. SHEFFIELD'S SECOND HAND ROSE

CH. SHEFFIELD'S SECOND HAND ROSE (Margery Shriver) CH.
WOLF'S LI'L JOE X CH. SHEFFIELD'S SURE FIRE (1980)
    CH. SHEFFIELD LITTLE NIGHT MUSIC
    CH. SHEFFIELD OLD FASHIONED GIRL
    CH. SHEFFIELD'S GREEN APPLE
    CH. SHEFFIELD'S ROSE TATTOO
    CH. SHEFFIELD'S WILD CLOVER

CH. SHEFFIELD'S SURE-FIRE

CH. SHEFFIELD'S SURE FIRE** (M. Shriver) CH. SHEFFIELD'S
SUNDAY PUNCH X CH. SHEFFIELD'S LUCY LOCKET SHOGO
(1979)
    CH. LI'L DAVEY OF SHEFFIELD
    CH. SHEFFIELD JOHNNY COME LATELY
    CH. SHEFFIELD'S CARELESS LOVE
    CH. SHEFFIELD'S CHARLATAN
    CH. SHEFFIELD'S DANCING TIGER
    CH. SHEFFIELD'S LAVENDAR BLUE
    CH. SHEFFIELD'S PENNY SERENADE
    CH. SHEFFIELD'S SECOND HAND ROSE
    CH. SHEFFIELD'S SHORTENING BREAD
    CH. SHEFFIELD'S SUNKIST
    CH. SHEFFIELD'S SWEETER THAN WINE

CH. SHEFFIELD'S WILD CLOVER (M. Shriver) CH. SHEFFIELD'S
SNEAKY PETE X CH. SHEFFIELD'S SECOND HAND ROSE (1983)
    CH. SHEFFIELD'S ALL THAT GLITTERS
    CH. SHEFFIELD'S COTTON EYED JOE
    CH. SHEFFIELD'S KITTEN ON THE KEYS
    CH. SHEFFIELD'S TRASHMASHER

CH. SHEFFIELD'S WILD CLOVER

SHEP'S GLOWING YO YO

Shep's Glowing YoYo (June Bradley and Collen Hertzler) CH. CHEN'S A
FAVORITE OF THE GODS X Shep's Li'l Tamu of Dunroamin, ROM
(1980)

      CH. LI'L GOLDEN SUMMER WIND

      CH. LI'L GOLDEN TI LEI OF SHANGRA LA

      CH. TOM'S LI'L GOLDEN RINKY DINK

SHEP'S LI'L TAMU OF DUNROAMIN

Shep's Li'l Tamu of Dunroamin' (J.L. Shepherd) CH. WOLF'S LI'L JOE
X Dunroamin' Dyna Might (1979)
    CH. PAR CAL'S HSIH HWANG TI OF SHEPS
    CH. SHEP'S BIG BAD LEROY BROWN
    CH. SHEP'S CHEESECAKE OF PUG PAK
    CH. SHEP'S LI'L TABBY CAT
    CH. SHEP'S MAD BOMBER OF PUG PAK
    CH. SHEP'S MAJOR TOP CAT
    CH. SHEP'S MISS TOM GIRL
    CH. SHEP'S SASSAFRAS COCA
    CH. SHEP'S LI'L GOLDEN SUNDAY NIP

CH. SHEP'S PEACH PUDDIN

CH. SHEP'S PEACH PUDDIN (James L. Shepard) CH. SHEP'S MAJOR
TOP CAT X Shep's Miss Georgia Peach (1984)
    CH. SHEP'S AFTERNOON DELITE
    CH. SHEP'S MAGIC MOMENT
    CH. SHEP'S SWEET INSPIRATION

CH. SHIRRAYNE'S BRASH BUFFI (Shirrayne Kennels) CH. WOLF'S
LI'L JOE X Pugtowne's Barbarella of Gore (1980)
      CH. SHIRRAYNE'S GOLDIGGER
      CH. SHIRRAYNE'S GOLDEN GAYMARK
      CH. SHIRRAYNE'S NAUGHTY NOVE
      CH. SHIRRAYNE'S TIGRESS TWIGGY

CH. SHIRRAYNE'S LOTSA LOVIN' (Shirrayne Kennels) Shirrayne's
Golden Gaymark X CH. GREENTUB'S BUSY BEE (1980)
      CH. SHIRRAYNE'S EGGER FIGARO
      CH. SHIRRAYNE'S ELIGIBLE FELIX
      CH. SHIRRAYNE'S LI'L MISCHIEF MAN
      CH. SHIRRAYNE'S LITTLE MOREEN
      CH. SHIRRAYNE'S SASSY SANDRA
      CH. SHIRRAYNE'S VIVID VANESSA
      CH. SHIRRAYNE'S VICTORIOUS VANCE

CH. SHIRRAYNE'S PERT PRIMADONNA (Donald & Anne Fischetti)
Anchorage Killer Joe X Shirrayne's Jazzy Jezebel (1983)
      CH. VANDONNA'S ADAM
      CH. VANDONNA'S ADORABLE AIMEE
      CH. VANDONNA'S BABY SNOOKS
      CH. VANDONNA'S BOJANGLES
      CH. VANDONNA'S BUBBLES

CH. SHIRRAYNE'S PERT PRIMADONNA

SILVERTOWN ONYX

Silvertown Onyx (Blk) (Doris Aldrich) AM. CAN. CH. SABBADAY
CAPTAIN'S KIDD X AM. CAN. CH. SABBADAY FAVOR (1981)
    CH. KENDORIC RAVENCROFT MIRANDA
    CH. KENDORIC'S GREAT ALEXEEV
    CH. KENDORIC'S PETER PELLETTE
    CH. KENDORIC'S SILVERTOWN NUGGET
    CH. SILVERTOWN JASPER

AM. CAN. CH. SILVERTOWN SUPRISE PACKAGE* (Polly J. Lamarine)
CH. SABBADAY CAPTAIN'S KIDD X CH. SABBADAY FAVOR
(1983) (1984*)
    CH. SILVERTOWN ANTICIPATION
    CH. SILVERTOWN BACK TALK
    CH. SILVERTOWN FRINGE BENEFIT
    CH. SILVERTOWN GRAND SLAM
    CH. SILVERTOWN KATRINA
    CH. SILVERTOWN SPOKESMAN
    CH. SILVERTOWN STUFF'N NONSENSE, C.D.

AM. CAN. CH. SURE SWEET HONEY BUN

AM. CAN. CH. SURE SWEET HONEY BUN (Royal & Mary Wenig)
CH. PANDA MISTERY JOEY OF HARDWAY X Sure Sweet Sucrose
(1983)
  CH. SURE SWEET CINNAMON TWIST
  CH. SURE SWEET MACAROON
  CH. SURE SWEET MAPLE BAR

(Photo by Bennett Associates)

CH. SURE SWEET SUCROSE

SURE SWEET SUCROSE (Mary & Royal Wenig) CH. CHARMILY'S
LI'L JOE'S DYN-A-MITE X Sunny's Sure Sweet Honey (1979)
  CH. SURE SWEET CANDY KISSES
  CH. SURE SWEET COOKIE
  CH. SURE SWEET HONEY BUN

Tori Lane You Are My Sunshine (Maryellen Castimore and Meb Bloxham) CH. GORE'S FANCI ADAM X CH. TORI LANE DADDY'S GIRL (1988)
      CH. TORI LANE APOLLO
      CH. TORI LANES I LOVE LUCY
      CH. TORI LANES OH ELIZABETH

Trafare's Traveling Lady 9/78 (Liane Dimitroff) CH. EWO'S TRAVELING MAN X CH. IVANWOLD PINAFORE OF HY WINDY (1982)
      CH. AKIRA VON SAN REMO
      CH. ALL THE WAY VON SAN REMO
      CH. BEE MY GIRL VON SAN REMO

TRAFARE'S TRAVELING LADY (on right)

CH. WANJO'S PADDY PUNKIN PIE

CH. WANJO'S PADDY PUNKIN PIE* (W. Hunter-J. Smida) Mr. C. of
Westchester X Carreca's Precious Punkin Pie (1980) (1981*)
    CH. CERRONIES MR DANTE
    CH. DINTY'S SWEET BRIDIE
    CH. J. PUGSLEY APPLESEED
    CH. WANJOS AS YOU LIKE IT
    CH. WANJOS MUCH ADO ABOUT NOTHING
    CH. WANJOS TAMING OF THE SHREW

WATERSIDE ROYAL JUBILEE, C.D.

CH. WENDY THE POO OF WISSELWOOD

Waterside Royal Jubilee C.D. (Carol L. Guttman) CAN. CH. BOHEMIAN JOEY OF KAEJAC C.D. X Waterside Royal Wind Song C.D. (1982)
   CH. HOWLAND BATTALION COMMANDER
   CH. HOWLAND CAHSMERE CLOWN
   CH. HOWLAND DELICATE DANDELION
   CH. HOWLAND MUPPET MUNCHKIN

CH. WENDY THE POO OF WISSELWOOD (Lorene Vickers) CH. NEUBRAA PAPAGENO (Eng. Imp.) X CH. HEATHER'S HONEY OF WISSELWOOD (1988)
   CH. PARAGON'S TENNESSEE TRAVELER
   CH. S-TELS VENUS OF PARAGON
   CH. WISSELWOOD MASKED MARVEL
   CH. WISSELWOOD MIGHTY-MOVER

WESTON'S BO-POPPIN'

Weston's Bo-Poppin' (Roland & Linda Buss) CH. WESTON'S BO-EDWARD X Weston's Sarah Koch (1986)
   CH. WINDY ACRE'S BUCK RODGER'S
   CH. WINDY ACRE'S HOLLY OF WODEMORE
   CH. WESTON'S TRADE MARK

CH. WESTON'S ISADOLL (Virginia Ritter) CH. BAYMEADOWS
ISABELLBOY X Weston's La Madelaine, ROM (1980)
    CH. RITTER'S BENJI OF MONACO
    CH. RITTER'S KERRI ON
    CH. RITTER'S MINI MUFFIN
    CH. RITTER'S NO NONSENSE

Weston's Isagenie (Mrs. Curtis R. Weston) CH. BAYMEADOWS
ISABELLBOY X Weston La Madelaine (1981)
    CH. HESTERS AMBER LADY
    CH. HESTERS ATTA BOY AMOS
    CH. HESTERS ATTA BOY ANDY

Weston's La Madelaine (Mrs. Curtis R. Weston) CH. WESTON'S LE FILS
FRANCOIS X Lady Amber Velvetina (1981)
    CH. WESTON'S HEARTS'N FLOWERS
    CH. WESTON'S ISADOLL
    CH. WESTON'S PRIDE'N JOY

WISEMAN'S BIZA D'ORZA

Wiseman's Biza D'Orza (Loretta Wiseman) CH. BLAYLOCK'S JIMMIE D.
X Ming-Toy of Lor La Dee (1979)
    CH. STEPHENS TOBETTA OF WISE LORE
    CH. WISE LORE'S JOMAHA
    CH. WISE LORE'S SHOWDOWN SHERMAN
    CH. WISE LORE'S U OTTA KNO WHO

CH. WISSELWOOD JOY BEE SHORTCAKE

CH. WISSELWOOD JAY BEE SHORTCAKE (Blk.) (Lorene Vickers-Smith)
    CH. JAY BEE'S MR. STUBBS (Blk) X Jay Bee's Little Complainer
(1988)
    CH. WISSELWOOD HORTON HERESA WHO
    CH. WISSELWOOD NIGHT MUSIC
    CH. WISSELWOOD WIZARD OF PUG-PAK

WISSELWOOD SILVER SLIPPER

CH. WISSELWOOD SILVER SLIPPER* (Charmaine Widmor) CH.
WISSELWOOD LEGACY OF PHIRCONE X Wohlford's Li'l Black
Beauty (Fawn) (1983) (1985*)
>   CH. BOLDERBUSTER OF FEATHERWOOD
>   CH. FEATHERWOOD NENAZADE STONE
>   CH. FEATHERWOOD STONE OF DESTINY
>   CH. WISSELWOOD FEATHERWOOD
>   CH. WISSELWOOD FEATHERWOOD KARA

SECTION IX

Bibliography & Index

- *Bibliography*
- *Index*

Bibliography

Periodicals

Allen, Michael (ed.), *American Cocker Magazine*, numerous articles from several issues.

Ardnt, T.K., "Breeders Forum." *Akita World*, December 1985.

Asseltyne, Claire, "Form Follows Function," *The Great Dane Reporter*, May–June, July–Aug., Sept.–Oct. 1980.

Bierman, Ann, "Feeding Your Puppy," *The Golden Retriever Review*, March 1987.

Bloore, Ruth, "How to Identify a Breeder," *Spot News*, October 1976.

Brown, Russell V., "Nutrition and Feeding of the Basenji," *The Basenji*, Feb. 1987.

Burnham, Patricia Gail, "Breeding, Litter Size and Gender," *American Cocker Review*, 1981.

Donnely, Mary, "Caesarian Section. . .The Home Care," *Min Pin Monthly*, March 1987.

Furumoto, Howard H., "Frozen and Extended Semen," *The ILIO*, Hawaii's Dog News, Oct. & Nov. 1986.

Gore, Louise V., "Care and Training of The Show Prospect," *Pug Talk*, March/April 1968.

Gore, Louise V., "Choosing that 'Show Potential Puppy'," *Pug Tails*, Sept./Oct. 1967.

Gore, Louise V., "Ears—Rose? Button? Flying? Flopping?", *Pug Talk*, July/August 1970.

Gore, Louise V., "Here Comes De Judge," *Pug Talk*, Vol. #3 1971.

Gore, Louise V., "How About That Line?", *Pug Talk*, Vol. #6 1971.

Gore, Louise V., "What I Hope the Year 1958 Will Do for the Pug," *Dog World*, February 1958.

Gore, Louise V., "What Is This Thing Called Gait?", *Pug Talk*, Vol. #9 1973.

Gore, Louise V., "When to Show our Pugs!!" *Pug Talk*, October 1972.

Grossman, Alvin, "The Basis of Heredity," *American Kennel Club Gazette*, April 1980.

Grossman, Marge, "To the Victors," *The American Cocker Review*, August 1966.

Hane, Curtis B., "Training Your Dog, A Consumers Guide," *The Great Dane Reporter*, March–April 1987.

Heathman, Marcy, "Pug Patter, Teeth In The Pug," *Pug Talk*, March/April 1988.

Mohrman, R.K., "Supplementation—May Be Hazardous To Your Pet's Health," *The Great Dane Reporter*, March–April 1980.

Paisley, Richard A., "Whelping A Pug," *Pug Talk*, April 1967.

Schaeffer, Ruth C., "The View From Here, A Breeder's Report On Collecting Frozen Sperm," *American Kennel Club Gazette*, November 1982.

Wittels, Bruce R., "Nutrition of Newly Born and Growing Individuals," *The Great Dane Reporter*, Jan./Feb. 1985.

Books

Benjamin, Carol L., *Mother Knows Best, The Natural Way to Train Your Dog*. New York: Howell Book House, 253 pgs., 1987.

Burnham, Patricia G., *Play Training Your Dog*. New York: St. Martin's Press, 1980.

Burns, Marsh A. & Fraser, Margaret N., *The Genetics of the Dog.* Farnham Royal Eng.: Commonwealth Agricultural Bureau, 1952.

Collins, Donald R., D.V.M., *The Collins Guide to Dog Nutrition.* New York: Howell Book House, Inc., 1973.

Evans, Job M., *The Evans Guide For Counseling Dog Owners.* New York: Howell Book House, Inc., 1985.

Fox, Michael W., *Understanding Your Dog.* New York: Coward, McCann & Geoghegan, 1972.

Holst, Phyllis A., *Canine Reproduction—A Breeder's Guide.* Loveland, Colorado: Alpine Publications, 1985.

Hutt, Fredrick B., *Genetics For Dog Breeders.* San Francisco: W.H. Freeman & Co., 245 pgs, 1979.

Little C.C., *The Inheritance of Coat Color In Dogs.* New York: Howell Book House, Inc. 194 pgs, 1973.

McAuliffe, Sharon & McAuliffe, Kathleen, *Life for Sale.* New Y rk: Coward, McCann & Geoghegan, 243 pgs, 1981.

Sabella, Frank & Kalstone, Shirlee, *The Art of Handling Show Dogs,* Hollywood: B & E Publications, 140 pgs, 1980.

Smith, Anthony, *The Human Pedigree.* Philadelphia: J.B. Lippincott Company, 308 pgs, 1975.

Tayton, Mark (revised and updated by Silk, Sheila T.), *Successful Kennel Management, Fourth Edition.* Taylors, South Carolina: Beech Tree Publishing Company, 248 pgs, 1984.

Whitney, Leon F., D.V.M., *How to Breed Dogs.* New York: Orange Judd Company, 1947.

Winge, Dr. Ojvind, *Inheritance in Dogs.* Comstock Publishing Company, Ithaca, New York: 1950.

Index